History's Mysteries:

Research, Discuss and Solve Some of History's Biggest Puzzles

Other Writing Books by Alphabet Publishing

Stories Without End
Taylor Sapp

What Would You Do?
Taylor Sapp

Outside the Box
Taylor Sapp

60 Positive Activities for Adults
Teresa X. Nguyen

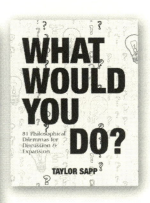

AlphabetPublishingBooks.com

History's Mysteries

Research, Discuss and Solve Some of History's Biggest Puzzles

Created by Taylor Sapp
with Catherine Noble, Peter Lacey,
Mina Gavell & Andrew Lawrence

ISBN: 978-1-956159-00-4 (print) 978-1-956159-01-1 (ebook)

1024 Main St. #172
Branford, CT 06405
USA

info@AlphabetPublishingBooks.com

www.AlphabetPublishingBooks.com

Discounts on class sets and bulk orders available upon inquiry.

Edited by Walton Burns

Interior and Cover Design by Red Panda Editorial Services

Country of Manufacture Specified on Last Page

First Printing 2021

Table of Contents

Section V - Aliens and Other Worlds

Section VI - Conspiracies and Secrets

Section VII - Screams, Murderers, Witches and Ghosts

Section VIII - A Miscellany

Supplementary Activities

How to Use this Collection

The purpose of these readings is to create history-themed topics for reading and also for research, creative writing, and discussion. The unique aspect of this book is that the reader is not just a passive observer of history but also a Historical Researcher and their job is to investigate and change history for the better. Each chapter presents an interesting historical mystery or controversial event students can get involved in solving. Some are about events that historians debate to this day, such as what happened to the Lost Colony of Roanoke or how the pyramids were built. Others are about popular conspiracy theories such as whether aliens created crop circles or whether Bigfoot exists.

Each chapter is organized the same way:

1. **Topic:** The topics chosen are all interesting or unique open-ended aspects of history. Some of these might be more well-known like Jack the Ripper's identity or JFK's assassination, while others are much more obscure, such as Project Serpo.

2. **Before you read**: Questions to introduce the topic.

3. **Vocabulary**: A preview of vocab for the reading along with 3 comprehension or discussion questions.

4. **Your Briefing**: A description of the historical event with the facts and areas of controversy of 300-800 words.

5. **Your Mission**: What does the student need to decide about? For example, in the chapter about JFK, students must decide how they can prevent the assassination?

6. **Comprehension Quiz**: 4-5 questions to check reading comprehension.

7. **Discussion Questions**: 3-5 discussion questions about the historical situation.

8. **Projects**: Each reading has 3 or more choices of extension activity:

   a. **Be a Part of History to Complete the Mission**: The reader should imagine themselves in this situation and write what they would do. This can be approached creatively as fiction, or the reader can do research and write with as much historical accuracy as possible, or both!

   b. **Other expansion topics**: These include research projects, interviews, art projects, and many more activities!

Dear Agent,

Congratulations, If you're reading this you have been chosen for the most prestigious of assignments, to work for the Historical Secret Agents! (HSA)

As an HSA member, you will have access to highly secretive information covering thousands of years of human history. Each mission will task you with studying the past carefully to find new solutions to old problems! This is not an easy job and each mission will place you into difficult situations.

For each mission you will have to be resourceful and come up with an effective plan to change - or protect - history for the better!

To say this is an important job is a severe understatement. As the quote says below, understanding our past is essential for the preservation and improvement of our history.

Sincerely,

T. J. Burns

General T.J. Burns, Director HSA

THOSE WHO FAIL TO LEARN FROM HISTORY ARE
CONDEMNED TO REPEAT IT

Section I - Monsters and Mysterious Creatures

What Happened to the Dinosaurs?

Before You Read

1. What do you know about dinosaurs?
2. What do you think happened to them?
3. What was the Earth like during the time of the dinosaurs?
4. What are the benefits of studying dinosaurs and their extinction?

Vocabulary Definitions:

Write the letter of the definition next to the matching word.

1. diverse (adj.) ____
2. fossil (n.) ____
3. extinct (adj.) ____
4. theory (n.) ____
5. massive (adj.) ____
6. adapt (v.) ____
7. plague (n.) ____
8. emissions (n.) ____
9. asteroid (n.) ____
10. compelling (adj.) ____

a. very large
b. a guess based on evidence
c. change to become better for a situation or environment
d. a widespread and dangerous disease
e. including many different kinds
f. a rock-like object orbiting the sun
g. the remains or impression of a very old creature
h. gases, light, or heat that are sent out or given off
i. convincing; difficult not to believe
j. no longer existing

Answers at the end of the book

Vocabulary Questions

Discuss with a partner.

1. Dinosaurs are one example of species that have become **extinct**. Do you know of any others?
2. What would you do if you had a **massive** headache? How would you deal with a **massive** amount of homework?
3. Have you ever needed to **adapt** to a new situation? What did you do to **adapt**

Your Briefing

524 Words - 810-1000L
Place: Earth
Time: 65.5 million years ago

For 160 million years, dinosaurs roamed, and ruled, the Earth. They were a *diverse* group of creatures as some were similar to our modern-day reptiles while others had more in common with birds. There were dinosaurs as small as a hummingbird and some that weighed up to 100,000 kilograms. Some ate plants and grasses, and others ate meat, including other dinosaurs.

When the dinosaurs first came into existence, there were no separate continents. The Earth was one large piece of land called Pangea. But as time went on, the plates of the Earth began to move, and the continents started to break apart and away from each other. The dinosaurs were witnesses to a great change in the Earth and perhaps also victims of this change.

Looking at the *fossil* record, scientists agree that about 65.5 million years ago, the dinosaurs became *extinct*. This is called the K-T event. Extinction is often a slow process, but scientists have evidence that the end of the dinosaurs came quickly. What happened to the dinosaurs is one of history's original mysteries.

Early theories:

As scientists first began to investigate the extinction of the dinosaurs, they came up with many *theories* about why they died off so suddenly. Many of these theories are related to the huge size of the dinosaurs. One idea is that there just wasn't enough food on the planet to feed these *massive* animals. Another is that their bodies grew but their brains did not, and so their small brains could not *adapt* to such a big body. These ideas are no longer credible as neither explains how these creatures could have been successful for millions of years and then died so suddenly.

Plague was another idea put forth to explain the K-T event but there is no evidence to support it. Also, it is unlikely that a plague would have killed all of the dinosaurs.

Deccan Traps:

This theory was popular at the end of the 20th century. The Deccan Traps are a large volcanic system in India. Some believed the *emissions* from these volcanoes blocked sunlight and/or created a greenhouse effect that warmed the Earth too much which killed off the plants. There is evidence that the Deccan Traps did have an effect on the Earth's climate, but was it enough to cause the K-T event?

Sudden impact:

The dinosaurs died suddenly. So perhaps there was a sudden event that caused it. One such idea is that an *asteroid* hit the Earth and caused severe and rapid changes. This idea was supported by the discovery of iridium, a substance that is very common in outer space but not on Earth. Others argued that if such a large asteroid struck the Earth, we would find evidence of it somewhere. Then in 1991, a huge crater, 100 miles (160 km) across, was found in Mexico. Such an asteroid would have been 2 million times more powerful than a nuclear bomb. Everything living nearby would have burned up immediately and most other life would have died eventually as the debris blocked out sunlight. Though this is a *compelling* theory, it is still only a guess.

Your Mission

Travel back in time and find out what happened to the dinosaurs.

Dinosaurs History Quiz

1. How long did the dinosaurs exist on Earth?

   a. 160 years

   b. 160,000 years

   c. 1,600,000 years

   d. 160 million years

2. According to the text, when the dinosaurs first appeared, the Earth ____.

   a. was exactly the same as it is now

   b. was much smaller

   c. had only one large continent

   d. had only a few cities

3. When did the K-T event occur?

   a. 160 million years ago

   b. 65.5 million years ago

   c. 100,000 years ago

   d. 1991

4. Some scientists thought the large bodies of the dinosaurs caused their extinction because ____.

   a. they overheated easily

   b. they couldn't find enough to eat

   c. their bones could not support their weight

   d. they could not adapt to environmental changes quickly

5. Scientists found a crater in ____ they believe proves how the dinosaurs became extinct.

   a. Pangea

   b. India

   c. Mexico

   d. an asteroid

Answers at the end of the book

Discussion Questions

1. Dinosaurs are a popular subject for both children and adults. Why do you think so many people are fascinated by dinosaurs?

2. Why do you think there are so many different theories about why the dinosaurs became extinct?

3. Extinction of species is actually quite common. What other species do you know of that has gone extinct? Why did this species go extinct?

4. Some scientists are interested in using genetic engineering to recreate living dinosaurs. What are the benefits and risks of this experiment?

Projects

1. **Be a Part of History to Complete the Mission:** Write about 1 page describing your visit to the time of the dinosaurs. What does the Earth look like? What's different from our current world? What adventures do you have?

2. Write an argumentative essay about what you think led to the extinction of the dinosaurs. Be sure to support your argument with solid reasons and examples.

3. Continue your research: The K-T extinction was not the only major extinction of species on Earth. What other extinction occurrences has the Earth experienced? Will there be another in our future? As you research, keep track of your sources and cite them. (See "Supplement 4: Finding Credible Sources" for more info**)**

4. Interview your classmates or friends and family:

Interview Question: What do you think happened to the dinosaurs? Why?		
Name	**Answer**	**Reason**
Mina	asteroid	It is logical and there is evidence of an asteroid

References

History.com Editors. (2010, March 24). *Why did the dinosaurs die out?* HISTORY. https://www.history.com/topics/pre-history/why-did-the-dinosaurs-die-out-1

Hotz, R. L. (2019, September 9). Scientists discover new evidence of the asteroid that killed off the dinosaurs. *The Wall Street Journal.* https://www.wsj.com/articles/scientists-discover-new-evidence-of-the-asteroid-that-killed-off-the-dinosaurs-11568055601

The Loch Ness Monster

Before You Read

1. Have you ever been surprised or startled by seeing a wild animal? Where were you and what happened?

2. How many undiscovered animal species do you think exist? Where are they? What might they look like? Why have we not discovered them yet?

3. Do you believe something is true if you see a photo? How do you know if a photo or video is fake? (See "Supplement 11: Fake News")

Vocabulary Definitions

Write the letter of the definition next to the matching word.

1. monster (n.) ____
2. creature (n.) ____
3. sighting (n.) ____
4. inspire (v.) ____
5. dinosaur (n.) ____
6. evidence (n.) ____
7. species (n.) ____
8. reptile (n.) ____
9. wake (n.) ____
10. hoax (n.) ____
11. ripple (n.) ____

a. to lead someone to act or believe in something
b. proof, facts to show something is true
c. the waves that follow a moving boat
d. an animal
e. one type of animal, plant, or living thing
f. a fake story meant to trick people
g. a large, scary, and dangerous animal or creature
h. a report of seeing something
i. cold-blooded animals with scales such as snakes, lizards, and turtles
j. large reptiles that died many, many years ago
k. small wave-like movement in water

Answers at the end of the book

Vocabulary Questions

Discuss with a partner.

1. What are the differences between **dinosaurs** and other **reptiles?**
2. What animal **species** can you find in your neighborhood? How often do you see them?
3. What things cause **ripples** on water?

Your Briefing

533 Words - 810-1000L
Place: Loch Ness, Scotland
Time: 1933

Imagine you are driving beside a large lake when you are suddenly surprised by strange movement in the water. It looks like a large animal. You think you can see a head and body, but you cannot recognize it as any animal you know. Before you have enough time to take a picture, the animal has disappeared under the water and all you can see are a few *ripples*. What would you believe you had seen? There are people who have had this kind of experience, and they believe they have seen a *monster*. In fact, there are reports of strange, mysterious *creatures* in large lakes all around the world.

One of the most famous lake monsters is the Loch Ness Monster. It is reported to live in Loch Ness, a large lake in Scotland. Although a few reports go back to the 1870s and possibly earlier, the monster first became widely famous from newspaper stories in the 1930s. Since then, many people have tried very hard to find the monster, and there has been an increase in reported *sightings*.

In 1933, George Spicer and his wife claimed to see the monster while driving beside the lake. The stories of their sighting *inspired* people to wonder about the existence of the monster. Then in 1934, a black-and-white photo taken by another man convinced many the creature was real. The photo shows something that looks like a *dinosaur* with a very long neck that is coming up out of the water, but not many other details. After the photo was reported, other sightings began to increase. However, the photo was later discovered to be fake, and there is still no clear photo or video that proves the monster is real. Nobody who has seen the monster is able to show *evidence*.

Scientists have searched deep in the lake using special equipment, but they have never found any strange animals. One recent study was a DNA search in 2018, but they again found nothing unusual. They say people are not actually seeing a monster. So then what about all the reports?

Some people think the monster is just a regular animal that has been seen unclearly. They say it might be a fish, seal, or otter. It has also been suggested that the monster is actually nothing but water, that the *wake* from large boats could look like an animal moving in the lake. However, some people still believe it is an undiscovered *species* —some kind of monster fish or very large *reptile*.

One other possibility is that the Loch Ness Monster is a total *hoax*. Maybe people lied about seeing the monster because they wanted to be famous or make money. After all, we know the photo from 1934 is fake. If this is true, though, why have so many people claimed to see a monster that doesn't exist? Furthermore, Loch Ness is not the only lake where people have reported strange creature sightings. Is it possible that there really is a strange creature hiding in Loch Ness or other lakes? If you could see clearly what George Spicer and others believe was the Loch Ness Monster, what do you think you would see?

Your Mission

Travel to Loch Ness in Scotland and discover the real Loch Ness Monster. Make sure you are able to record what you find so that others will believe you.

Loch Ness Monster History Quiz

1. Where is the Loch Ness Monster reported to live?

    a. England

    b. the United States

    c. Scotland

    d. The ocean

2. What is Loch Ness?

    a. a newspaper

    b. a lake

    c. a country

    d. an animal

3. When did reports of the Loch Ness Monster begin to increase?

    a. the 1930s

    b. the 1950s

    c. the 1870s

    d. 2018

4. What explanation do non-believers give for the reported monster sightings?

    a. It is a normal animal seen unclearly.

    b. It is the wake from a boat.

    c. It is a hoax.

    d. All of the above.

5. Who has clear evidence that the Loch Ness Monster is real?

    a. newspapers

    b. George Spicer

    c. scientists

    d. no one

Answers at the end of the book

Discussion Questions

1. Do you believe there might be a monster or undiscovered species living in Loch Ness? What do you think the animal really looks like?

2. Why is it so hard for people to get good evidence of the monster?

3. Do you know any stories about mysterious creatures from your country similar to the Loch Ness Monster?

   a. Where is the creature reported to live?

   b. What does it look like?

   c. Is there any good evidence it exists?

   d. Do you think it might be real? Explain.

4. Do you know about any famous hoaxes?

   a. If so, explain what happened. What was the lie?

   b. How many people believed the hoax and why?

   c. What happened to the people who made up the hoax? Did they get in trouble?

5. Why would somebody want to make a hoax?

   a. Is there such a thing as a safe hoax or a fun hoax?

   b. In what ways could a hoax be dangerous?

   c. What should happen to somebody who creates a hoax that many people believe?

6. How can newspapers and media avoid sharing hoaxes and false information?

   a. Do you think there are hoaxes reported in the news these days? Explain and give an example.

Projects

1. **Be a Part of History to Complete the Mission:** Visit Loch Ness in Scotland and discover what George Spicer and others saw. Use modern technology to gather evidence and prove what is true about the Loch Ness Monster.

   a. What do you see in Loch Ness in 1933? Is it a monster or not? Describe it carefully.

   b. Is George Spicer trustworthy? Can you help him tell his story, or do you need to tell a different story to the newspapers?

   c. Will you become famous for revealing the truth?

2. Research a single species that is newly discovered by scientists and make a presentation.

   a. When and where was this creature discovered?

   b. Describe its appearance and behavior.

   c. How did scientists find the new species, and why did it take them until recently to discover it?

   d. What is your reaction to learning about this new species?

3. Present about a mystery creature or monster legend. Use a slideshow or other visual aid for a presentation.

    a. Where is the creature reported to live and who claims to have seen it?

    b. What is the creature supposed to look like? Create your own artwork to show what it might look like.

    c. Is there any good evidence it is real? Evaluate your sources. (See "Supplement 4: Finding Credible Sources".)

    d. What is your opinion?

4. Use "Supplement 2: Create Your Own Mystery" to create your own mystery and introduce a creature or monster legend from your region or culture.

5. Visit, observe, and report about a local natural area. Travel to a lake, forest, or mountain near you and take notes on what you find.

    a. Explore the area. What kind of activities can people do there?

    b. What kind of animals do you see there?

    c. Are there any areas where other animals might be hiding? What kind of animals do you think might be there that you cannot see?

    d. Write a report or blog post about your exploration. Do you recommend others visit?

6. Interview your classmates or friends and family:

Interview Question: Where is the best place to find new, undiscovered animal species?		
Name	**Answer**	**Reason**
Peter	The bottom of the ocean	Humans have not done as much exploration there.

References

BBC News. (2019, September 5). *Loch Ness monster may be giant eel, say scientists.* https://www.bbc.com/news/uk-scotland-highlands-islands-49495145

Campbell, S. (2013, April 14). Steuart Campbell: Say goodbye to Loch Ness mystery. *The Scotsman.* https://www.scotsman.com/news/opinion/columnists/steuart-campbell-say-goodbye-loch-ness-mystery-1579700

Greshko, M. (2018, May 23). *Scientists Are Hunting for DNA in Loch Ness-Get the Facts.* National Geographic. https://www.nationalgeographic.com/science/article/loch-ness-monster-scotland-environmental-dna-science.

Lyons, S. (1999, January 12). *The legend of Loch Ness.* PBS: Public Broadcasting Service. https://www.pbs.org/wgbh/nova/article/legend-loch-ness/

National Geographic. (n.d.). *Loch Ness monster hoax* [Video]. Video Home - National Geographic. https://video.nationalgeographic.com/video/00000144-0a3a-d3cb-a96c-7b3fe4780000

The Elusive Ivory-billed Woodpecker

Before You Read

1. How often do you visit natural places near your home?
2. What's your favorite outdoor activity?
3. Are you worried about losing natural places near your community?
4. How important is it to protect wild plants and animals

Vocabulary Definitions

Write the letter of the definition next to the matching word.

1. extinct (adj.) ____
2. conservation (n.) ____
3. species (n.) ____
4. swamp (n.) ____
5. habitat (n.) ____
6. binoculars (n.) ____
7. conclusive (adj.) ____
8. elusive (adj.) ____
9. remote (adj.) ____
10. catch a glimpse (v.) ____

a. type of animal, plant, or other living thing
b. to see for just a second
c. removing doubt and providing answers
d. no longer existing
e. action to protect animals and nature
f. natural area an animal needs to live
g. tool for looking closely at something far away
h. far from people and difficult to reach
i. difficult to find or catch
j. land partly filled with water

Answers at the end of the book

Vocabulary Questions

Discuss with a partner.

1. What kinds of things do people watch with **binoculars**?
2. What animal **species** can you find at a **swamp**?
3. Is your neighborhood a good **habitat** for animals? Explain.

Your Briefing

500 Words - 1010-1200L
Place: The Singer Tract, Louisiana, USA.
Time: 1935

Bird watching is an activity many people enjoy. Anyone can hang a bird feeder outside their window and watch neighborhood *species* visit their yard. Goldfinches, song sparrows, and blue jays are common in many yards in the United States. Serious bird watchers like to go outside to natural places like forests or wetlands to find a wider variety of species. They take *binoculars* and an identification book with them and usually keep a list of what they see. However, the most serious birders like you travel to *remote* locations to search for rare, *elusive* species.

In North America, the most elusive species is the ivory-billed woodpecker. It is a big black and white bird with a long, powerful bill and a crest of red feathers on its head. Like other woodpeckers, it climbs trees and hammers against wood to find food. It is the largest woodpecker in North America, and people have nicknamed it "the Lord God bird."

Unfortunately, experts believe the ivory-billed woodpecker is *extinct* because it has not been photographed since the 1930s, and the last sure sighting was from Cuba in the 1980s. This does not stop bird watchers from searching for it, though. They think there is a chance some are still alive in remote regions of Arkansas, Louisiana, or Florida. Although several people have reported possible sightings in recent years, no one has been able to provide *conclusive* evidence.

Ivory-billed woodpeckers were not always so rare. They previously lived in *swampy* forests in many parts of the southeast

United States, but their *habitat* was destroyed over time. People cut down the trees the woodpeckers needed for nests and food. By the 1930s, bird watchers knew only one piece of land in Louisiana where they could see them. It was called the Singer Tract. They asked the company that owned the land to protect the birds, but this company decided against *conservation*, and the habitat was eventually ruined. Now, although people continue to search for the woodpeckers, nobody knows for sure whether there are any still alive.

As a serious bird watcher, you are determined to be the one who finally gets conclusive evidence. You have the equipment: binoculars for getting a closer look, a kayak for navigating swamps, clothing to keep dry and protect from insects, and a camera to record your sighting. You know ivory-billed woodpeckers need old forests with large dead trees far away from human activity, so you have traveled to a very remote part of the southeast United States. It may take you months just to *catch a glimpse* of the elusive bird, but if you can get photo evidence, the world will celebrate your discovery.

However, it may really be too late. The only sure way to find the ivory-billed woodpecker and help other people see it is to go back in time to the Singer Tract and protect the habitat. Are you ready to fight for the survival of one of the most beautiful and fascinating North American species?

Your Mission

Explore remote habitat to discover where Ivory-billed woodpeckers are living and convince officials to protect the area for conservation.

References

Bales, S. (2010, August 31). A close encounter with the rarest bird. Smithsonian Magazine. https://www.smithsonianmag.com/science-nature/a-close-encounter-with-the-rarest-bird-54437868

Cornell Lab of Ornithology. (n.d.). Ivory-billed woodpecker identification. All about Birds. https://www.allaboutbirds.org/guide/Ivory-billed_Woodpecker/id

Cornell Lab of Ornithology. (n.d.). Ivory-billed woodpecker life history. All about Birds. https://www.allaboutbirds.org/guide/Ivory-billed_Woodpecker/lifehistory

Donahue, M. (2017, January 25). Possible ivory-billed woodpecker footage breathes life into extinction debate. Audubon. https://www.audubon.org/news/possible-ivory-billed-woodpecker-footage-breathes-life-extinction-debate

Sibley, D. A. (2014). The Sibley guide to birds (2nd ed.). Knopf.

U.S. Fish and Wildlife Service. (n.d.). Tensas River National Wildlife Refuge: The Singer Tract and "last stand" for the Ivory-Billed Woodpecker. https://www.fws.gov/ivorybill/pdf/IBW%20Singer%20Tract%20Fact%20Sheet.pdf

Ivory-billed Woodpecker History Quiz

1. What is the Singer Tract?

    a. an organization for woodpecker conservation

    b. the musical sound woodpeckers make

    c. the last piece of land ivory-billed woodpeckers nested on

    d. a tool for watching birds

2. Where do people search for ivory-billed woodpeckers?

    a. all over North America

    b. on the internet

    c. in large cities with many people

    d. in the southeast USA.

3. When was the last photograph taken of an ivory-billed woodpecker?

    a. never

    b. the 1930s

    c. the 1980s

    d. 2017

4. When and where was the last sure sighting of an ivory-billed woodpecker?

    a. Arkansas

    b. Cuba

    c. Louisiana

    d. Florida

5. What kind of habitat do these woodpeckers need?

    a. old forests with large, dead trees

    b. backyards full of bird feeders

    c. remote deserts

    d. tropical beaches

6. Why are these woodpeckers so rare now?_____

_____

Answers at the end of the book

Discussion Questions

1. Do you believe the ivory-billed woodpecker is still alive somewhere? If so, where?

2. Do you know any animal species that have become extinct in modern times?

    a. Where did they used to live?

    b. Why did they become extinct?

3. Is it possible that other species we believe are extinct might still exist somewhere? If they do, why can't we find them?

4. What are some ways we can protect animals from extinction?

5. What would it have been like to live during the time when different animals were on Earth?

Projects

1. **Be a Part of History to Complete the Mission:** Try to find the ivory-billed woodpecker. Describe the sights and sounds of the habitat and explain the challenges you face. Are you successful in your search and will anybody believe you?

2. Imagine it is your job to ask the company to save the habitat for the ivory-billed woodpecker. What can you tell them to convince them it is the right thing to do?

    a. Argue on behalf of saving the woodpeckers' habitat. Make sure to use strong logic. (See "Supplement 9: Logic and Logical Fallacies".)

3. Research an organization in your area that does conservation work.

    a. What animals or habitats do they want to protect near you?

    b. Make a presentation to teach your class about the organization's work.

4. Research a recently extinct or currently endangered species.

    a. Make a multimedia presentation or poster to share facts with your classmates.

5. Hang a bird feeder in your yard and keep a journal by your window to record the bird species that you see.

    a. Describe the birds' appearance and behaviors.

    b. Which ones are your favorites?

6. Interview your classmates or friends and family:

Interview Question: What is your favorite wild animal near your home?		
Name	**Answer**	**Reason**
Peter	Coyote	I enjoy listening to them howl at night.

Bigfoot: Ancient Ape of The Northwest

Before You Read

Across history and cultures, there have been stories about strange and fantastic beasts which may or may not be real. Bigfoot, also known as Sasquatch, is just one of them. Bigfoot is often described as a large, muscular, ape, standing about 6–9 feet (1.8–2.7 m) tall, and covered with thick hair. Its footprints may be as large as 24 inches (60 cm) long and 8 inches (20 cm) wide. For centuries, starting with the Native Americans, there have been stories of this mythical ape-man in the Pacific Northwest. Is it real?

1. Do you know any stories about monsters or strange creatures from your country/culture?
    a. What usually happens in these stories?
    b. Where do most people hear the stories from?
    c. What cultural purpose do these stories have, if any?
2. What makes you believe, or not believe, in these stories?
    a. Were people in the past more likely to believe in stories like this?
    b. Why or why not?
    c. Do you?

Vocabulary Definitions

Write the letter of the definition next to the matching word.

1. creature (n.) ____
2. footprint (n.) ____
3. swing (v.) ____
4. hoax (n.) ____
5. plaster cast (n.) ____
6. crouch (v.) ____
7. creek (n.) ____

a. the mark in the ground where something was walking
b. to move from one direction to another, usually in a pattern
c. an animal or being, possibly imaginary
d. to bend the knees and get low to the ground
e. a model of something that left an impression in the ground
f. a fake story meant to trick people
g. a small river or stream

Answers at the end of the book

Vocabulary Questions

Discuss with a partner.

1. What is the scariest creature you can think of? What makes it so frightening?
2. Are there any famous hoaxes that tricked many people in your country? What makes people believe?
3. Describe a creek. What are the sounds, smells, sights, etc. that you think of?

Your Briefing

241 Words - 1010L -1200L
Place: Bluff Creek, in the Six Rivers National Forest, California - USA
Time: Early afternoon Friday, October 20, 1967

You find yourself in the bright midday sun of the Northern California wilderness, next to a small creek. You see two men riding horses, looking much like cowboys, rounding a large tree that had been turned over by a previous flood, its roots sticking like outstretched arms high into the air. Suddenly, the men become excited and start yelling. One pulls out a video camera and begins recording as they jump off their horses and start running. It's then that you see it - a large, hairy *creature*, standing at least six feet (1.8 meters) tall, *crouching* by the stream. The men are close to it now, no more than 25 feet (7.6 meters) away. The animal begins to walk quickly away, its large, strong arms *swinging* by its side. As it disappears into the forest, it turns and looks at the men. The men make a *plaster cast* of two of the creature's *footprints*, before riding away.

For many years, these two men, Roger Patterson and Bob Gimlin, claimed that their minute-long film proved the existence of Sasquatch and inspired generations of believers who are still searching for Bigfoot to this day. Others, however, insist that the film was a *hoax*: that the images show nothing more than a tall man in a gorilla costume running around in the woods. They claim that Patterson and Gimlin made up the whole thing to get fame and riches. What do you think?

Your Mission

Determine whether the Patterson-Gimlin film really shows a Bigfoot, or if it's all made up.

References

Encyclopedia Britannica. (n.d.). Sasquatch. In *Britanica.com*. Retrieved May 17, 2020 from https://www.britannica.com/topic/Sasquatch

Long, G. (2004). *The making of Bigfoot: The inside story*. Prometheus Books. Accessed from https://books.google.com/books?id=ZbuUHlRcEWYC

OPB. (2019, April 12). *The film that made Bigfoot a star* [Video]. YouTube. https://www.youtube.com/watch?v=xVo6Vj0_Xbo

Bigfoot History Quiz

1. When Patterson and Gimlin saw the creature, they began
   - a. taking photographs
   - b. trying to kill it
   - c. recording it on video
   - d. trying to capture it

2. Some people think that the film really shows
   - a. a new species of ape
   - b. a person in a costume
   - c. an actor filming a movie
   - d. a plaster statue

3. When the men see the creature, it ____ .
   - a. attacks them
   - b. hides in the water
   - c. walks away quickly
   - d. makes loud noises

4. Before the men go, they take ____ .
   - a. hair samples
   - b. pictures of the ground
   - c. a water measurement
   - d. casts of footprints

5. Another common name for Bigfoot is ____ .
   - a. Sasquatch
   - b. Gimlin
   - c. Patterson
   - d. Yeti

Answers at the end of the book

Discussion Questions

1. What are some other explanations for what the men claimed to have seen that day?

2. Have you ever seen, heard, or felt anything very strange while in nature? Describe what happened, and what you think it was.

3. How would this event be reported differently today, with all the advances in technology and communication? Do you think this takes away any mystery?

Projects

1. **Be a Part of History to Complete the Mission:** Write a first-person story about what you would do in this situation. Explain your reasons.

2. What do you think actually happened that day? Why? What steps could you take to check the facts? Make a list of three or more facts and three that you think are fiction. Use "Supplement 12: Using Wikipedia" to help you separate fact from fiction.

3. Think of a similar creature you know about from a story in your culture, or another. Compare and contrast it with Bigfoot.

Bigfoot

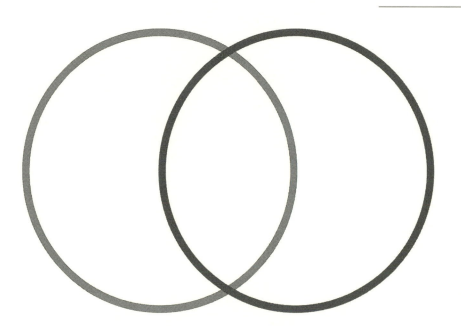

4. Go online and watch the famous Patterson-Gimlin Bigfoot clip (OPB 2019, https://www.youtube.com/watch?v=xVo6Vj0_). What is your first thought? Could it be real, or is it definitely a hoax? Show it to several other people and survey them on their reactions:

Interview Question: Could this film clip be evidence for the existence of Bigfoot?		
Name	**Answer**	**Reason**
Andrew	Yes	Because I've seen one before!

It's a Bird? It's a Plane? It's a Picasso

According to PabloPicasso.org, the *Chicago Picasso* may be one of Chicago's most famous outdoor sculptures. At 50 ft (16.2 meters) and 160 tons, this giant rules over Daley Square, but what is it exactly?

Before You Read

1. What "animals" do you see in front of the building?
2. Do public spaces need art? Why or why not?
3. What do you know about Pablo Picasso?

Vocabulary Definitions

Write the letter of the definition next to the matching word.

1. revolutionized (v.) ____
2. gifted (adj.) ____
3. tones (n.) ____
4. ocher (adj.) ____
5. atypical ___
6. puzzling (adj.) ____
7. complement (v.) ____
8. unveiling (n.) ____
9. booed (v.) ____
10. refused (v.) ___

a. intensity of a color
b. light yellow-brown color
c. making one think
d. showed disapproval
e. "I didn't want to."
f. to go well with another thing
g. changed dramatically
h. uncovering of a work of art
i. not representative of a type
j. having exceptional natural ability

Answers at the end of the book

Vocabulary Questions

Discuss with a partner.

1. In which subject are you **gifted**?
2. What in nature is **ocher**?
3. When was the last time you **refused** to do something?

Your Briefing

491 words - 810 - 1000L
Place: Chicago, Illinois, USA
Time: August 15, 1967

Pablo Picasso (1881-1973) was a genius who *revolutionized* painting and sculpture. From a young age, he was a *gifted* artist. In his early work, he played with the emotions of color. His painting *Brooding Woman* (1904-1905) communicates feelings through *tones* of sky-blue, cerulean and ice-blue. After his Blue Period, he continued with a Rose Period, then experimented with gray, beige, and *ocher*.

Later, his art challenged our way of seeing. In *The Three Dancers* (1925), the figures are *atypical*. An eye is vertical instead of horizontal, a hole in a stomach offers a view of the heavens, and two of the characters are missing their feet. As he aged, his work became more open to interpretation. *The Charnel House* (1944) is a collection of body parts and geometric shapes. In spite of—or maybe because of—his *puzzling* intentions, Picasso became one of the most famous artists in history.

In history, the 1960s was a time of change in the United States. Classic structures and traditions were giving way to more modern thinking. In Chicago, Illinois, USA, three architects asked the revolutionary Pablo Picasso to create a statue to *complement* the building in Daley Plaza, a large square in the city center. Picasso had never visited Chicago, but he was interested in the city's reputation as the home of 1920s gangsters such as Al Capone. He agreed to the job but turned down the $100,000 fee. The statue was his gift to the city.

The statue was still expensive, however. The process required several models and the use of a steel factory in another state. Three charitable foundations contributed $351,959.17 ($2.7 million in today's dollars) to build the statue. Many thought the money should go to another project.

Before anyone had even seen the statue, people complained. They wanted Daley Plaza, the site of the statue, to remain a place for summer festivals and concerts. On August 15, 1967, 50 thousand residents awaited the *unveiling* of Picasso's newest work. As Mayor Richard J. Daley pulled the cord on the curtain covering the statue, the crowd was impatient. When the material dropped to the ground, some people clapped; others *booed*. What were they looking at?

The statue, 50ft (16.2 meters) tall and 160 tons, had a large, strange face, two eyes, rib cage and two matching back panels. What was this thing? Why was it so confusing? Shouldn't statues be celebrations of famous people from history? Shouldn't statues at least be recognizably human? In the same way that different people can see various shapes in clouds, visitors to Daley Plaza saw a dog, a bird, a baboon. Some viewers thought it looked like a cow sticking out its tongue; others saw women from Picasso's past. Children seemed to like the statue. The rib cage was fun to climb on and the back panels —hair? wings?—were great for sliding down.

Picasso boldly *refused* to explain what he meant the statue to represent.

Your Mission

Imagine you are traveling back in time to Chicago, Illinois, on August 15, 1967, to present an explanation of the Chicago Picasso that the crowd of 50 thousand Chicagoans will accept.

It's a Picasso! History Quiz

1. Pablo Picasso's art was revolutionary in the way it used...

    a. color and shape

    b. space and location

    c. fabric and paper

    d. lights and shadow

2. Choose the sentence that is **not** correct.

    a. Picasso's art can be very famous.

    b. Picasso's art is typical.

    c. Picasso's art may be puzzling.

    d. Picasso's art included unusual faces.

3. The *Chicago Picasso* cost:

    a. nothing

    b. $100,000.

    c. $351,959.17

    d. $2.7 million.

4. Why were most people bothered by the statue?

    a. They didn't know what it meant.

    b. They didn't like animals.

    c. They didn't like how it was made.

    d. They thought it was frightening.

5. According to the passage, some viewers thought the statue looked like...

    a. a baboon sticking out its tongue

    b. a cow sticking out its tongue

    c. a woman sticking out her tongue

    d. an artist sticking out his tongue

Answers at the end of the book

Discussion Questions

1. In order to discuss art, you need to know some vocabulary for colors, textures, and shapes. By yourself, with a partner, or in a group complete the following chart

Colors	Textures	Shapes
Write the ones you know, and then check	Write the ones you know, and then check	Write the ones you know, and then check
https://bit.ly/namecolors	https://bit.ly/nametextures	https://bit.ly/nameshapes
to learn new ways to describe colors.	to learn new ways to describe textures.	to learn new ways to describe shapes.
blue	smooth	circle

2. In order to discuss the Chicago Picasso, you might use vocabulary for animals. By yourself, with a partner, or in a group, please complete the chart of animals by continent

Africa	Antarctica	Asia	Australia/ Oceania	Europe	North Amer- ica	South Amer- ica
lion	krill	panda	koala	wolf	cougar	sloth

3. In order to discuss the Chicago Picasso, you may want to review anatomy (parts of the body). By yourself, with a friend, or in a group, complete the chart.

head			
skull			
torso			
torso			
limbs (legs, arms, hands, feet)			
instep			

4. In order to discuss the Chicago Picasso, it might be important to be able to label objects in space. Write the names for the compass points around the compass rose.

Draw small boxes **above, below, to the left of, to the right of, behind,** and **in front of** the cube:

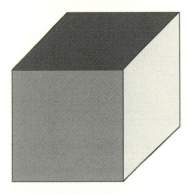

On a piece of unlined, plain paper, draw the *Chicago Picasso*.

Projects

1. **Be a Part of History to Complete the Mission:** Explain the Chicago Picasso using the vocabulary of color, texture, shape, anatomy, and location. Using your own drawing of the statue, make your case for your ideas. Be ready to present your interpretation to the 50,000 people in Daley Plaza on August 15, 1967 (or to a partner, a group, or the class).

2. Do you like the statue? If yes, what would you say to encourage the artist? If you don't like the statue, how would you tell Picasso that he might want to change his design? Remember to be kind. Look at "Supplement 8: Opinions vs. Facts" to review what part of the information in the briefing is opinion and what part is fact.

3. Although the statue is known by the name the *Chicago Picasso*, this name did not come from the artist. Picasso did not name his statue. Now that you know the statue very well, what name do you think it should have. Be ready to defend your answer! (Fill in the blanks.)

The statue should be called _____ because

_____

_____

and _____

_____

and _____.

4. Many people were angry about the statue for its cost, its look, and its location. Write 1 page from the point of view of the statue. Did it feel bullied? How did it feel about the children climbing on it? How did it identify?

5. Interview your classmates or friends and family:

Interview Question: What is your favorite work of art?		
Name	**Answer**	**Reason**
Catherine	y	The painting shows a tsunami that is bigger than Mt. Fuji in Japan. Even though the picture is not realistic, the details and brushstrokes show the exciting action of the wave.

References

Artner, A. G. (2007, Dec 19). Chicago's Picasso sculpture. Chicago Tribune. https://www.chicagotribune.com/nation-world/chi-chicagodays-picasso-story-story.html

Lopez, R. (2018, August 9). The story behind the 'controversial' Picasso sculpture that became a symbol of Chicago. The Art Newspaper. https://www.theartnewspaper.com/news/the-story-behind-the-controversial-picasso-sculpture-that-became-a-symbol-of-chicago

PabloPicasso.org. (n.d.). Chicago Picasso, 1962-64 by Pablo Picasso. https://www.pablopicasso.org/chicago-picasso.jsp

Public Delivery. (2021, Jan 30). Why did some hate Pablo Picasso's Chicago sculpture? https://publicdelivery.org/pablo-picasso-chicago/

City of Chicago. (n.d.). Richard J. Daley Center. https://www.chicago.gov/city/en/sites/retrofitchicago/home/participants/richard-j-daley-center.html.

Section II - Heroes and Villains

Genghis Khan: Villain or Hero

Before You Read

1. What do you know about Genghis Khan?
2. There are many warriors throughout history. Why are some very famous?
3. How should a winning army treat a losing army after the war is over?
4. Why do different countries often tell different versions of the same historical event?

Vocabulary Definitions

Write the letter of the definition next to the matching word.

1. blacksmith (n.) ____
2. cruelty (n.) ____
3. contiguous (adj.) ____
4. abolish (v.) ____
5. feats (n.) ____
6. descendants (n.) ____
7. genocide (n.) ____
8. massacre (n.) ____
9. abound (v.) ____
10. plagues (n.) ____
11. bloodlust (n.) ____
12. innovator (n.) ____

a. to end or get rid of
b. a family's or group's children, grandchildren, and so on
c. behavior that causes pain or suffering
d. serious illnesses that kill many
e. great accomplishments of strength or courage
f. connected, without any breaks
g. the killing of a large group of people of one nationality or ethnicity
h. a person who makes or fixes iron objects by hand
i. to be many
j. the killing of many people in a very cruel way
k. person who finds new, better ways of doing things
l. love of killing and violence

Answers at the end of the book

Vocabulary Questions

Discuss with a partner.

1. Think of a famous hero, real or imaginary. What are some of their famous *feats*?
2. What types of fruit and vegetables *abound* in your country?
3. Who are some famous *innovators*?

Your Briefing

608 Words 1010-1200L
Place: Northeast Asia
Time: Mid 12th-13th century

Sometime in the mid-12th century, on the great grasslands of Mongolia, a baby was born to a noble family. He was named Temüjin, meaning blacksmith. He would grow up to be given the name Genghis Khan (great emperor), a name that would come to be linked to power and cruelty. Through his own efforts and those of his heirs, the Mongol Empire would become the largest contiguous empire ever known. Only the British Empire was bigger. The khanates, or geo-political territories established by Genghis Khan, continued throughout the centuries until the last one was abolished in 1931. His descendants include the great Kublai Khan and Tamurlane as well as 0.5% of all men living today. While much of what Genghis Khan accomplished is not in doubt, whether these feats should be viewed positively or negatively is highly debatable.

Villain?

There are many reasons to see Genghis Khan as a villain. First of all, many historians believe he and his army killed over 40 million people, about 11% of the world's population at that time. We know this because records show huge population declines in China and Iran while they were at war with the Mongols.

What's worse is that Genghis Khan is accused of committing genocide. There are numerous reports of the Mongol army entering cities in which women and children were massacred along with the soldiers. All the buildings were razed, and the surrounding farms and fields burned. Very few people today know about the Western Xia culture of China because its people and cities were so completely destroyed by the Mongols.

The reported way in which Genghis Khan and his army killed people is another reason why we associate him with cruelty. Stories abound of the ways Khan tortured his victims, especially powerful ones who refused to surrender to him.

Hero?

While no one argues that Genghis Khan was responsible for many deaths, there is some debate about how many were killed and how. Some historians argue that many of those who died in China and Iran during Khan's time actually died from natural disasters and plagues. They also make the argument that the Mongols often destroyed whole cities as a strategy. When neighboring cities heard about the terrible destruction, they quickly and peacefully surrendered. It could be argued that the destruction of one city allowed many others to survive. A final argument regarding Khan's blood lust is that the Mongol religion, which worshiped "the eternal blue sky" found the sight of blood to be shameful. Though it was necessary in war, it should be shed quickly or avoided altogether.

Many of these historians argue that Genghis Khan should be viewed as an innovator, not a destroyer. He was able to unite all of the tribes of Mongolia into one society that valued ability over nobility. The nation of Mongolia considers Genghis Khan to be the father of their nation. In Ulaanbaatar, the capital of Mongolia, they have built a giant statue and complex celebrating Genghis Khan. Under him, democratic values thrived, religious freedom was enforced, and global trading grew because of increased road building and the widespread use of paper money.

In fact, most early records and writing, including Chaucer's Canterbury Tales, give a very positive view of Genghis Khan. It was not until the 18th century when anti-Asian feelings started to grow that the Khan gained a negative reputation. In fact, babies born with certain birth defects are described as mongoloids and said to look like Mongols, though this is not polite. It is quite possible that later historians presented Genghis Khan in a way that reflected their own ideas rather than facts of history.

Your Mission

Meet with Genghis Khan and those who encountered him.
Decide whether he was a hero or a villain.

Genghis Khan History Quiz

1. Genghis Khan lived during the _____ centuries.
    a. 5th and 6th
    b. 8th and 9th
    c. 12th and 13th
    d. 16th and 17th

2. What country was not part of the Mongolian Empire?
    a. Russia
    b. Great Britain
    c. China
    d. Iran

3. What is **not** mentioned as a possible reason why so many people died during Genghis Khan's time?
    a. disease
    b. war
    c. natural disasters
    d. poisoning

4. The Mongol religion viewed ____ as something that should be avoided.
    a. blood
    b. war
    c. trading
    d. money

5. Those who have a positive view of Genghis Khan credit him with making progress in the areas of religion, democracy, and _____.
    a. art
    b. commerce
    c. philosophy
    d. medicine

Answers at the end of the book

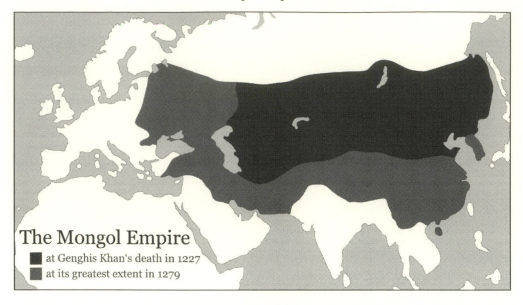

The Mongol Empire
- at Genghis Khan's death in 1227
- at its greatest extent in 1279

Discussion Questions

1. It is not uncommon for different groups to have different versions of historical events or figures. Can you think of an example from your part of the world? What are the two versions? Why do you think there is disagreement about what actually happened?

2. Genghis Khan was known for rewarding skilled and talented people rather than only his friends and family. Why was this considered important? What are the dangers of only rewarding friends and family?

3. The increased use of paper money is considered an important factor in the growth of trade during Mongol reign. What advantages does using paper money have? What do people have to agree on in order to use paper money?

4. One explanation for Genghis Khan's extreme cruelty toward some cities was that it helped him avoid war with other cities. Is this a justified reason?

Projects

1. **Be a Part of History to Complete the Mission:** Go back in time and visit part of the Mongolian Empire. Interview some members of his army as well as citizens of cities he has conquered. Do they think he is a good leader? Are people happy with how their life has changed since the Mongols arrived?

2. Imagine you are a close friend of Genghis Khan. What is his personality like? What are his hobbies? How does he act when he is with his family?

3. Research: Look at the map of the Mongol Empire. Choose a country and research its relationship with Genghis Khan and his descendants. Was it a positive, negative, or neutral relationship? As you read, think about the critical thinking questions from "Supplement 13: Critical Questions for Media Literacy". Share your findings with your class.

4. Create Genghis Khan's family tree: His genes spread very far throughout Asia, Central Asia, Eastern Europe, and the Middle East. Draw a family tree as far as you can. How far does it spread geographically? How far into modern history does it go? Is there a point where it connects or comes close to your family?

5. Interview your classmates or friends and family:

Interview Question: Do you think Genghis Khan has had a more positive or negative impact on civilization?		
Name	**Answer**	**Reason**

References

HistoryASM. (2011, January 30). The last khanate. HistoryASM. https://historyasm.blogspot.com/2011/01/last-khanate.html

Andrews, E. (2014, April 29). 10 things you may not know about Genghis Khan. HISTORY. https://www.history.com/news/10-things-you-may-not-know-about-genghis-khan

Genghis Khan, a prolific lover, DNA data implies. (2003, February 14). National Geographic. https://www.nationalgeographic.com/news/2003/2/mongolia-genghis-khan-dna/

Weatherford, J. (2005). *Genghis Khan and the making of the modern world*. Broadway Books.

The Children's Crusade

Before You Read

1. How old do you have to be to join the army in your country?
2. Did you ever or would you ever join the army?
3. What could be some of the positive or negative effects of strong religious beliefs? Give an example of each.
4. Do you believe some people receive special messages from God? Explain.

Vocabulary Definitions

Write the letter of the definition next to the matching word

1. crusade (n.) ____
2. ill-fated (adj.) ____
3. Christian (n.) ____
4. the Holy Land (n.) ____
5. Muslim (n.) ____
6. the pope (n.) ____
7. miracle (n.) ____
8. convert (v.) ____
9. inspire (v.) ____
10. disastrous (adj.) ____
11. beg (v.) ____
12. slave (n.) ____
13. peasant (n.) ___

a. someone whose religion follows teachings of Jesus Christ
b. the leader of the Catholic Church
c. poor farmer
d. to cause a strong belief
e. a religious war or mission
f. someone who follows the Islam religion revealed by Muhammad
g. Israel and Palestine, where Jesus Christ lived
h. having a bad ending, unsuccessful
i. to ask with strong feelings
j. to change someone's religion
k. someone owned by another person who works without pay
l. causing a lot of damage, having many problems
m. impossible or unexplainable gift from a god

Answers at the end of the book

Vocabulary Questions

1. Do you believe in **miracles**? Have you ever experienced one? Explain.
2. Have you ever made a plan that ended with **disastrous** results? What went wrong?
3. Do you have any **Muslim** or **Christian** friends? What have they told you about their religion?

Your Briefing

580 Words - 810-1000L
Place: Cologne Germany; Paris France
Time: 1212 AD

Because children cannot do very much real work, they often have more free time than adults. Nowadays, lucky children usually spend this time playing with friends or entertaining themselves at home. However, in one of the strangest events in history, thousands of European children gathered for a very difficult and dangerous journey to war. Historians call it the Children's Crusade, and it was definitely not fun and games. Somewhere between 20,000 and 90,000 children participated in this ill-fated event.

The Children's Crusade was actually just one of many crusades. Between the years 1096 and 1291, European Christians went on many missions to the Holy Land to take control of the city Jerusalem from the Muslims who were living there. These were religious wars. Many people were killed, and neither side was able to keep peaceful control. Nevertheless, the pope and other European leaders regularly called together armies to fight for Jerusalem, and when the Children's Crusade happened in 1212, the crusades had been ongoing for over one hundred years. In other words, the idea of fighting for God in the Holy Land was not new or unusual. In fact, the Children's Crusade was started by ordinary people and not by the pope or government leaders.

Obviously, a religious war is not a safe activity for children. So how did the Children's Crusade happen? According to historians, two different people started the crusade by claiming that God himself had spoken to them and would provide miracles. In Germany, Nicholas of Cologne called people to travel to Jerusalem and convert the Muslims to Christianity. He claimed God would help them walk through the sea on dry land. In France, a 12-year-old boy named Stephen of Cloyes also inspired people by making similar claims about God and miracles. Neither Nicholas nor Stephen had support from official leaders, but they both took large groups of children on long journeys to the Mediterranean Sea, which they needed to cross to get to the Holy Land.

These trips were disastrous. The children had to walk hundreds of miles during a hot summer. More than half of Nicholas's followers died on the way from Germany to Italy. Stephen's followers had to beg for food, and some also died traveling across France. Unsurprisingly, many people in both groups decided to quit. When the remaining children finally reached the Mediterranean Sea, they did not receive any miracle from God. The sea did not open for them, and Stephen and Nicholas's crusades failed before they ever left Europe.

Unfortunately, that is not the end of the story. Although some children returned home, there were others that still believed in the mission and boarded ships to continue to the Holy Land. There is no record of what happened to them, and they were never seen again. Historians guess they were probably tricked and sold as slaves in northern Africa. Some might have died at sea. Whatever happened, it was not the ending promised by Nicholas and Stephen.

Historians are not sure how much is true in the story of the Children's Crusade. Some think it was actually poor people and peasants who followed Nicholas and Stephen across Europe. It is also possible that parts of the story were created as a warning against unofficial crusades.

If you traveled back to Europe in 1212, who would you see following Nicholas and Stephen? What would happen if you joined them on their journey? Could you convince anyone that it was a bad idea?

Your Mission

Travel to Cologne Germany or Paris France in the year 1212 and find out the truth about the Children's Crusades. If necessary, convince the participants that their plan is foolish and dangerous.

Children's Crusade History Quiz

1. When did the Children's Crusade happen?

    a. 1096

    b. 1212

    c. 1291

    d. 2012

2. What was the goal of the European crusades?

    a. to control Jerusalem and the Holy Land

    b. to conquer Europe

    c. to convert children to Islam

    d. to make peace between religions

3. Who started the Children's Crusade?

    a. The pope

    b. The Muslims in Jerusalem

    c. Two people from France and Germany

    d. The governments of France and Germany

4. How many people participated in the Children's Crusade?

    a. 12

    b. about 500

    c. between 20,000 and 90,000

    d. more than 1 million

5. What was the result of the Children's Crusade?

    a. Some of the children died on the way.

    b. Some of the children quit before they reached the Holy Land.

    c. Some of the children disappeared at sea.

    d. All of the above.

Answers at the end of the book

Discussion Questions

1. Do you believe the story of the Children's Crusade is true? Explain your opinion.

2. How can religious beliefs sometimes cause wars?

3. Does age, gender, or health matter when choosing who should join the army to fight wars? Explain.

4. Have you ever been inspired by somebody's speech to do something?

5. Have you ever been converted to a new belief or opinion? Explain.

6. Have you ever been on a very difficult journey? Where did you go and what happened?

Projects

1. **Be a part of history to complete your mission:** Visit the year 1212 and describe what you find in France and Germany.

    a. Who is actually following Nicholas and Stephen? Talk to them about why they believe in the crusade.

    b. What can you say to convince the children or peasants against going on the dangerous journey?

2. Imagine you join the last remaining child crusaders on a ship across the Mediterranean Sea. Describe the journey.

    a. Where do you go and what happens to you?

    b. Do you ever make it to Jerusalem, do you escape, or do you arrive in a strange new culture?

3. Research a current or recent war. Make a presentation to show classmates what you have learned.

    a. Who is fighting and what do they believe?

    b. Use "Supplement 4: Finding Credible Sources" to evaluate your sources on the war.

    c. What do you think is the best way to avoid this kind of war?

    d. Finish your presentation with an argument for or against the war. Make sure to use strong logic. (See "Supplement 9: Logic and Logical Fallacies".)

4. Pretend you are a travel agent and advertise a vacation to the Holy Land.

    a. Research famous landmarks that tourists would want to visit.

    b. Make a poster or visual presentation to advertise locations and activities in Jerusalem.

    c. What will you recommend tourists see and do?

5. Research how organizations like UNICEF and Child Soldiers International are working to protect children from becoming soldiers.

    a. Where are children still used as soldiers today, and what can we do to help?

    b. Write down your personal reaction to the information you learn.

6. Interview your classmates or friends and family:

Interview Question: How did you spend your free time when you were a child?		
Name	**Answer**	**Reason**
Peter	I caught frogs, snakes, and turtles in the creek by my house.	I liked animals and exploring nature

References

Gary, the Archivist (Host). (2016, September 6). The children's crusade 1212 (No. 71) [Audio podcast episode]. In *Medieval Archives Podcast.* https://medievalarchives.com/2016/09/06/map-childrens-crusade/

Hansbery, J. (1938). The children's crusade. *The Catholic Historical Review, 24(1)*, 30-38. http://www.jstor.org/stable/25013654

Meseguer, E. (2020, May 28). The children's crusade set out for the Holy Land in 1212. It never arrived. *National Geographic.* https://www.nationalgeographic.com/history/magazine/2020/05-06/children-crusades-set-out-holy-land-1212-never-arrived/

Artist or Monster? Stop Adolf Hitler

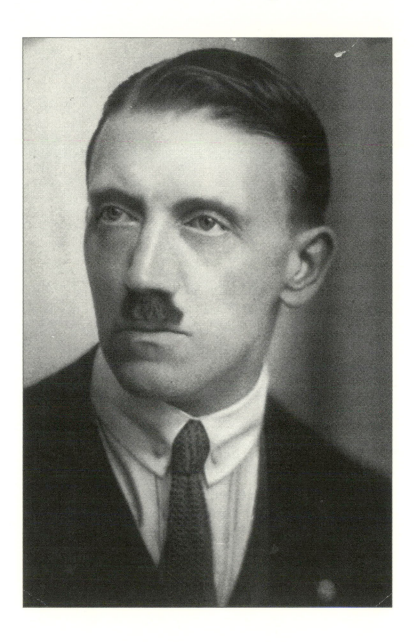

Before You Read

1. Read this quote by Walter Langer about the former German leader Adolf Hitler: "If you tell a big enough lie and tell it frequently enough, it will be believed."

    a. What does this quote mean?

    b. Do you agree or disagree with this statement? Why?

2. Adolf Hitler is commonly considered one of the most, if not the most, dangerous, and evil leaders in world history. What are the terrible things Hitler did?

3. What else do you know about Hitler?

Vocabulary Definitions

Write the letter of the definition next to the matching word

1. pursue (v.) ____
2. rhetoric (n.) ____
3. decorated (adj.) ____
4. Nazi (n.) ____
5. coup (n.) ____
6. anti-Semitism (n.) ____
7. nationalism (n.) ____
8. dictatorship (n.) ____
9. Axis (n.) ____
10. genocide (n.) ____

a. prejudice and racist discrimination against Jewish people
b. persuasive language
c. a political focus on patriotism and placing one's own country above all others
d. the alliance of Germany and Italy formed before and during World War II, later extended to include Japan and other countries
e. a one-party rule with a single leader at the top
f. awarded
g. the killing of a large group of people of one nationality or ethnicity
h. Short for National Socialist German Workers Party, the political party of Adolf Hitler and his German rule from 1933-1945
i. to follow a path or goal with motivation
j. To take power from the government by force

Answers at the end of the book

Vocabulary Questions

Discuss with a partner.

Discuss with a partner.

1. What is something important you have **pursued**? Did you succeed?
2. What are the positives of **nationalism?** What are the negatives?
3. Can you think of a **coup** in any other country? Have you ever had one in your home country or area?

Your Briefing

730 Words 1210 -1400L
Place: Vienna, Austria
Time: December 1, 1907

Adolf Hitler was born in Austria on April 20, 1889. In his childhood, he showed great interest in the arts. In 1907, Hitler left Linz to live and study fine art in Vienna, financed by his mother. He was very unsuccessful in his art career as he was twice rejected by the

Academy of Fine Arts Vienna.

On December 21, 1907, his mother died of breast cancer at the age of 47, and without financial support, Hitler was sometimes forced to live on the streets and earn money as a casual laborer and by

House at a lake with mountains by Adolf Hitler, 1910

painting and selling watercolors of Vienna's sights.

During his time in Vienna, he *pursued* a growing passion for two other interests: architecture and music. He also first became exposed to racist *rhetoric*. Hitler read local newspapers such and read writings by *anti-Semitic* leaders such as Karl Lueger and Georg Ritter von Schönerer that encouraged prejudice and played on Christian fears of being invaded by Eastern European Jewish people.

Hitler moved to Germany in 1913 and was *decorated* for his service in the German Army in World War I. In 1919 Hitler joined the NSDAP (National Socialist German Workers Party), more commonly known as the *Nazi* party. In 1923, he attempted to seize power in a failed *coup* in Munich and was imprisoned. While in jail, he dictated the first volume of his autobiography and political *manifesto Mein Kampf* ("My Struggle"). After his release from prison in 1924, Hitler gained popular support by furthering his support of German *nationalism* He also falsely denounced international capitalism and communism as being part of a Jewish conspiracy. The Nazi party slowly gathered power during the 1920s becoming the second largest party in Germany by 1929.

By 1933, the Nazi party was the largest elected party in the Germany. This led to the Enabling Act of 1933, which transformed the government into Nazi Germany, a one-party *dictatorship*. Hitler aimed to eliminate Jews from Germany and establish a New Order to counter what he saw as the injustice of the post-World War I international order dominated by Britain and France. His first six years in power resulted in rapid economic progress, while his message of antisemitism was a precursor to war.

Hitler sought *Lebensraum* ("living space") for the German people in Eastern Europe, meaning Germany should conquer Europe or even the world and non-German people should be killed. He began military action and on September 1, 1939 invaded Poland, resulting in Britain and France declaring war on Germany, the beginning of World War II. In June 1941, Hitler ordered an invasion of the Soviet Union. By the end of 1941, German forces and the European *Axis* powers occupied most of Europe and North Africa. In December 1941, he formally declared war on the United States, bringing them directly into the conflict. Failure to defeat the Soviets and the entry of the United States into the war forced Germany onto the defensive and it suffered a series of escalating defeats. In the final days of the war during the Battle of Berlin in 1945, he married his long-time lover, Eva Braun. Less than two days later on April 30, 1945, the two committed suicide to avoid capture by the Soviet Red Army and their corpses were burned.

Under Hitler's leadership, the Nazis' were responsible for the *genocide* of at least 5.5 million Jews and millions of other victims whom he and his followers deemed *Untermenschen* ("sub-humans") or socially undesirable. Hitler and the Nazi regime were also responsible for the killing of an estimated 19.3 million civilians and prisoners of war. In addition, 29 million soldiers and civilians died as a result of military action in the European theater. The number of civilians killed during the Second World War was unprecedented in warfare and the casualties constituted the deadliest conflict in human history.

After your briefing, you find yourself suddenly transported to a bar in 1910 Germany. Hitler, a struggling artist, is sitting alone in a booth unhappily drinking after having his work rejected by Jewish businessmen. He is now an innocent artist; he has not hurt anyone...yet. You have your weapons (a small gun and a knife as well as a jar of poison) in your pocket. It's your choice whether you choose to kill him, trick him, or talk to him. How will you choose to stop Hitler from his future atrocities?

Your Mission

Stop Hitler by any means necessary from causing millions of future deaths!

References

Adolf Hitler. (2021, March 16). In *Wikipedia*. https://en.wikipedia.org/w/index.php?title=Adolf_Hitler&oldid=1012541721

Lukacs J. (1998). *Adolf Hitler*. In *Britannica.com* Retrieved 16 March 2021. https://www.britannica.com/biography/Adolf-Hitler

Johnson, B. (2014). *Inside the army's spectacular hidden treasure room*. Buzzfeed News. https://www.buzzfeed.com/bennyjohnson/inside-the-armys-spectacular-hidden-treasure-room

Pappas, S. (2016, April 18). *Hitler's rise: How a homeless artist became a murderous tyrant*. Live Science. https://www.livescience.com/54441-how-hitler-rose-to-power.html

Stop Hitler History Quiz

1. Adolf Hitler was the Chancellor of ____ .
    a. the USA
    b. Austria
    c. Germany
    d. England

2. Before becoming a politician, Hitler was working as a(n.) ____ .____
    a. artist
    b. architect
    c. musician
    d. all of the above

3. Adolf Hitler was responsible for starting World War I.
    a. true
    b. false

4. Hitler's government focused on horrific words and actions of Anti-semitism, which is discrimination against which ethnic group?
    a. Jews
    b. Poles
    c. African Americans
    d. Asians

5. The failure to successfully invade the Soviet Union was one of the main causes for Hitler and Germany's defeat in World War II.
    a. True
    b. False

Answers at the end of the book

Discussion Questions

1. What are the biggest challenges of this assignment? Would you be willing to do it?

2. It is claimed by some that Hitler faked his own death. Do you think that's possible? Why or why not?

3. Think of another leader in history with an evil reputation? How is that leader similar or different to Hitler?

4. Read the following quote by Hitler. What do you think it means? Do you agree or disagree?"

"Those who want to live, let them fight, and those who do not want to fight in this world of eternal struggle do not deserve to live."

Projects

1. **Be a Part of History to Complete the Mission!** Write the story of meeting Hitler! Write about 1 page. Here are some questions to consider as you write:

    a. What will you say to Hitler?

    b. How can you stop him? Through persuasion or force?

2. Find a quote by Adolf Hitler, write it down, and answer the following:

    a. When/where did he say the quote?

    b. Describe what it means.

    c. Do you agree or disagree? Why?

3. Research about Hitler: Write about 1 page - answer 1 or both questions below (See Supplements 4 and 5 for help finding sources) What were his most dubious or evil achievements? How did Hitler's rule in Germany affect or change world history?

4. More research: Research another leader in history similar to Hitler. (For example: Mussolini or Stalin) and describe how they were similar or different.

5. Interview your classmates or friends and family: Afterward, compare their answers. How are they the same or different? What do you think about the results?

Interview Question: Who do you think was the most dangerous leader in history?		
Name	**Answer**	**Reason**

Lyuh Woon-hyung and the Division of Korea

Before You Read

1. Why are North and South Korea separate countries?

2. Have political disagreements affected your country or your culture?

3. Do you think it's possible North and South Korea might join together again someday in the future? Explain your opinion.

Vocabulary Definitions

Write the letter of the definition next to the matching word.

1. liberated (adj.) ____
2. Soviet (adj./ n.) ____
3. expansion (n.) ____
4. independence (n.) ____
5. committee (n.) ____
6. provisional (adj.) ____
7. recognize (v.) ____
8. from scratch (prep. phrase) ____
9. executed (adj.) ____
10. assassinated (adj.) ____
11. permanently (adv.) ___
12. killed by political ene-mies

a. killed as punishment
b. received freedom
c. becoming bigger
d. forever
e. from the very beginning
f. only for now, before a final decision
g. group for making plans and decisions
h. an alliance made up of several communist states (including Russia) that existed from 1922-1991.
i. being in charge of yourself and your decisions, no outside control
j. (here) say something is legal or true

Answers at the end of the book

Vocabulary Questions

Discuss with a partner.

1. Was your country ever **liberated** from another country? When and how did it receive **independence**?
2. What crimes are people **executed** for? Do you think it's a fair punishment?
3. Which countries were part of the **Soviet** Union (U.S.S.R.)? How many can you name?

Your Briefing

471 Words - 810-1000L
Place: Hyehwa-dong; Seoul, Korea
Time: 1947

Who was going to run the government in newly liberated Korea? This was a question nobody could answer in 1946 when they won freedom from Japan. The country was divided in the middle by foreign powers. The Soviets had arrived from the north and wanted to support someone who agreed with their politics. The Americans had arrived from the south with very different politics and a fear of Soviet expansion. Was there anyone in Korea both could trust? No, it seemed unlikely, but it wasn't because there were no Korean leaders ready to lead their own country.

Like other Korean leaders, Lyuh Woon-hyung had been preparing for Korean *independence* for many years. As World War II was ending in 1945, he had organized a *committee* with other Korean leaders like Cho Man-sik to get ready for liberation. Then he had created a *provisional* government, the People's Republic of Korea, and worked to smoothly take over power from the Japanese Empire. He had the support and cooperation of many Korean people, and like every other leader in Korea, he knew it was important for all of Korea to stay together as one nation. Despite all his preparations, he had to find a way to convince the Soviets and Americans that he and his government were trustworthy to lead a new nation. That turned out to be an impossible task.

When the Americans arrived, they refused to recognize Lyuh's government and decided to build a totally new government from scratch. They thought he was too friendly with the Soviets. However, the Soviets also had their own plans. When Cho Man-sik disagreed with their plan to stay in Korea and guide the new government for a long period, he mysteriously disappeared. Some people believe he was executed. It was a dangerous time to be a leader in Korea.

Although Lyuh continued to work to create a united and independent Korean government, he was losing power to groups working for the Soviets and Americans. The possibility of peacefully uniting all of Korea under one government was disappearing. But after working for so many years, Lyuh Woon-hyung did not just give up. He continued to try to get cooperation from different groups and to unify the Korean people. If anyone had a chance to save Korea from being permanently divided, maybe it was him.

In the end, he did not have a chance. He was assassinated by a 19-year-old activist in the Hyehwa neighborhood of Seoul in 1947. The attacker was reported to be part of a right-wing extremist group, but historians are not sure of the truth. Soon, the Soviet and American division of Korea became permanent and eventually led to the Korean War in 1950. But what if Lyuh Woon-hyung had survived? Could he have eventually found a way to prevent all of the suffering that happened during and after the war?

Your Mission

Travel to 1947 Korea, protect Lyuh Woon-hyung from assassination in Hyehwa-dong Seoul, and help prevent the Korean War between a divided Korea.

References

Kim, H. (1988). The American military government in South Korea, 1945-1948: Its formation, policies, and legacies. *Asian Perspective, 12*(1), 51-83. http://www.jstor.org/stable/42703907

Krishnan, R. R. (1984). Early history of US imperialism in Korea. *Social Scientist, 12*(11), 3. https://doi.org/10.2307/3516875

Park, R.(2016, October 19). Remembering Godang Cho man-sik (1883-1950). *The Korean Herald*. https://www.koreaherald.com/view.php?ud=20161019000638

Stueck, W. (1995). The United States, the Soviet Union, and the division of Korea: A comparative approach. *The Journal of American-East Asian Relations, 4*(1), 1-27. http://www.jstor.org/stable/23612581

Tae-Jong, K. (2007, July 19). Mongyang allegedly killed by S. Korean Communist Party. *The Korea Times*. https://www.koreatimes.co.kr/www/nation/2019/12/113_6822.html

Wilson Center Digital Archive. (1947, July 19). *Modern Korean History Portal*. https://digitalarchive.wilson-center.org/theme/modern-korean-history-portal/timeline?year=1947#

Korean Division History Quiz

1. When did World War II end?

    a. 1945

    b. 1946

    c. 1947

    d. 1950

2. Which country was Korea liberated from?

    a. the United States

    b. the Soviet Union

    c. Japan

    d. China

3. Why did the Americans not recognize Lyuh Woon-hyung's provisional government?

    a. They thought he was not an experienced leader.

    b. He could not speak English.

    c. They did not know about his government.

    d. They thought he was too close to the Soviets.

4. What happened to Cho Man-sik?

    a. He disappeared after he disagreed with the Soviets.

    b. He was assassinated by a teenager in Seoul.

    c. The Americans put him in prison.

    d. He became the leader of North Korea.

5. Who divided Korea?

    a. Japan

    b. the Soviets and Americans

    c. Lyuh Woon-hyung

    d. Cho Man-sik

Discussion Questions

1. Is it sometimes necessary for foreign powers to make decisions about other countries' governments? What are the pros and cons of foreign intervention?

2. Is assassination ever a justifiable action? Explain your opinion.

3. Why do you think the teenage activist assassinated Lyuh Woon-hyung? Do you think he might have been supported by foreign powers, or did he act alone?

4. What should the Americans and Soviets have done differently about Korea?

5. Many countries have had civil wars. Is there ever a good reason for one part of a country to fight another part of the same country?

Projects

1. **Be a Part of History to Complete the Mission:** Help Lyuh Woon-hyung survive assassination and write about how he tries to keep Korea united.

   a. Can he successfully keep Korea united?

   b. Does he decide to help the Americans or Soviets?

   c. You know the Korean War will be terrible, so what do you suggest to him is the best solution?

   d. How will Korea be different if you keep it united?

2. Do you enjoy Korean food, music, drama, or fashion? Prepare a presentation on your favorite aspect of Korean culture.

3. Research another country that has been divided (e.g. Sudan, Yugoslavia, Ireland, Czechoslovakia) and write a short report about the causes and effects.

   a. Was there a civil war?

   b. Were any foreign powers involved?

   c. Do you think reunification is possible or important?

4. Research and report on the current relationship between North and South Korea.

   a. What kind of violence and arguments have happened since the Korean War? Is either country safe to live in today?

   b. Compare and contrast what the two governments say about reunification. Is there any evidence that they might work together?

   c. Find news stories from both North Korean and South Korean media about their politics. What statements do they make about each other? How do you know if the information is true or false? (See "Supplement 11: Fake News")

5. Interview your classmates or friends and family:

Interview Question: Do you believe North and South Korea will ever reunite?		
Name	**Answer**	**Reason**
Peter	Yes	Many people on both sides want to reunite. However, I think it may take a long time.

Who Killed Tupac?

Before You Read

1. Has anyone ever told you that you looked like someone else? Who? How did it make you feel?

2. Have you ever wanted to run away from your life? Why?

3. What is rap music? What rap songs do you know? Why are rap songs popular?

4. Listen to this famous song, "Keep Ya Head Up", by rapper Tupac (2Pac) Shakur at https://www.youtube.com/watch?v=fAJfDP3b5_U. Who is Tupac singing to?

    a. Mothers are many things. Can you give examples? How do you help your mother?

Vocabulary Definitions

Write the letter of the definition next to the matching word.

1. the music industry (n.) ____
2. ambushed (v.) ____
3. The Strip (n.) ____
4. colleagues (n.) ____
5. paramedics (n.) ____
6. political activist (n.) ____
7. controversial (adj.) ____
8. brutality (n.) ____
9. marginalized (adj.) ____
10. refuge (n.) ____

a. attacked
b. the music business
c. co-workers
d. safe place
e. belonging to a non-dominant group or culture
f. essential medical workers
g. causes disagreement
h. a street of hotels in Las Vegas
i. change maker
j. violence

Answers at the end of the book

Vocabulary Questions

Discuss with a partner.

1. What do you know about *The Strip* in Las Vegas?
2. Why are **paramedics** important?
3. Who is a **political activist** in your country? What are they fighting for?

Your Briefing

352 words - 810-1000L
Place: Las Vegas, Nevada
Time: September 7, 1996

Tupac Shakur, or 2Pac, was robbed and shot five times on November 30th, 1994. He didn't die. As a result, he believed others in the music industry wanted to kill him.

Two years later, on September 7, 1996, Tupac Shakur was ambushed for a second time. At 11:15pm, on Las Vegas Boulevard (the Strip), Shakur was riding in a black BMW with colleagues. At a stoplight, a white Cadillac lined up with Shakur's sedan. Shots were fired. Police and paramedics raced Shakur to a nearby hospital. Shakur was seriously injured with gunshots to his chest, lung, arm, and thigh. At 4:03 a.m., six days later, a 25-year-old Tupac Shakur died.

Tupac Amaru Shakur, also known as Tupac Shakur, later known as 2Pac, was born Lesane Parish Crooks on June 16, 1971. His mother had changed her name from Alice Faye Williams. She chose Afeni, meaning a "lover of people" in Yoruba (a language originating in western African countries) and Shakur, the Arabic word for "light." As a political activist, she joined the controversial Black Panther Party, an organization for social programs and against police brutality.

Afeni changed her baby's name to Tupac Amaru Shakur after important fighters against South American slavery. In his teen years, Tupac Amaru Shakur became 2Pac, a well-respected rapper and actor, famous for championing the marginalized. He rapped with a mixture of anger and empathy, examining difficult truths about poverty, crime, and sexuality in the United States. And, like his revolutionary predecessors, Tupac Shakur died a violent death.

Or did he?

Some people believe that 2Pac is still alive. Assata Shakur, Tupac's godmother, is the only woman to escape from a maximum-security prison in New Jersey. She lives in Cuba where she is still a fugitive. Cuba could have also been a refuge for Tupac, who feared other musicians were jealous and angry at him. One man claims that he was part of the security force that smuggled 2Pac, alive, out of the hospital.

Search on the internet and find pictures that people claim are of Tupac after his death. Do you think these pictures could be Tupac?

Your Mission

Find out who killed Tupac

Who Killed Tupac History Quiz

1. Who was angry with Tupac Shakur, in his opinion?

    a. The Black Panther Party

    b. Tupac Amaru and Tupac Amaru II

    c. Rappers and industry executives

    d. Exploited and marginalized people

2. Why is Assata Shakur famous?

    a. She's 2Pac's mom.

    b. She escaped from prison.

    c. She sang with 2Pac.

    d. 2Pac wrote a song about her.

3. What happened on The Strip?

    a. A black BMW hit a white Cadillac

    b. A white Cadillac got in front of the black BMW

    c. The black BMW pulled up to the white Cadillac

    d. The white Cadillac had an accident with the black BMW

4. What is 2Pac famous for?

    a. Singing songs about his community

    b. Being robbed and shot

    c. Fighting police brutality

    d. Being a political activist

5. Which family member did 2Pac sing about?

    a. his wife

    b. his godmother

    c. his father

    d. his mother

Answers at the end of the book

Discussion Questions

1. Why might 2Pac want people to think he is dead?

2. Why is Cuba a good hiding place for 2Pac? Research Cuba's relationship with the US This article is useful: https://www.newsweek.com/cuba-wont-extradite-american-fugitives-294516. Check Supplement 4: Finding Credible Sources. Complete the checklist to identify possible bias.

3. 2Pac had many relatives who were in the Black Panther Party. How could they have helped him escape? Read about the Black Panther Party at www.britannica.com/topic/Black-Panther-Party.

4. There are other celebrities whom people have seen after they died, for example, Elvis Presley and Juan Gabriel. Are these celebrities hiding? Why do people see them? 5. What are five things that a person should do to disappear? What are five things a person **should not** do?

Projects

1. **Be A Part of History to Complete the Mission:** Who wanted 2Pac killed? Why?

   a. Listen to 2Pac's song, "All Eyez on Me"

   b. What is 2Pac saying? What do you think of the language of the song? Does the song make you angry? Was 2Pac angry? What does the song say about jealousy?

   c. Work with a partner or a group to write a 1-page profile of 2Pac's killer(s). Could it have been another rapper? A record company executive jealous of his money? An old girlfriend angry at his ideas about women? Moms angry that their children admired a Black man who lived "a Thug Life?" What do you think?

2. If 2Pac is hiding in another country, he would have first had to escape from the hospital. How did he do this? Did someone who worked at the hospital hide him? Did he escape alone or did his friends help him? With a partner, use the map of the hospital where 2Pac went after he was shot to show him escape. https://www.umcsn.com/Getting-Around-UMCSN/Documents/UMCSN-Parking-and-Building-Map.pdf

3. How is 2Pac's shooting connected to the shooting of Biggie Smalls (The Notorious B.I.G.)? Use this Venn diagram to discuss the differences and similarities between the two rappers:

TuPac   **Biggie Smalls**

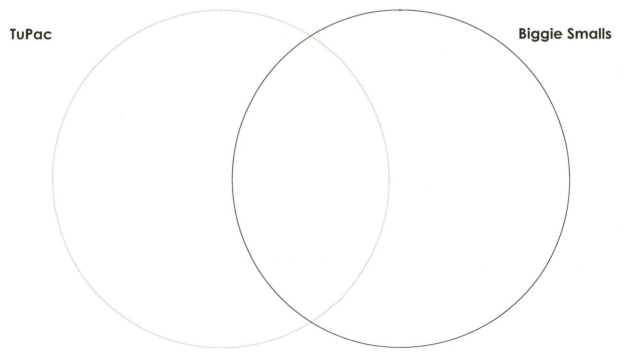

4. Interview your classmates or friends and family. You may have to tell them a little bit about 2Pac's story before they can answer.

Interview Question: Could Tupac still be alive?		
Name	**Answer**	**Reason**
Catherine	No	2Pac loved to write and record music. We would have seen him on YouTube if he were still alive.

References

Holmes, C. (2020, February 11). One man believes Tupac is alive in New Mexico -- And plans to make a movie about it. *Rolling Stone*. https://www.rollingstone.com/music/music-news/tupac-alive-movie-951140/

Ross, M. (2020, February 13). Tupac is alive! And living with the Navajo, new film will argue. *The Mercury News*. https://www.mercurynews.com/2020/02/12/tupac-is-alive-and-living-with-the-navajo-new-film-will-argue/

Tahir, T. (2020, September 13). Tupac is alive after faking his own autopsy, claim conspiracy nuts. *The Sun*. https://www.thesun.co.uk/news/12656822/tupac-alive-faking-autopsy-picture-coroners-report/

Section III - Famous Unsolved Crimes and Criminals

Who Was Jack the Ripper?

Before You Read

1. Have you heard of Jack the Ripper? If so, what do you know about him?

2. Look at the picture and read the letter below allegedly written by Jack the Ripper. What can you guess about this person from the letter?

3. Do you think this was written by the real Jack the Ripper? Why or why not?

4. A **Ripperologist** is someone devoted to solving the mystery of Jack the Ripper. Why do you think regular people would be so interested in murders from hundreds of years ago?

Vocabulary Definitions

Write the letter of the definition next to the matching word.

1. serial killer (n.) ____
2. squeal (v/n) ____
3. mutilated (v.) ____
4. anatomy (n.) ____
5. prostitute (n.) ____
6. perpetrator (n.) ____
7. hoax (n.) ____
8. vigilant (adj.) ____
9. dastardly (adj.) ____

a. a fake story meant to trick people
b. strongly damaged
c. a person who carries out a harmful, illegal, or immoral act
d. a person who murders people repeatedly
e. a high-pitched cry or scream.
f. a study of the structure of the human body.
g. a woman, who engages in sexual activity for payment.
h. cruel and wicked.
i. watching carefully for possible danger.

Answers at the end of the book

Vocabulary Questions

Discuss with a partner.

1. Do you know any infamous *serial killers*? Describe them.
2. What is a situation that has made you *squeal*? Describe it.
3. Give an example of when a person should be *vigilant*.

Your Briefing

507 Words - 1210-1400L
Place: London, England
Time: August 1888

An unknown killer, named Jack the Ripper murdered four women (all *prostitutes*) between August and November 1888 in the Whitechapel area of London.

The five victims historians have determined to be victims of the ripper are:

1. Mary Ann Nicholls: August 31, 1888
2. Annie Chapman: September 8
3. Elizabeth Stride and Catherine Eddowes: September 30
4. Mary Jane Kelly: November 9

In addition, Martha Tabram, stabbed to death on 6 August 1888, is considered by some Ripperologists (experts who study the crimes) to be the first victim, although unlike the rest, she was not mutilated, so she has not been officially considered a victim.

Over the years, the identity and even gender of the Ripper has been widely disputed. It has been suggested that he or she was a doctor or butcher based on the evidence of weapons and the mutilations that occurred, which showed a knowledge of human anatomy. Many theories have been put forward suggesting individuals who might be responsible:

- Prince Albert Victor, Duke of Clarence. Queen Victoria's grandson. Some claim his murderous ways were protected by his family.
- Walter Sickert - A renowned painter who had made sketches and paintings of the Ripper crimes that were almost too accurate....

- James Maybrick - Considered the #1 suspect by many Ripperologists, due to a mysterious diary uncovered in 1992 where Maybrick claimed to be the Ripper. Strangely, he was poisoned by his own wife and there are many theories about whether his diary could be real evidence or just a hoax
- Jill the Ripper - 'the mad midwife' Some claim Jack could have been a woman with medical knowledge, such as a midwife. This might explain why the killer was able to move easily and was never caught.

Some people think there was no Jack the Ripper. Violence to prostitutes was not uncommon at this time and there were many instances of women being brutalized. But the nature of these murders strongly suggests a single perpetrator.

The murderer is also thought to have sometimes written letters to several public figures. These letters have never been proved to be authentic and may have been hoaxes.

For example, in September of 1888 a letter was submitted to the police signed Jack the Ripper. It was released by police and caused widespread fear and panic. This was the letter that inspired the name Jack the Ripper and the police released it hoping that making the story public would aid in catching the Ripper.

However, Jack the Ripper was never caught, though he is not thought to have killed again after November 1888. Some believe he could have been stopped by vigilant citizens, while others believe he had completed whatever his dastardly goals were.

The legacy of these brutal murders is still seen today with the rise of the Ripperologist, an individual who has made it their mission to provide the 'definitive solution' to the murders. One thing is for sure, finding the identity of this killer would be solving one of history's greatest mysteries!

Your Mission

Can you discover Jack the Ripper's identity and stop him?

Letter submitted to the police by Jack the Ripper

with original spelling and punctuation mistakes) from BBC America Editors, 2012.

25th September 1888

Dear Boss,
I keep on hearing the police have caught me but they wont fix me just yet. I have laughed when they look so clever and talk about being on the right track. That joke about Leather Apron gave me real fits. I am down on w****s and I shan't quit ripping them till I do get buckled. Grand work the last job was. I gave the lady no time to squeal. How can they catch me now?

I love my work and want to start again. You will soon hear of me with my funny little games. I saved some of the proper red stuff in a ginger beer bottle over the last job to write with but it went thick like glue and I can't use it. Red ink is fit enough I hope ha. ha. The next job I do I shall clip the lady's ears off and send to the police officers just for jolly wouldn't you. Keep this letter back till I do a bit more work, then give it out straight. My knife's so nice and sharp I want to get to work right away if I get a chance. Good Luck.

Yours truly,
Jack the Ripper
Don't mind me giving the trade name.
P.S. Wasn't good enough to post this before I got all the red ink off my hands, curse it. No luck yet. They say I'm a doctor now. Ha ha.

Jack the Ripper History Quiz

1. How many confirmed victims did Jack the Ripper have?

    a. 4

    b. 5

    c. 6

    d. 7

2. Which statement about a person suspected of being Jack the Ripper is true?

    a. Walter Sickert took detailed photographs of the scenes of Jack the Ripper's crimes.

    b. James Maybrick confessed to the crimes but then said he was joking.

    c. Prince Albert Victor, grandson of Queen Victoria, is one suspect.

    d. Some DNA evidence suggests a woman named Jill Kelly was the real killer.

3. Jack the Ripper's victims were....

    a. male

    b. female

4. Where did the nickname "Jack the Ripper" come from?

    a. the police

    b. a newspaper

    c. the public

    d. a letter claimed to be written by the killer.

5. True or False - Jack the Ripper had no confirmed victims after November 1888.

    a. true

    b. false

Discussion Questions

1. The story of Jack the Ripper has remained so popular for hundreds of years that it has even created *Ripperologists* - those devoted to solving the mystery.

    a. Would you like to be a *Ripperologist*? Why or why not?

2. Which of the possible identities of Jack the Ripper sounds the most believable?

3. What do you think the Ripper's motivation was? Why did he only kill female prostitutes?

4. Jack the Ripper is believed to have killed only between August and November of 1888.

5. Why do you think Jack the Ripper stopped?

6. Do you know of any infamous serial killers from your home city or country? Describe them. Were they ever caught? How were they caught?

7. There have been many movies, TV shows, and books about serial killers. Why do you think many people are so interested in learning about them? Have you seen or read about any serial killers? What did you learn?

Projects

1. **Be a Part of History to Complete the Mission!** Write 1 page. Choose one or more of these questions to consider as you write:

    a. What was Jack the Ripper's real identity?

    b. b.   How will you catch Jack the Ripper?

    c. c.   How will the public react to him being caught?

2. Research Jack the Ripper and answer the following:

3. What other theories about the Ripper's identity do you think are possible? Why?

4. Imagine you are the police trying to catch Jack the Ripper.

5. Design a poster that you would put up to warn/get help from the public!

6. Research police methods on catching killers. **(**See "Supplements 4: Finding Credible Sources" and "5: Citing Sources" for help on using sources)

    a. Which methods do you think are most effective?

    b. What would you do if you were the police trying to catch a killer?

    c. Which methods would you use?

7. Interview your classmates or friends and family: How would you catch a serial killer?

Interview Question: Imagine you are the police: What's the best way to catch a serial killer?		
Name	**Answer**	**Reason**
Taylor	Behavior Analysis	Check out the book Mindhunters

References

BBC America. (2012, December 14). *The origin of the name Jack the Ripper.* https://www.bbcamerica.com/blogs/the-origin-of-the-name-jack-the-ripper--51225

BBC America. (2013, January 13). *The 5 craziest Jack the Ripper theories.* https://www.bbcamerica.com/shows/ripper-street/blog/2013/01/the-5-craziest-jack-the-ripper-theories

History.com Editors. (2010, November 8). *Jack the Ripper.* HISTORY. https://www.history.com/topics/british-history/jack-the-ripper

Kilday, A. & Nash, D. (2018) *The Ripper of our nightmares: 5 theories about Jack the Ripper's identity.* History Extra. https://www.historyextra.com/period/victorian/jack-the-ripper-identity-theories-nightmares/

The Osage Indian Murders

Delegation of the Osage tribe with President Coolidge, 1924

Before You Read

1. What do you know about the Native American Indians?

2. Do you know about indigenous people in your part of the world?

3. What can we learn by studying the traditions of indigenous cultures?

4. Wealth has many benefits but also can lead to problems. What sorts of problems arise when people have a great deal of money?

Vocabulary Definitions

Write the letter of the definition next to the matching word.

1. tribe (n.) _____
2. migrated (v.) _____
3. reservation (n.) _____
4. uprooting (v.) _____
5. unscrupulous (adj.) _____
6. passed down (v.) _____
7. guardian (n.) _____
8. deceased (adj.) _____
9. remains (n.) _____
10. appealed (v.) _____
11. overshadowed (v.) _____

a. moved from one place to another
b. asked for something in a serious way
c. a close group of people linked by family, societal, religious, or economic ties
d. to be made less important than something or someone else
e. having no or low moral values
f. a person who takes responsibility for another
g. given from one person to another, usually from an older generation to a younger
h. no longer alive
i. land set aside for native people to live on
j. moving from a comfortable place such as a home
k. what is left of a dead body

Answers at the end of the book

Vocabulary Questions

Discuss with a partner.

1. Are there any native **tribes** in your country or region? Were there in the past?
2. Have you ever done or witnessed something **unscrupulous**? How did you feel about it?
3. Give an example of something that was **passed down** in your family.

Your Briefing

593 words -1010 -1200L
Place: Osage County, Oklahoma
Time: 1921-1925

1897 found the *tribe* of Osage Native American Indians living in the northeastern part of Oklahoma. As was the case with many Native American tribes, though the Osage had originated in the eastern part of the United States, wars, migration, and the government kept them moving west until they were forced to move onto a *reservation* in Kansas. Later, they agreed to sell this land to the government and resettle on a reservation in Oklahoma. This could not have been an easy or pleasant experience for them as they had to keep *uprooting* their homes and moving to new areas, most often on foot. Moreover, the new area in Oklahoma was poor land for farming.

Fortunately, in 1897, oil was discovered on the Osage land. As a result, by the 1920s, the Osage were taking in hundreds of millions of dollars a year (by today's standards) and were known to be the richest people on Earth. Unfortunately, all this wealth attracted the attention of the government and many *unscrupulous* people.

Even though the Osage owned their land and the money made from its oil belonged to them, this was done through a system called "headrights". Headrights, or the ability to collect money from oil on the land, could be *passed down* to children or other relatives even if they were not Osage. In 1921, the US government passed a law that required every person with these headrights who was more than 50% Osage to have a *guardian*. These guardians would manage the money for the Osage and prevent them from spending all of it. However, the guardians, who were always white men, were able to keep some of the money for themselves and often prevented the

Osage from spending their money as they liked. The guardians also had a lot of influence over who would inherit the headrights of *deceased* Osage. Around this time, some suspicious things started to happen with the Osage landowners.

The early 1920's was referred to as the "Reign of Terror" for the Osage people. During that time, over 20 people were murdered in Osage county—18 of them were Native American and several were all from one family. In May of 1921, hunters found the *remains* of an Osage woman named Anna Brown. After an investigation, her death was ruled to be accidental and her headrights passed to her mother, Lizzie Q. Kyle, who died a few months later. Over the next few months, two of Anna's cousins were shot dead and her sister died when a bomb exploded in her house. Clues pointed to a business associate, a white man named William Hale. Interestingly, Hale's nephew was married to an Osage woman, Mollie Kyle. In addition to her own headrights, she had inherited those of her murdered sisters, mother, and cousin. During the trial of William Hale and his nephews, it was revealed that Mollie was slowly being poisoned.

As the deaths piled up, local officials and the Office of Indian Affairs seemed incapable of, or uninterested in, solving the crimes. Out of desperation, the Osage *appealed* to the newly formed Federal Bureau of Investigation (FBI). It was their first murder case. Hale and his accomplices were convicted of murder and conspiracy. In 1925, Congress changed the law allowing only Osage people to inherit headrights. However, by then over 100 suspected murders had occurred and very few were ever solved. It was a devastating time for the Osage people and the notoriety of the "Reign of Terror" *overshadowed* their general reputation as a peaceful and hard-working people.

Your Mission

Prevent the murders of the Osage people.

Osage Indian Murders History Quiz

1. The Osage tribe first formed in _____ .

    a. Kansas

    b. Oklahoma

    c. the Eastern United States

    d. various areas

2. Oil was discovered on Osage lands in _____ .

    a. 1897

    b. 1921

    c. 1925

    d. 1997

3. The official reason Osage were given guardians to help them with _____ .

    a. drilling oil

    b. education

    c. saving their money

    d. farming

4. _____ was one of the first Osage victims of the "Reign of Terror".

    a. Mollie Kyle

    b. Lizzie Q. Kyle

    c. Anna Brown

    d. William Hale

5. The Osage asked the FBI to help them because _____ .

    a. the FBI was very famous

    b. the FBI offered to help

    c. the FBI was responsible for helping native people

    d. no one else would help them

Answers at the end of the book

Discussion Questions

1. Why do you think the United States government implemented the guardian program for the Osage Indians?

2. Only people who were more than 50% Osage were required to have a guardian. What role do you think our "blood" or genetics play in who we are as people? What role can stereotypes about people's ethnicities play in how they are treated?

3. The Osage case was the first time the FBI tackled a murder case. Do you know of any famous cases the FBI has solved or been unable to solve?

4. The Osage felt their reputation was highly damaged by the "Reign of Terror". Why or how is a community affected when they suffer from negative publicity, even when it is not their fault?

Projects

1. **Be a Part of History to Complete the Mission:** Travel back to 1920 when the oil is pumping, the Osage are getting rich, and none have been murdered yet. How will you stop the "Reign of Terror"? Will you start by talking to the Osage people themselves or to the people who want to take their money? You know about William Hale and his nephews, but there are other people to watch out for too.

2. Continue the story- After some of those guilty of murdering the Osage were put in prison and the government changed the law allowing only Osage to inherit headrights, did life return to normal? Write about 1-2 pages from the perspective of an Osage person living during this time.

3. Research the Osage Indians-What are some other ways we can remember them other than for the "Reign of Terror"?

4. Research an indigenous group from your area of the world- Where did they come from? What were their accomplishments? What was/is their relationship with the national government of their area? As you read, use "Supplement 6: List of Sources or References") to help you determine how biased or unbiased the information is.

5. Write a letter to the United States government asking them to change the law requiring the Osage landowners to have guardians. Be sure to include two or three strong reasons why the law should be changed.

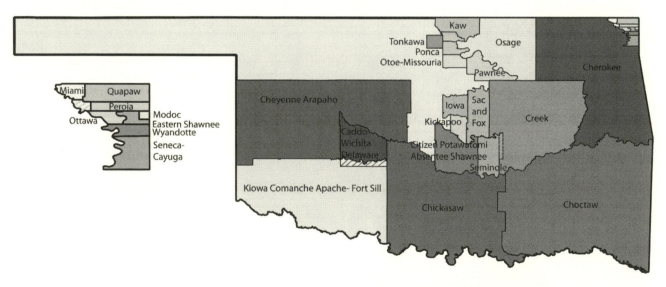

Map of the tribes of Oklahoma's territory, 2012. Wikimedia Commons.

References

Grann, D. (2017). *Killers of the flower moon: The Osage murders and the birth of the FBI*. Vintage.

Howell M. (2014, January 12). Greed, collusion lead to Osage murders. (2014, January 12). *The Oklahoman*. https://www.oklahoman.com/article/3923054/stories-of-the-ages-greed-collusion-lead-to-reign-of-terror-against-osage-nation

Encyclopedia Britannica. (n.d.). Osage. (n.d.). In *Britannica.com* Retrieved 17 May 2021 from https://www.britannica.com/topic/Osage

D. B. Cooper, Skyjacker

Police Sketches of DB Cooper. FBI.

Before You Read

1. Read this quote from the man commonly known as D. B. Cooper: "Miss, you'd better look at that note. I have a bomb."

    a. What kind of person would say a quote like this? In what situation?

    b. What would you do if a person said this to you?

    c. What do you think this person wants?

2. Are there any famous criminals in your country's history? What made them famous?

3. Why do people sometimes root for criminals?

4. What makes some crimes interesting?

5. Do you know any famous crimes that have never been solved?

6. Is there a "perfect crime"?

Vocabulary Definitions

Write the letter of the definition next to the matching word

1. hijack (v.) ____
2. ransom (n/v) ____
3. parachute (n/v) ____
4. police sketch (n.) ____
5. wilderness (n.) ____
6. sniper (n.) ___

a. a device that allows you to safely jump from an airplane
b. to illegally take control of a vehicle by force or intimidation
c. a place, like a forest, that is empty of people and very wild
d. a drawing made from the memories of people who saw a criminal
e. to demand you get something, usually money, before you release something/someone to safety
f. a person trained to shoot people from a long distance

Answers at the end of the book

Vocabulary Questions

Discuss with a partner.

1. Would you ever jump out of an airplane wearing a **parachute**? Why or why not?
2. What if you were asked to describe someone for a **police sketch**? Do you think you would be good at remembering the details? Think of a stranger you saw recently (at the store, on the street, etc.) and describe them to your partner to draw. Compare their work with your memory!
3. How long do you think you could survive in the **wilderness** by yourself? What supplies would you want to have?

Your Briefing

676 Words - 1010L - 1200L
Place: 10,000 ft (3,000 m) in the air above Southwestern Washington State - USA
Time: November 24, 1971

It's the night before Thanksgiving, 1971, at Portland International Airport in Oregon. A man in his mid-40's wearing a black business suit, white shirt, and black tie pays $20 in cash for a one-way ticket to Seattle, Washington. Northwest Orient Airlines flight 305 takes off on time for its 30-minute flight, climbing into the afternoon sky over the Columbia River and dense, dark forest to the north. The Boeing 727-100 levels off, and the man in seat 18C hands a note to the head flight attendant, Florence Schaffner, who puts it away in her purse, thinking the man with sharp, brown eyes is trying to give her his phone number.

Before she could walk away the man, who gave his name as

"Dan Cooper" on his ticket, leaned in and whispered, "Miss, you'd better look at that note. I have a bomb." Cooper opened his dark briefcase, which contained eight red cylinders and a battery. The man, who remained calm, polite, even pleasant, throughout the flight, demanded $200,000 in US dollars ($1.3 million in 2020 dollars), four *parachutes*, and a fuel truck to be ready in Seattle: he had *hijacked* the airplane.

Money recovered from the DB Cooper heist

The pilots radioed the demands to the airline, which agreed to pay the ransom immediately, and to the FBI. All the while, the other passengers were unaware; they were told that a "minor mechanical difficulty" was causing their delay as they circled above the Puget Sound just west of Seattle for almost two hours. During this time, the company rushed to get the cash, and the FBI found acceptable parachutes at a local skydiving school. All the while, Cooper, now wearing dark sunglasses, sat in his seat quietly smoking cigarettes and sipping his second whiskey and soda. The flight finally landed at 5:39 p.m., and Cooper ordered that all the window shades be closed, to avoid the possibility of the FBI snipers shooting him while the plane was parked. After the parachutes and 10,000 unmarked $20 bills were delivered in a plain backpack, Cooper released the 36 other passengers, leaving only him, Schaffner, and the pilots. The silver jet was now full of fuel. At 7:40 p.m. Cooper told the crew to take off and head toward Mexico City.

Behind Cooper's plane, above and below, out of sight, two F-106 fighter jets followed the plane through the black night as it headed south, back over the vast *wilderness* below. Cooper had told the pilots to fly as slow as possible and also very low. Suddenly, the pilot saw a red warning light which told him that the rear airstairs had been opened. A few minutes later, at 8:13 p.m., the crew felt a bump: Cooper had jumped into the freezing rainstorm above the empty pine and fir forests southwest of Mt. St. Helens. He was never seen, dead or alive, again.

Many say that Cooper couldn't have opened his parachute in time from that altitude, and that he died as soon as he hit the ground that night. Even if he did, the remote location, bad weather that night, and Cooper's lack of proper clothing or supplies all would have made it difficult for him to survive for long in the forest. On the other hand, there have been people over the years who have claimed to be D.B. Cooper, or to know who he was. So far, though, none of these have proven true, and the FBI closed the case in 2016. Some of the most convincing theories about the skyjacker's identity have included army veterans with parachuting experience, lifelong criminals, and people who worked for the airlines.

Nine years after the crime, a boy was digging in the sand on a beach just down the river from Portland when he discovered three packets of the ransom money totaling $5,800. The money was badly damaged, but the serial numbers matched. The rest of the money has never been found. Did D. B. Cooper survive the jump? How did the money get there and what happened to the rest? Who was D. B. Cooper?

Your Mission

Find out the true identity of D. B. Cooper, and what really happened to him. Determine if you should stop the hijacking before it begins.

D. B. Cooper History Quiz

1. D. B. Cooper's flight started in ____ .

    a. Seattle

    b. Portland

    c. Vancouver

    d. Washington

2. Cooper said that he had a ____ .

    a. gun

    b. parachute

    c. parachute

    d. bomb

3. Cooper's escape was notable because

    a. he hijacked a jet fighter

    b. he hid in a fuel tanker

    c. he parachuted from the plane

    d. he disguised himself as a flight attendant

4. What did Cooper NOT demand as part of his ransom?

    a. money

    b. parachutes

    c. guns

    d. fuel

5. None of the ransom money was ever found.

    a. true

    b. false

Answers at the end of the book

Discussion Questions

1. What do you think actually happened to Cooper? Why do you think this?

2. Is there ever a good reason to commit a crime such as skyjacking? Give examples to support your opinion.

3. Look up the song "D. B. Cooper" by Todd Snider. Do you agree with the interpretation in the lyrics? How does it compare with the facts of the story? (See "Supplement 8: Opinions vs. Facts".)

Projects

1. **Be a Part of History to Complete the Mission:** Travel back to November 1971 at the departure gate at Portland International Airport. D.B. Cooper is about to board the plane. What do you do?

2. Write a first-person story about what you think happened on November 24, 1971, from the perspective of Cooper. What is he thinking? Why is he doing this? What is his story?

3. Many people see D. B. Cooper as a folk hero, a person who is liked a lot by people for something they did that was illegal or controversial. Do you agree? Like in the song, do you hope that Cooper is never caught? Why or why not?

4. Interview your classmates or friends and family:

Interview Question: Do you think D. B. Cooper is a folk hero? Why or why not?		
Name	**Answer**	**Reason**
Andrew	No	Because he was a criminal

References

Miss Cellania. (2019, August 26). 11 theories on the true identity of D.B. Cooper. Considerable. https://www.considerable.com/entertainment/history/who-was-db-cooper/

Crime Museum. (2018, August 6). D. B. Cooper. https://www.crimemuseum.org/crime-library/cold-cases/d-b-cooper/

Federal Bureau of Investigation. (2016, May 18). D. B. Cooper hijacking. https://www.fbi.gov/history/famous-cases/db-cooper-hijacking

Snider, T. (2000) D. B. Cooper [Song]. on Happy to Be Here [Album]. Oh Boy Records.

Usborne, D. (2008, January 3). The unsolved crime of the century: the hunt for D B Cooper. The Independent. https://www.independent.co.uk/news/world/americas/the-unsolved-crime-of-the-century-the-hunt-for-d-b-cooper-767808.html

Elizabeth Stewart Gardner Museum Heist

Empty frames in the Isabella Stewart Gardner Museum still hang where stolen items used to be

Before You Read

1. Have you ever visited an art museum? Where? What did you see?
2. Can you think of some famous artists?
3. How much are famous artworks worth? Why do you think they're often so valuable?
4. Do you think it is easy to solve art thefts? Why do you think so

Vocabulary Definitions

Write the letter of the definition next to the matching word.

1. heist (n.) ____
2. renowned (adj.) ____
3. will (n.) ____
4. stipulation (n.) ____
5. winding down (v.) ____
6. devastating (adj.) ____
7. absconding (v.) ____
8. recover (v.) ____
9. resolution (n.) ____
10. at hand (adv.) ____
11. anonymous (adj.) ____

a. condition or requirement that is part of an agreement
b. slowly coming to an end
c. a robbery
d. known by many people
e. causing great shock or sadness
f. of an unknown name or identity
g. leave quickly and secretly
h. about to happen
i. a legal document stating what to do with one's money and possessions after death
j. an answer to a problem or difficulty
k. to find something stolen or lost

Answers at the end of the book

Vocab Questions

Discuss with a partner.

1. If you were writing your *will*, what would you leave and to whom?
2. How do you like to *wind down* at the end of the day?
3. Brainstorm some reasons why a person would want to write an *anonymous* letter or make an *anonymous* phone call.

Your Briefing

500 words - 1010L-1200L
Place: Boston, Massachusetts
Time: March 18, 1990

On January 1, 1903, Elizabeth Stuart Gardener opened a museum in Boston, Massachusetts containing many valuable paintings by *renowned* artists such as Rembrandt, Vermeer, and Botticelli. She and her husband had collected these during the many years they had spent traveling the world. In her *will*, she left money to maintain the museum but with the *stipulation* that the museum not be changed.

For over 65 years, the museum remained as Gardner had left it. Then in the early hours of March 18, 1990, as the people of Boston were *winding down* their St. Patrick's Day celebrations, the Elisabeth Stewart Gardner Museum experienced a *devastating* change. Two men dressed as police officers asked to be let into the museum. Once inside, they handcuffed the two security guards, Rick Abath and Randy Hestand. Thanks to motion detectors in the museum, we know the thieves first entered the Dutch Room at 1:48 a.m. where they took several paintings as well as an ancient Chinese *gu*, a special kind of drinking vessel. Next, the two men headed to the Short Gallery where they took more paintings and an eagle sculpture from the top of a Napoleonic flag. A Manet painting was also taken from the Blue Room although the motion detector did not record any movement in that room during the 81-minute robbery. Finally, the thieves checked on the guards before *absconding* with 13 works of art estimated to be worth over $500 million.

Despite the efforts of the FBI and a $100 million reward for the return of the missing art (and an additional $10,000 for the Chinese *gu*), the art was never returned and the mystery was never solved.

So, who was responsible for America's most famous art theft and where are the missing art pieces? Was it the security guard, Rick Abath? Early on the night of the crime, he had opened and shut the side door of the museum. He claimed this was part of his nightly routine to make sure the door was locked, but security footage showed this was untrue. Was it Whitey Bulger, the powerful head of the Winter Hill Gang? In terms of crime, nothing happened in Boston without him knowing about it. Or perhaps it was another gang in Boston such as the Merlino gang who had been working on a plan to rob the museum back in 1981?

Police and the FBI questioned many suspects but could make no arrests nor *recover* any work. A *resolution* seemed to be *at hand* in 1994 when an *anonymous* letter was sent to the museum. The writer claimed to know where the missing pieces were and offered to return them for $2.6 million. The letter directed the museum to communicate its answer through a secret code printed in the newspaper. Though the museum agreed, the letter writer seemed to change their mind and no deal was made. To this day, empty frames on the walls of the museum wait for the return of their missing contents.

Your Mission

Solve the crime! Find out who was responsible for the theft of the art. More importantly, find the missing pieces and return them to their home.

Elizabeth Stewart Gardener History Quiz

1. In what year did Elizabeth Stewart Gardener open her museum?

     a. 1903

     b. 1981

     c. 1990

     d. 1994

2. How many guards were on duty the night of the robbery?

     a. 2

     b. 3

     c. 4

     d. 5

3. The security guards let the robbers in because the robbers were dressed as _____.

     a. security guards

     b. police officers

     c. electricians

     d. tourists

4. What is strange about the art stolen from the Blue Room?

     a. The door to that room was locked.

     b. Nothing in the Blue Room was very valuable.

     c. The alarms showed no one went in there during the robbery.

     d. The Blue Room was known to be haunted.

5. Why was the crime boss Whitey Bulger considered a suspect?

     a. He had made other plans to steal art.

     b. He was seen near the museum the night of the heist.

     c. He told someone he had done it.

     d. He knew about all crimes committed in the area.

Answers at the end of the book

Discussion Questions

1. Though art can be very valuable, it is not easy to sell without getting caught. Why do you think some criminals choose to steal art rather than other items that may be less difficult to sell?

2. Many people were interviewed about this crime and police followed many leads. Yet 30 years after the theft, the whereabouts of the missing works is still a mystery. What problems do you think the police encountered while trying to solve this crime?

3. Experts estimate that the total of the missing art pieces is $500 million. Why do you think they are worth so much? Would you spend millions of dollars on a famous piece of art if you could?

4. During the years prior to the theft, the Elizabeth Stewart Gardner Museum received tips about various plots to break in and steal art. Is there something the museum should have done differently to prevent the theft?

Projects

1. **Be a Part of History to Complete the Mission:** Write about 1 page describing where the thieves went after they left the museum and what they did with the art.

2. Create a code. In 1994, the director of the Elizabeth Stewart Gardner Museum received a letter offering to return the art in exchange for $2.6 million. She was directed to put all her communications in code and publish them in the newspaper. Decide if you will accept the offer and create a code letting the thieves know your decision.

3. Do some research. There have been many famous art heists; some were solved and some were not. Research a famous art heist. Where did it occur? What was stolen? How did the thieves get in? Was the art recovered? As you conduct your research, use the See "Supplement 4: Finding Credible Sources" in order to ensure your sources are credible. Share your findings with your class.

4. Interview the robbers: If you had a chance to interview the two men who committed the art heist, what would you ask them? Create some questions and role play the interview with a partner.

Questions	Answers
Ex. Had you ever met Rick Abath before the night of the theft?	Ex. No! Of course not!
Ex. What did you do with the stolen art?	Ex. Well....

References

FBI Boston. (2013, March 18). *FBI provides new information regarding the 1990 Isabella Stewart Gardner Museum art heist.* https://archives.fbi.gov/archives/boston/press-releases/2013/fbi-provides-new-information-regarding-the-1990-isabella-stewart-gardner-museum-art-heist

Isabella Stewart Gardner Museum (n.d.). *Learn about the theft.* https://www.gardnermuseum.org/about/theft

Kurkjian, S. (2013, March 10). Guard who opened the door to robbers in notorious Gardner Museum heist under suspicion 23 years later. *Boston Globe.* https://www3.bostonglobe.com/metro/2013/03/10/guard-who-opened-door-robbers-notorious-gardner-museum-heist-under-suspicion-years-later/1TUiDyi1GbcnBgQT64olSP/story.html

Floating Feet

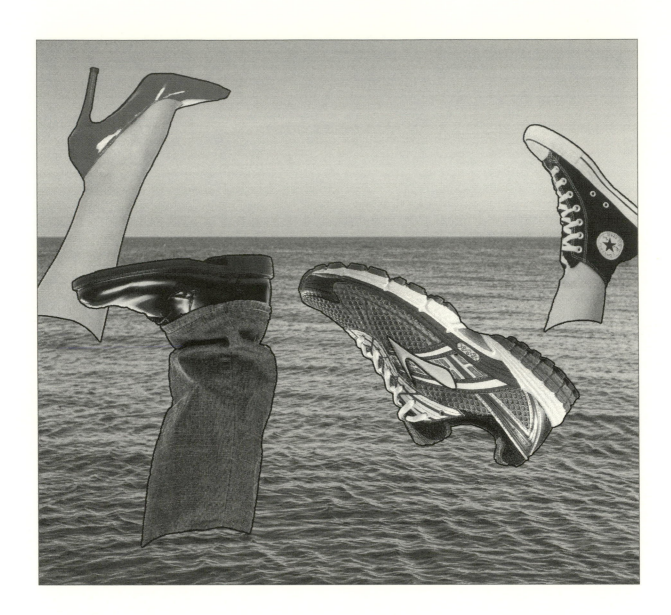

Before You Read

1. Have you ever found anything strange or interesting while walking on the beach, or in another natural place?

   a. What was it?

   b. Did you pick it up? Why or why not?

   c. Where do you think it came from?

   d. Who do you think it belonged to?

   e. How do you think it got there?

Vocabulary Definitions

Write the letter of the definition next to the matching word

1. driftwood (n.) ____
2. shoreline (n.) ____
3. cozy (adj.) ____
4. unidentified (adj.) ____
5. phantom (adj/n) ____
6. currents (n.) ____
7. tides (n.) ____
8. uninhabited (adj.) ____
9. respectively (adv.) ____
10. encased (v.) ____
11. precedent (n.) ____
12. speculated (v.) ____
13. remains (n.) ____
14. hoax (n.) ____
15. serial killer (n.) ____

16. up and down movement of water caused by the moon's gravity
   a. the area where a body of water meets the land
   b. comfortable, nice
   c. in the order already mentioned
   d. a fake story meant to trick people
   e. wood that floats in water and sometimes wash up on the beach
   f. an example in the past to support a statement
   g. no one is living there
   h. water in motion from one place to another, side to side
   i. unknown person or thing
   j. guessed, without strong evidence
   k. a person who murders people repeatedly
   l. mysterious
   m. covered, surrounded
   n. the physical parts of a body left behind after death

Answers at the end of the book

Vocabulary Questions

Discuss with a partner.

1. What is the most *uninhabited* place you've been to? What was it like there?
2. What happens to most people's *remains* after they die in your country? Compare and contrast with other countries and/or cultures.
3. Are there any famous *serial killers* in your country? Were they ever caught?

Your Briefing

643 Words - 1010L - 1200L
Place: Gabriola Island, British Columbia, Canada
Time: August 26, 2007

You sit on a large piece of driftwood, staring down at your foot as it draws circles in the cool sand. You look up across the Strait of Georgia toward Vancouver, some 80 km away across the steel blue waters of the Salish Sea. A couple is hiking along the shoreline, laughing, and holding each other close, enjoying the sun and warmth that only last for a short time in this part of Canada. You look down at your feet again, cozy in the soft, gray sand, when you hear a scream. The woman is covering her mouth, backing away while pointing at some small, white thing near the water, while the man is poking at it with a stick. A minute later, the woman starts talking on her cell phone, saying something like: "Hello, police? My husband and I are on the beach and we found a white Reebok sneaker. What? Oh, and there are bones sticking out of it..."

The foot the couple found that day was the second in what would be more than 20 that washed up on the shores around the Salish Sea, which separates Washington State from British Columbia. While some have been identified through DNA and other methods, the majority remain unidentified. So, while there are official explanations for some of these phantom feet, who do the rest belong to? Where are they coming from? What (or who) killed them? And where are the other parts of the bodies?

The waters in this part of the world are cold and feature fast moving currents and large tides. There are also more than 400 islands and nearly 7,500 km of coast, much of it remote and uninhabited. However, at the north and south ends of this water are the cities of Vancouver, B.C. and Seattle, Washington, respectively, with a combined metro population of close to 7 million people. And of those who die in this region, some obviously end up in the water. But why? Fishing accidents and suicides have been positively linked to several of those missing feet, with the boot-encased foot of one fisherman found floating nearly 25 years after he went missing.

But how do the feet stay afloat and intact for so long? One Canadian official stated that the feet could have separated naturally at a joint, weak points during decomposition. The shoes helped the feet to both be preserved and float in the strong currents of the Pacific Ocean.

There is a precedent for sneakers traveling over large distances, both of time and space. In 1990 a container ship heading from Seoul, South Korea to Seattle lost some of its cargo in a storm, including some 40,000 pairs of Nikes. For years, these shoes would wash up all along the West Coast of the US, with people collecting them off the beach and attending meetups to find matching pairs to wear and sell. The Nikes have also continued to follow the currents, being found in

Hawaii, Australia, and back "home" in Asia.

Could this help prove that some of the mystery feet of the Salish Sea came from the Pacific Ocean? Some have speculated that the remains could have come from shipwrecks in the open ocean, or as far away as Asia, perhaps including victims of the 2004 tsunami. The many feet appearing on the beaches of Washington and British Columbia have made local beachgoers both scared and curious. There have even been hoaxes where people have put animal bones in shoes and left them on the beach to scare others. Some have even said that this could be the work of a serial killer.

In the end, each of these floating feet came from a person who is no longer with us. Can you help solve the mystery, and bring *closure* to families whose relatives have been missing, maybe for years?

Your Mission

Go to the Salish Sea and interview locals, police, and others. Use science and reasoning to figure out where the unidentified feet are coming from, and why. Is the answer sad, yet simple, such as suicides or accidents? Or is the real reason bigger - or maybe darker - than officials have been telling us?

References

CBC News. (2007, August 31). *Discovery of unattached human feet baffles B.C. police*. CBC. https://www.cbc.ca/news/canada/british-columbia/discovery-of-unattached-human-feet-baffles-b-c-police-1.671205

CBC News. (2008, June 19). *'Foot' hoax on B.C. south coast despicable: police*. CBC. https://www.cbc.ca/news/canada/british-columbia/foot-hoax-on-b-c-south-coast-despicable-police-1.711228

CTV News. (2011, August 30). *Another foot washes ashore -- this time in Vancouver*. CTV. https://bc.ctvnews.ca/another-foot-washes-ashore-this-time-in-vancouver-1.690474

Kassam, A. (2017, December 14). Human foot found on Canada shoreline – the 13th such discovery in a decade. *The Guardian*. https://www.theguardian.com/world/2017/dec/13/canada-human-foot-british-columbia

Mckie, R. (1992, November 22). Oceanographers find lessons in the great Nike shoe spill. *The Seattle Times*. https://archive.seattletimes.com/archive/?date=19921122&slug=1526004

PMF IAS. (2018, July 31). *Pacific Ocean currents | Phytoplankton and fishing*. https://www.pmfias.com/pacific-ocean-currents-phytoplankton-fishing-zones/

Postmedia News. (2012, February 17). Severed foot found in B.C. lake belonged to missing fisherman, police say. *National Post*. https://nationalpost.com/news/canada/severed-foot-found-in-b-c-lake-belonged-to-missing-fisherman-police-say/

The SeaDoc Society. (n.d.). About the Salish sea. https://www.seadocsociety.org/about-the-salish-sea

Floating Feet History Quiz

1. The floating feet washed up from the waters of _____.

    a. Lake Washington

    b. The Columbia River

    c. The Salish Sea

    d. Seattle Harbor

2. More than _____ feet have been found so far.

    a. 10

    b. 20

    c. 30

    d. 40

3. The oldest foot was found more than _____ years after the person went missing.

    a. 10

    b. 15

    c. 20

    d. 25

4. 40,000 _____ fell off of a ship in 1990.

    a. feet

    b. boots

    c. bones

    d. Nikes

5. _____ of the feet's identities have been discovered.

    a. None

    b. Some

    c. Most

    d. All

Answers at the end of the book

Discussion Questions

1. Have you or anyone you know ever found something strange or mysterious? Describe it, and what happened.

2. What would you do if you found a human foot in a shoe on a beach?

    a. Would you examine it closely?

    b. Would you touch it?

    c. Who would you call?

    d. Do you think it would be better just to leave it and not tell anybody? Why or why not?

    e. How do you think it could have gotten there?

Projects

1. **Be a Part of History to Complete the Mission**: What do you think is the best explanation for the floating feet? What is the most logical answer? What could be a logical fallacy that someone might make when thinking of this mystery? See "Supplement 9: Logic and Logical Fallacies."

2. Have you ever heard of a "message in a bottle"? What is it?

    a. Why do people write them?

    b. Imagine you are standing on a beach, holding a bottle with a cork, pen, and paper. Write a message in a bottle and "float" (send) it to a friend or family member.

3. Interview your classmates or friends and family:

Interview Question: What would you do if you found a human foot in a shoe on a beach?		
Name	**Answer**	**Reason**
Andrew	Sell it.	Could make a lot of money for it on eBay!

Section IV - Disappearances

Prepared by Agent Andrew Lawrence

Why Did the Olmecs Disappear?

The Olmecs were able to carve detailed sculptures like these gigantic heads, all without the use of metal tools. These are one of the few traces left today of this once powerful civilization.

Before You Read

1. Do you know any famous civilizations that collapsed or disappeared?

    a. Who were they?

    b. What are they famous for?

    c. What contributions did they give to future civilizations?

    d. How did they collapse/disappear? Do we know for sure?

2. What do you know about the ancient people of Mesoamerica (the area of Central Mexico down through Central America)?

    a. Have you heard of the Aztecs or Mayans? What about the Olmecs?

    b. What do you think life was like 2,500 years ago in this part of the world?

    c. Tell your partner what you think these people did for food, shelter, art, war, and so on.

    d. What was life like in your country at this time?

Vocabulary Definitions

Write the letter of the definition next to the matching word

1. ruins (n.) ____
2. descendants (n.) ____
3. monuments (n.) ____
4. mighty (adj.) ____
5. sacrifices (n.) ____
6. tablet (n.) ____
7. pictograms (n.) ____
8. reliance (n.) ____
9. decline (v.) ____
10. peninsula (n.) ____

a. a family's or group's children, grandchildren, and so on
b. the killing of an animal or person for religious or cultural reasons
c. powerful, advanced
d. the broken and abandoned remains of buildings or other structures from the past
e. small drawings that represent words or ideas, such as found in ancient Egypt
f. something that was built to remember a special event or person
g. having a very strong need for something
h. a piece of land surrounded by water on three sides
i. to reduce in power or number gradually, over time
j. a piece of stone with writing or other images carved into it

Answers at the end of the book

Vocabulary Questions

Discuss with a partner.

1. Have you ever visited any ruins? Where were they? Who built them? What was it like?
2. What are some important monuments in your city/country? What do they represent?
3. Would you like living on a peninsula? Why or why not?

Your Briefing

442 Words - 1210L - 1400L
Place: San Lorenzo, South Coast of The Gulf of Mexico
Time: 400 BCE

When you see famous *ruins* like the Colosseum in Rome, The Great Wall of China, or Egypt's pyramids what do you think about? Do you ever wonder about the people who built and used them so far in the past? With many of these sites, we know exactly what happened and why, thanks to written evidence. But what about a culture that disappeared long, long ago, without leaving us any writings to tell their story? How can we know what happened to them? This is the case with the Olmecs, an advanced culture that thrived on the Gulf Coast of present-day Mexico before vanishing more than 2,400 years ago.

Considered the "mother culture" of the more famous Mayan and Aztec peoples of the region, it's likely that many people who live in the area today are descendants of the mysterious Olmec. They built large and complex cities and *monuments* without the use of metal tools, including giant stone heads which could measure 10 ft (3 m) high and 15 ft (4.5 m) around. Clearly, this was once a *mighty* civilization, one which constructed pyramids in their cities that reached heights of 110 ft (34 m), atop which human *sacrifices* may have been carried out. Their calendar, religion, artwork, sports, farming techniques, and writing system were all likely adopted and adapted by the cultures that followed their decline.

However, no books have yet been found, only one stone *tablet* containing *pictograms* has been found so far. The Cascajal Block (drawing on the left), dated to roughly 700 BCE, represents the oldest system of writing in the Western Hemisphere. The block's 62 symbols contain images of fish, eyes, insects, weapons, and corn, which was one of the Olmec's primary crops, along with squash and sweet potatoes.

Some think that their *reliance* on just a handful of crops could have left the Olmecs vulnerable to disasters that affected their farms, such as volcanic eruptions, droughts, hurricanes, or even climate change. Could a lack of food have led to their disappearance? After peaking around 1,000 BCE with the great cities of San Lorenzo and La Venta (not the original names, which have been lost to time), the civilization *declined* starting around 400 BCE, nearly 2,000 years before the arrival of Europeans.

Archaeologists know this because pottery, jewelry, and sculptures with Olmec images and designs were no longer produced after this time. Could warfare have played a part? Or something else entirely? To be sure, the Olmec people did not simply disappear overnight, but no major civilization would thrive in the Yucatan *Peninsula* until the Mayans some 650 years later. The mystery remains: What happened to the Olmecs Rome

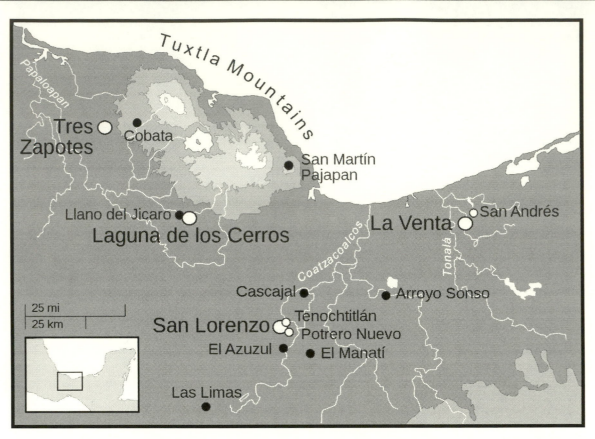

A map of the Olmec heartland, at the peak of Olmec civilization. White dots are known Olmec villages and towns. Black dots are places artifacts and monuments have been found.

Your Mission

Imagine you could go back in time and become the head advisor to the Olmec king. What advice would you give him to avoid the civilization's collapse?

Olmecs Quiz

1. The Olmec civilization was mainly located in what is now _____.

    a. China

    b. Egypt

    c. Italy

    d. Mexico

2. The Olmec civilization began to decline in ____.BCE.

    a. 400

    b. 700

    c. 2,000

    d. 2,400

3. The Olmecs are famous for their giant ____

    a. stadiums

    b. books

    c. heads

    d. farms

4. Which has *not* been suggested as a reason for the disappearance of the Olmecs?

    a. crop failure

    b. warfare

    c. disease

    d. natural disasters

5. The Olmecs left behind _____ writing.

    a. no

    b. very little

    c. much

    d. all of their

Answers at the end of the book

Discussion Questions

1. Discuss what may have happened to the Olmecs.

2. What ancient civilizations existed in your country in the past? Talk with a classmate, friend, or family member from your same country/region about these questions, then share with the class:

    a. What was its name?

    b. What do you know about them?

    c. What were they like at their peak?

    d. What happened to them?

    e. Are parts of their culture still present in your country today, such as in language, art, or religion?

Projects

1. **Be a Part of History to Complete the Mission**: What do you think really happened to the Olmecs? What sources would you use to make your argument? See "Supplement 4: Finding Credible Sources". Use at least two sources to write a short essay explaining your theory.

2. Compare and contrast an ancient civilization from your country with your culture today. Use a *Venn diagram* or write a short paragraph.

   a. Compare your work with a partner from another country. Whose culture today has more similarities with its past? Why do you think this is? Give a short presentation with your partner explaining this.

3. Imagine that you travel far into the future and are standing in the ruins of your own city. What could have led to its decline, and why? Write this down on the first line below. After that, interview your classmates or friends and family: Later, choose one response and write a short paragraph in which you consider whether you believe this is likely or not, and why.

Name	City	Reason

References

Bitto, R. (2020, May 12). *Olmec colossal stone heads.*Mexico Unexplained. http://mexicounexplained.com/olmec-colossal-stone-heads

Cartwright, Marc. *Aztec sacrifice.* (2018, May 3). Ancient History Encyclopedia. https://www.ancient.eu/Aztec_Sacrifice/

Cartwright, Marc. (2014, March 21). *Olmec colossal stone heads.* Ancient History Encyclopedia. https://www.ancient.eu/article/672/olmec-colossal-stone-heads/

Minster, C. (2018, September 18). *Why did the ancient Olmec civilization disappear?* ThoughtCo. https://www.thoughtco.com/the-decline-of-the-olmec-civilization-2136291

Ojus, D. (2007, February 11). *Olmec writing: The oldest in the Western Hemisphere — Journal of young investigators.* Journal of Young Investigators. https://www.jyi.org/2007-february/2007/2/11/olmec-writing-the-oldest-in-the-western-hemisphere

Nan Madol: Pacific Megalith Mystery

Before You Read

1. Do you know about the origin of your home city? How old is it and who built it?

2. Have you ever visited an ancient cultural site? Where was it and how was the experience?

3. What kind of ancient knowledge did people in the past have that we no longer have?

Vocabulary Definitions

Write the letter of the definition next to the matching word.

1. megalith (n.) ____
2. monument (n.) ____
3. statue (n.) ____
4. marvel (v.) ____
5. ritual (n.) ____
6. archaeologist (n.) ____
7. astronomy (n.) ____
8. canal (n.) ____
9. dynasty (n.) ____
10. priest (n.) ____
11. tomb (n.) ____
12. precisely (adv.) ____
13. magician (n.) ____
14. skeptical (adj.) ____
15. isolated (adj.) ____

a. a person who studies ancient sites
b. a human made waterway
c. a family of rulers that has power for generations
d. a person who does things science cannot explain
e. carefully and exactly, without mistakes
f. an activity in religion or culture for a special time or event
g. 3D art of a person or animal
h. a building made for a dead body
i. studying the stars
j. to look at or think about with amazement
k. something that was built to remember a special event or person
l. a person who leads religious activities
m. not trusting, doubting
n. an ancient construction with large stones
o. to be alone, without connections

Vocabulary Questions

Discuss with a partner.

1. Do you participate in any *rituals* from your culture? Explain what they are and what you do.
2. Are there any famous *monuments* in your city? What do people remember when they see it?
3. Are you a *skeptical* person? What kind of information do you find hard to trust?

Your Briefing

448 Words - 1010-1200L
Place: Island of Pohnpei, Federated States of Micronesia
Time: 1180

moai

Megaliths are ancient *monuments* that were built with very large stones. These monuments can be found in many countries around the world. Some of them are made from just one rock carved to look like a human face, such as the moai *statues* on Easter Island. Others are simple structures, such as dolmens that mark gravesites in Europe and Asia. The best-known megalith is probably Stonehenge in England which averages 800,000 visitors per year. People like to *marvel* at these sites and imagine the *rituals* of ancient life.

Historians and *archaeologists* study these sites to understand ancient cultures, but megaliths keep many mysteries. It's not always clear why they were built. Different sites may have been used for *astronomy*, religion, or communication. Furthermore, it is incredible that such very large stones could have been carved, transported, and lifted into the air without any modern machinery.

dolem

We still don't know exactly how it was done at many sites. Some people wonder if these ancient cultures had advanced technology that we don't have anymore.

One of the most interesting megalithic sites is in the middle of the Pacific Ocean on the small jungle island of Pohnpei. There you will find Nan Madol, a megalithic city built from large pieces of black stone. The stones are stacked into walls and buildings that form artificial islands and *canals*. Visitors today can enter Nan Madol and walk through some of the structures, but nobody has lived there for hundreds of years. Historians think Nan Madol was built close to 1000 years ago. They believe some buildings were for special *priests* and some for the *tombs* of rulers. However, just like Stonehenge or the pyramids of Egypt, nobody can figure out exactly how it was built.

How could the ancient islanders have cut the rock so *precisely* and moved piece after piece into place without the help of modern machines? It seems even more difficult when you realize they were a small civilization that was *isolated* in the middle of the ocean. They didn't have very much land or manpower. The city is such an amazing achievement that some people believe the construction was magic. There are old stories that *magicians* made the rocks float through the air. Of course, historians are very *skeptical* of those stories, but they do not have information that explains the real way the city was built.

Is it possible the ancient islanders saw the large rocks flying over the top of the jungle mountains like airplanes? Did their priests have special powers? Or is it more likely they used special technology or skills that are forgotten? Only the ancient Pohnpei citizens know the answers for sure.

Your Mission

Visit ancient Pohnpei and discover the people and methods that built Nan Madol. Describe their technology and make sure it is not lost for us in the future.

References

Pohnpei Visitors Bureau. (n.d.). *Nan Madol | Federated States of Micronesia.* https://www.nan-madol.com

History.com Editors. (2019, February 21). *Stonehenge.* HISTORY. https://www.history.com/topics/british-history/stonehenge

National Park Service. (2020, January 6). *Nan Madol.* https://www.nps.gov/places/nan-madol.htm

Pala, C. (2009, November 3). Nan Madol: The city built on coral reefs. *Smithsonian Magazine.* https://www.smithsonianmag.com/history/nan-madol-the-city-built-on-coral-reefs-147288758

UNESCO World Heritage Centre. (n.d.). *Nan Madol: Ceremonial centre of eastern Micronesia.* https://whc.unesco.org/en/list/1503

Nan Madol History Quiz

1. Where can you find a megalith?

    a. Asia

    b. Easter Island

    c. England

    d. all of the above

2. Where is Nan Madol?

    a. England

    b. Pohnpei

    c. Egypt

    d. Europe

3. Which is the best description of Nan Madol?

    a. stone buildings and canals

    b. a jungle island

    c. a rock carved to look like a face

    d. a story about magic

4. Why is Nan Madol mysterious?

    a. We don't know where it is.

    b. We don't know how it was built.

    c. We don't know who lives there.

    d. We don't know if it is real.

5. How old is Nan Madol?

    a. about 800,000 years old

    b. about 1000 years old

    c. about 500 years old

    d. about 100 years old

Discussion Questions

1. How do you think Nan Madol was likely constructed?

    a. How many different theories can you brainstorm?

    b. How could somebody solve the mystery of its construction?

2. Do you know any ancient stories from your culture or in your community? If so, do you believe them? Why or why not?

3. Is it possible that ancient people had advanced technology or skills that we don't have now?

    a. If so, how was it lost?

    b. Could the mysteries of megaliths be proof of magic?

    c. What kind of things are you skeptical about? Why do you have trouble believing them?

Projects

1. **Be a Part of History to Complete the Mission:** Visit ancient Pohnpei and discover the methods used to build Nan Madol.

   a. Who is doing the construction and what technology is being used?

   b. Do you see magic happening?

   c. Write a description of what you observe and solve the Nan Madol mystery.

2. Research an example of a megalith from your country and prepare a short presentation. ("See Supplement 4: Finding Credible Sources")

   a. Where is it and how big is it?

   b. Do historians know how or why it was built?

   c. f it is possible, visit the site.

3. Construct miniature models of three different types of megaliths.

   a. Use them as a visual aid to present about megaliths around the world and the mysteries of their construction.

   b. Describe where you can find each type of megalith and explain what historians do and don't know.

4. Imagine you are one of the workers constructing Stonehenge, the Egyptian pyramids, or Nan Madol.

   a. Write a diary entry that describes one day in your life.

   b. What work did you do and how did you feel?

5. Research the history of your city or a city you know well to make a timeline of major events.

   a. Who were the rulers?

   b. What were the major events?

   c. How did life change over time?

   d. What information do you want to know that you can't find?

6. Interview your classmates or friends and family:

Interview Question: Do you believe in magic?		
Name	**Answer**	**Reason**
Peter	No	People only believe in magic if evidence of truth is lost or hidden. That's why magicians have to keep secrets, because it's not magic without secrets

The "Lost Colony" of Roanoke Island

Before You Read

1. What is the most important thing you've ever lost? How did you lose it? Did you ever find it?

2. Have you ever gotten lost? Where were you? What did you do?

3. Why do people move to new countries?

Vocabulary Definitions

Write the letter of the definition next to the matching word.

1. hostile (adj.) ____
2. clues (n, pl) ____
3. ashore (n.) ____
4. dismantle (v.) ____
5. post (n.) ____
6. refer to (v.) ____
7. antagonistic (adj.) ____
8. sensitive (adj.) ____
9. dig (v.) ____
10. evidence (n.) ____

a. the supporting part of a fence
b. showing opposition
c. direct to something
d. facts or information that show something is true
e. respond to slight changes
f. information to solve a mystery
g. remove earth from a hole
h. on shore from the sea
i. unfriendly
j. take apart into pieces

Answers at the end of the book

Vocabulary Questions

Discuss with a partner.

1. What makes a person *hostile* to someone?
2. Why does a fence need a *post*?
3. What tools do you need to *dig* a hole?

Your Briefing

546 words - 610 - 800L

Place: Roanoke Island, North Carolina, USA

Time: 1603

In 1587, a group of 87 men, 17 women and 11 children came *ashore* to Roanoke Island. The English were determined to live on this beautiful island. This was the third visit by English men, and this time they brought strong, adventurous women to build a community. The colony was uncivilized: finding food, building shelter and basic everyday survival is a frightening challenge. They wanted to farm, but farming is very difficult. John White, one of the settlers, decided to go back to England for supplies. When he returned, three years later, there were no people. Where were the settlers who had come to Roanoke Island in 1587? And where was his granddaughter, Virginia Dare, the first English child born in a New World colony? There were Spanish settlers who hated the English, *hostile* tribes who hated the English and bad weather which seems to hate the English.

There was no blood, nothing was broken, and the houses had been neatly *dismantled*. John White found two clues: on a tree, there were three letters, CRO, and on a fence *post*, White read the word, "CROATOAN."

What does this word mean? Did it *refer to* the Native American tribe with the same name? Or did it point to a nearby island, also with the same name?

John White was not able to continue the search, but now, 13 years later, Bartholomew Gilbert, a British ship captain, has three ideas. He wants to visit the island of Croatoan. He reminds everyone that an earlier rescue party failed to reach Croatoan because of bad weather. He asks if someone is familiar with the weather patterns of the region.

He also wants to talk to Native Americans and other settlers. He warns everyone to be careful because some Native American tribes are *antagonistic* to Europeans. On the other hand, witnesses reported white faces among the brown ones. Could the 115 settlers be living with Native Americans? He suggests learning about the tribe before making contact.

Also, there are Spanish settlers nearby. The Spanish might know something about the disappearing settlers, but they are unhappy because of their country's war with England a few years before. Gilbert warns everyone to be *sensitive* when interviewing the Spanish settlers and Native American residents. He also instructs a small group of crew members to stay on Roanoke Island and *dig* for *evidence*. Perhaps the 115 missing settlers left behind something underground.

There is something spooky about the island. Are supernatural forces at work here? What Gilbert cannot know is that the word, "Croatoan," might be evil. There are rumors that Edgar Allen Poe, Black Bart, Ambrose Bierce, and Amelia Earhart were all connected to the word "Croatoan" before they died. There is also a story from 1921 of a "ghost ship" that crashed on the outer banks of North Carolina, very close to Roanoke Island. The tale describes the ship as empty of sailors, with no explanation for their disappearance. On the last page of the logbook, someone had written the word: "Croatoan." Are these unverified stories true or urban legends? In 1603, Bartholomew Gilbert and his crew are searching for any clues to the disappearance of the original settlers. Say a prayer that bad weather and evil spirits spare their lives. And yours.

Your Mission

Join Bartholomew Gilbert and his crew and find the missing settlers. It is 1603, and you return to the Roanoke Island Colony in the New World with British ship captain

Bartholomew Gilbert and his crew. You want to understand why, 26 years earlier, 115 people disappeared from the island.

The "Lost Colony" of Roanoke Island History Quiz

1. The 1587 trip was the third attempt to settle Roanoke Island. What was different about the group this time?

    a. They were English, not Spanish.

    b. They included Spanish settlers.

    c. They included women.

    d. They excluded women.

2. What year did John White first return to the colony from England?

    a. 1587

    b. 1590

    c. 1603

    d. 1921

3. "Croatoan" means

    a. a kind of tree

    b. a New World colony

    c. a Native American group in North Carolina

    d. a city in North Carolina

4. Which of the following hazards did the Roanoke Colony potentially face?

    a. a curse from Native Americans

    b. war with England

    c. hostile Spanish

    d. a lack of men

5. Who is Virginia Dare?

    a. The first English baby born in the Colonies

    b. The first female sea captain in England

    c. John White's daughter

    d. a Croaton Indian

Answers at the end of the book

Discussion Questions

1. Listen to (and sing along with) @mrclassbetts "Roanoke Colony Song:" https://www.youtube.com/watch?v=Nusuzs1qKDo.

    a. What song does it remind you of?

    b. Do you better understand the story of the "Lost Colony"?

2. What does Croatoan mean? Read "Croatoan Indians": https://www.ncpedia.org/croatoan-indians.

    a. What does the meaning of the word "Croatoan" tell you about the culture of the Croatoan Indians?

    b. What kind of people were they? What did they value in their society? How did they make decisions?

3. Read "Archaeologists find new clues to "Lost Colony" Mystery" (https://www.history.com/news/archaeologists-find-new-clues-to-lost-colony-mystery).

    a. What did the archaeologists find? Why are these items important to solving the mystery?

    b. What do the archaeologists think happened to the "Lost Colony"?

    c. Why might Virginia Dare's relatives become angry to find out that Virginia became part of a Native American tribe?

4. Watch Stephanie Harlowe's YouTube channel's episode, "The Lost Colony of Roanoke Island: When 115 People Disappear in Thin Air" at https://www.youtube.com/watch?v=yxTSZuOsckA.

    a. What new information do you learn about Virginia Dare?

    b. Look at "Supplement 13: Critical Questions for Media Literacy". After watching Stephanie Harlowe's explanation of the Roanoke mystery, answer the supplement's five questions about the author and who may or may not look good in her telling of the story.

    c. What do you think Harlowe wants you to believe?

5. What do you think happened to Bartholomew Gilbert and his crew? Discuss with a partner or in a small group.

Projects

1. **Be a Part of History to Complete the Mission**: Solve the mystery of the disappearance of the 115 Roanoke Island residents by interviewing neighbors. With a partner, decide what five questions to ask people in the area of the "Lost Colony?" Discuss how your questions differ if you are interviewing:

    a. Croatoans?

    b. Spaniards?

    c. How would you make sure you were polite to the two groups? How would you be different with each group?

2. What do you think happened to the "Lost Colony?" Write 1 page from the point of view:

    a. of a settler of the "lost colony"

    b. of a member of a friendly tribe

    c. of a member of a hostile tribe

    d. of a storm cloud

3. 3. Research one of the famous people who might have said or written, "Croatoan" before their death. Why did they say this word, in your opinion? Write down three reasons and share with a partner, a small group or with the class.

    a.

    b.

    c.

4. Other civilizations have disappeared. Here is one list: https://www.toptenz.net/top-10-civilizations-that-mysteriously-disappeared.php Research one of these civilizations and discuss what you learned with a partner or in a group. You can also read about the Olmecs in this same unit.

5. Interview your classmates or friends and family:

Interview Question: If you could only leave one word behind after you die, what would it be? Why?		
Name	**Answer**	**Reason**
Catherine	Time	I think time is an interesting concept. What is it? Can we travel back/forwards? Also, "time" is what the ref calls at the end of the game, and death is the end of the game

References

Harlowe, S. (2018, October 31). *The lost colony of Roanoke: when 115 people vanish into thin air* [Video]. YouTube. https://www.youtube.com/watch?v=yxTSZuOsckA

History.com Staff. (2012, October 2). *What happened to the "lost colony" of Roanoke?* HISTORY. https://www.history.com/news/what-happened-to-the-lost-colony-of-roanoke

Lawler, A. (2017, April 7). The mystery of Roanoke endures yet another cruel twist. *Smithsonian Magazine.* https://www.smithsonianmag.com/history/mystery-roanoke-endures-yet-another-cruel-twist-180962837

The Dyatlov Pass Incident

Before You Read

1. What kinds of things would you need to pack on a long hiking trip in the winter?
2. What kinds of dangers do people face when they go hiking or camping?
3. Why do people choose to do dangerous sports?
4. Many people who have lost loved ones say their grief is increased by not knowing how they died? Why do you think this is?

Vocabulary Definitions

Write the letter of the definition next to the matching word.

1. summiting (v.) ____
2. attain (v.) ____
3. hypothermia (n.) ____
4. autopsies (n.) ____
5. fractured (v.) ____
6. avalanches (n.) ____
7. pitch (v.) ____
8. accident-prone (adj.) ____
9. hallucinate (v.) ____
10. bizarre (adj.) ____

a. to see or sense something that is not real
b. an examination done on a dead body to find the cause of death
c. to reach the top of a mountain
d. a condition involving a dangerously low body temperature
e. to get something through hard work or achievement
f. very strange and unusual
g. the dangerous falling of snow and/or rock down a mountain
h. broken or cracked
i. tending to have unintentional problems or damage
j. (here) to set up a tent

Answers at the end of the book

Vocabulary Questions

Discuss with a partner.

1. Are you interested in summiting a mountain? Why or why not?
2. Why do you think some people are more accident-prone than others?
3. What are some reasons why a person might hallucinate?

Your Briefing

583 Words-810L-1000L
Place: Northern Ural Mountains, U.S.S.R.
Time: January-February 1959

On January 27th, 1959, nine members of a backpacking club from the Ural Polytechnic Institute set off on a very difficult hike to climb Holatchahl Mountain during their winter holiday. The seven men and two women were close friends and experienced hikers. By *summiting* this mountain, they would *attain* the highest hiking certification. Unfortunately, when the winter holiday ended and teachers and students returned to the university, the hikers did not.

Because of miscommunication, it took a few weeks before a search party was organized to find the missing hikers. Friends and family prayed that the group was delayed by injury or illness but still alive. However, on February 26th, the search party found a disturbing sight. The tent was standing on the side of a mountain, torn on one side but otherwise okay. Inside the tent, the searchers found all the hikers gear including their boots. Wherever the hikers were, they had no shoes.

Following sets of footprints, the searchers eventually found the bodies of all nine hikers in three separate areas. None were alive. The rescuers were confused because all the hikers were wearing light clothing that was not suitable for the harsh winter climate. Why would they come outside into the freezing cold without their boots and coats?

It seemed that most of the hikers had died of *hypothermia*, but some also had terrible injuries. *Autopsies* showed that two hikers died from severe chest injuries and one from a *fractured* skull. Despite numerous investigations, the case remained open for 60 years and the government kept many of the documents secret. To this day, we aren't exactly sure what happened to the hikers. Possible explanations include:

Attack by other humans: A group of native people, the Mansi, lived nearby the campsite. Were they angry that the hikers were on their land? Other hikers in the area reported strange orange lights in the sky. Did the hikers discover a top-secret military experiment? Both suggestions seem unlikely as the Mansi were peaceful people and had even hosted the hikers for tea. Moreover, only nine sets of footprints were found at the campsite.

Avalanche: Avalanches have taken the lives of many hikers and skiers. Could such an event have forced the hiking club out of their tent and then pushed them down the mountain? After over 60 years of investigations, this is the conclusion of the Russian government. However, many people argue that these experienced hikers would know better than to *pitch* a tent in an *accident-prone* area. In fact, the location of the tent was found to be in a very safe area even if there were an avalanche. Moreover, though the tent was torn and collapsed on one side, it was still mostly standing.

Hypothermia: When humans become very cold, it doesn't only affect their bodies. They can begin to have very strange thoughts and even *hallucinate*. They can even begin to feel very hot and want to take their clothes off. Is this why the hikers left the tent without their coats and boots? Were they trying to cool off? Considering the experience of the hikers, this also doesn't seem like a likely occurrence. They were probably keeping warm enough and if one or two of the hikers began to hallucinate, the others would have kept them safe.

Supernatural forces: The case is so *bizarre* and no explanation seems to make sense. Perhaps something unimaginable occurred in that tent on the night of February 1, 1959, something beyond our experience and understanding.

Your Mission

Find the hikers at the Dyatlov Pass and lead them back to safety. S

Dyatlov Pass Incident History Quiz

1. Why were the hikers on Holatchahl Mountain?

    a. They were on vacation.

    b. They were lost.

    c. They were rescuing other hikers.

    d. They were trying to get a certification.

2. How many of the hikers were women?

    a. 1

    b. 2

    c. 3

    d. 4

3. Most of the hikers died because they were too ____.

    a. hungry

    b. ill

    c. cold

    d. injured

4. One possible reason why the hikers left their tent mentioned in the text is

    a. snow and rocks falling down the mountain

    b. bear attack

    c. hunger

    d. an argument

5. Which statement is true according to the text?

    a. The hikers were probably involved in an avalanche.

    b. More experienced hikers would have survived.

    c. Hiking in the mountains during winter is dangerous.

    d. UFOs were seen on the night the hikers died.

Answers at the end of the book

Discussion Questions

1. Why do you think the nine hikers wanted to attempt such a difficult and dangerous trip?

2. Why do you think the Soviet government was so secretive about the details of the case?

3. Do you think this case will ever be solved? What would an investigator need to do in order to solve the case?

Projects

1. **Be a Part of History to Complete the Mission**: The hikers took turns keeping a journal during their trip. Imagine you are one of the hikers. Write a page or two about the last night on the mountain.

2. Make a list of supplies and equipment you would take for a trip like the hikers took. Now imagine you can only fit half of these items in your backpack. Which are the most important? Compare your list with a classmate.

Packing List

1. Tent
2. Flashlight
3.
4.
5.
6.

3. Write about your own experience! Have you ever gone on a hiking or camping trip? What supplies did you bring with you? Did you have everything you needed? Were there any other challenges you experienced?

4. Disappearances of hikers, campers, and other adventurers are not totally uncommon. Using "Supplement 2: Create Your Own Mystery", write your own mystery about a disappearance.

5. Interview your classmates or friends and family:

Interview Question: What do you think happened to the hikers?		
Name	**Answer**	**Reason**
Mina	supernatural forces	I think aliens took them.

References

Devitt, P. (2020, July 11). *Russia blames avalanche for 1959 Urals mountain tragedy, RIA agency reports.* Reuters News Agency. https://www.reuters.com/article/us-russia-accident-idUSKCN24C0IE

Eichar, D. (2013). *Dead mountain: The untold true story of the Dyatlov Pass incident.* Chronicle Books.

Mead, D. (2017, September 5). *Russia's Dyatlov pass incident, the strangest unsolved mystery of the last century.* VICE. https://www.vice.com/en/article/wjj9yb/russias-dyatlov-pass-incident-the-strangest-unsolved-mystery-of-the-last-century

Help MH370!

Before You Read

1. What can you tell your partner about the map?
2. What countries do you see?
3. Why is the map important?
4. Why do planes crash?

Vocabulary Definitions

Write the letter of the definition next to the matching word.

1. disappeared (v.) ____
2. pilot (n.) ____
3. transponder (n.) ____
4. steered (v.) ____
5. invisible (adj.) ____
6. ash (n.) ____
7. windshield (n.) ____
8. crash (v.) ____
9. crew (n.) ____
10. butt (n.) ___

a. violently hit something
b. cannot be seen
c. dust left over from fire
d. gone
e. a group of people who work on a plane
f. the person who controls the plane
g. guided the movement of something
h. front glass window of a car
i. a device that receives and sends a signal
j. informal term for the backside of an animal

Answers at the end of the book

Vocabulary Questions

Discuss with a partner.

1. What are some reasons why someone might have *disappeared*?
2. Which of these have you *steered*: a bicycle, a car, a boat, a plane?
3. Would you like to be *invisible*? Why or why not?

Briefing

393 words - 810-1000L
Place: The Indian Ocean
Time: 12:41am, March 8, 2014

At 12:42am, on March 18, 2014, Flight MH370, a Boeing 777-200ER, *disappeared* on a flight from Kuala Lumpur, Malaysia to Beijing, China. Its *pilot*, Captain Zaharie Ahmad Shah, 53, said, "Good night, Malaysian 370," as he *steered* the plane toward Vietnam. Seconds later, the plane's *transponder* turned off, and the plane became *invisible* to radar. Did Captain Zaharie turn it off? If so, why? The captain had flown for over 20 years. He was a senior pilot. Although he didn't live with his wife and children, he still talked to them. Some may say he wanted to disappear. Did he? Or did someone hijack the plane? Or could there have been a fire?

There are many reasons for a plane to crash. There could be a problem with the engines. A plane could fly into a storm. *Ash* from an erupting volcano can damage the plane's electrical systems. High-flying birds can hit the *windshield*. And, sometimes, the pilot can *crash* the plane on purpose. There is no proof that Captain Zaharie crashed the plane; however, his marriage had ended. He was lonely, and officials believe he wanted to die.

But where is the plane?

Even though a Boeing 777 is 242.4 ft (73.9 m) long, the length of six school buses, the Indian Ocean is 6200 miles (10,000 km) wide. Looking for the lost plane is like trying to find an ant on the *butt* of an elephant. Twenty-five countries searched for the plane. The search cost $200 million, but the searchers found nothing. In 2016, the cabin panel of a Boeing 777, washed up on a beach near Madagascar in the

Indian Ocean. In 2017, part of a Boeing 777 engine cooling system was found on a beach in South Africa. The largest piece of MH370 is a piece of the wing that was found on a beach on the island of Réunion, also in the Indian Ocean.

On board MH370, at least one couple was on their honeymoon. Two of the passengers were flying with stolen passports. An Australian engineer told his wife before he got on the plane, if anything happened to him, to give his ring to his oldest and his watch to his younger son. The flight *crew* were all Malaysian and the passengers came from 12 different countries.

The 227 passengers and 12 crew members remain missing.

Your Mission

Explain what happened to the flight.

MH370! History Quiz

1. Flight MH370 went missing above:

   a. Kuala Lumpur, Malaysia

   b. Beijing, China

   c. the Indian Ocean

   d. Vietnam

2. Why did the plane become invisible to radar?

   a. It had stealth technology.

   b. The transponder stopped working.

   c. The radar stopped working.

   d. Airports in Asia don't use radar.

3. How big is the Indian Ocean?

   a. The length of six school buses

   b. 73.9 meters

   c. 200 million

   d. 10,000 kilometers

4. What is one thing that was *not* mentioned as a cause of an airplane accident?

   a. birds

   b. terrorism

   c. volcanoes

   d. storms

5. How many people were killed as a result of the plane crash?

   a. 212

   b. 227

   c. 237

   d. 239

Answers at the end of the book

Discussion Questions

1. How does a plane fly? Watch this cute video for kids that explains how planes fly: https://www.youtube.com/watch?v=UUBk_vmgRXY. Listen for the definitions of airplane parts.

    a. Work in groups of three. Each student should choose one of the lists below. Listen for the definition and write notes to share your information with the other members of your group.

Student #1	Student #2	Student #3
fuselage	wings	landing gear
flight deck	throttle	yoke
instrument panels	flaps	slats
elevators	aileron	spoilers
stabilizers	rudder pedals	rudder

2. How does a pilot fly a plane? Look at this information from NASA: www.grc.nasa.gov/www/k-12/UEET/StudentSite/dynamicsofflight.html Discuss with a partner.

3. Is it possible that Capt. Zaharie crashed the plane? Before Capt. Zaharie disappeared, he may have felt alone. How do you help a lonely person? How could you be Capt. Zaharie's friend and help him if he were depressed?

4. What is stress? Why do people feel stress in a job? What are stressful parts of being a pilot?

5. Everyone feels stress at some time in life. What do you do when you feel stress? Whom do you talk to?

    a. Go to https://www.webmd.com/ and search for 'Stress Management'. There you can find 13 ways to fight stress. Do you agree? Discuss with your partner.

Projects

1. **Be a Part of History to Complete the Mission**: Create a strategy to find out what happened to the plane.

    a. With a partner, write five questions to ask the pilot, Capt. Zaharie.

    b. With a partner, write five questions to ask the Malaysian government official in charge of the investigation.

    c. With a partner, write five questions for passengers on the plane.

2. Write 1 page explaining what you think happened on flight MH370.

3. Who were Daedalus and Icarus? Research the story. Check "Supplement: 4 Finding Credible Sources" for information on paraphrasing.

    a. Tell your partner, group, or class the story.

    b. Would you like to have wings? Tell your partner or the group why or why not.

4. Helping a friend feel better is a great skill to have. Interview your classmates or friends and family

Interview Question: What is the best way to cheer up someone who is unhappy?		
Name	**Answer**	**Reason**
Catherine	Taking someone to a restaurant or shopping.	If you tell your unhappy friend that you have a plan for them and this plan shows that you thought about the things that they like to do, it shows that you care.

References

Fedschun, T. (2019, June 17). Malaysia Airlines flight 370 'disintegrated into confetti': report. *New York Post.* https://nypost.com/2019/06/17/malaysia-airlines-flight-370-disintegrated-into-confetti-report/

Langewiesche, W. (2019, June 17). What really happened to Malaysia's missing airplane. *The Atlantic.* https://www.theatlantic.com/magazine/archive/2019/07/mh370-malaysia-airlines/590653/

Harlowe, S. (2019, March 12). *Mystery Monday: MH370: A flight that disappeared into thin air?* [Video]. YouTube. https://www.youtube.com/watch?v=ykErm0mmLAE

Steinbuch, Y. (2019, July 12). MH370 pilot was in control of plane 'until the end': investigators. *New York Post.* https://nypost.com/2019/07/12/mh370-pilot-was-in-control-of-plane-until-the-end-investigators/

Section V - Aliens and Other Worlds

Who Built the Pyramids?

Before You Read

1. Above is a picture of the pyramids from Ancient Egypt. How do you think they were made? What purpose do they serve?
2. Do you believe there is life on other planets?
3. If so, do you think aliens have visited Earth? Why or why not?

Vocabulary Definitions

Write the letter of the definition next to the matching word.

a. pyramid (n.) _____
b. pharaoh (n.) _____
c. mastaba (n.) _____
d. circa (prep) _____
e. sentinel (n/v) _____
f. mortuary (n.) _____
g. carpentry (n.) _____
h. ancient (adj.) _____
i. infamous (adj.) _____
j. decry (v.) _____

k. a ruler in ancient Egypt
l. a large structure usually with a square base and sloping sides that meet in a point at the top
m. around the time of
n. a place where dead people are kept
o. well-known, but not for a good reason
p. very old
q. A kind of Egyptian tomb
r. to speak badly about someone or something
s. the job or activity of making or repairing things such as houses or furniture with wood
t. a guard that keeps watch

Answers at the end of the book

Vocabulary Questions

Discuss with a partner.

1. Have you ever visited a *mortuary*? If so, why did you go?
2. Are you good at *carpentry*? Why or why not?
3. Who is someone *infamous* in your home country or region? Why are they *infamous*?

Your Briefing

670 Words - 1010-1200L
Place: Giza, Egypt
Time: ~2560 BCE

How the *pyramids* at Giza were built is one of Egypt's, and the world's, biggest mysteries.

Egypt's *pharaohs* expected to become gods in the afterlife. To prepare for the next world, they built temples to the gods and massive pyramid tombs for themselves. These tombs were filled with all the things each ruler would need to guide and sustain himself in the next world, including treasures, carvings, and paintings.

There are more than 100 surviving pyramids in Egypt, with the oldest known pyramid built around 2630 BCE at Saqqara, for the third dynasty's King Djoser. Known as the Step Pyramid, it began as a traditional *mastaba* before being redesigned.

But generally, the most famous is the Great Pyramid of Giza in Egypt standing at over 450 feet. Pharaoh Khufu began the first Giza pyramid project, *circa* 2550 BCE. His Great Pyramid is the largest in Giza and measures 481 feet (147 meters) high. Each of its 2.3 million stone blocks weigh an average of 2.5 to 15 tons. Khufu's son, Pharaoh Khafre, built the second pyramid at Giza, circa 2520 BCE which included the Sphinx, a mysterious limestone statue with the body of a lion and a pharaoh's head. It's believed that the Sphinx may be a sentinel for the pharaoh's entire tomb complex. The third and last of the Giza Pyramids is considerably smaller than the first two. Built by Pharaoh Menkaure circa 2490 B.C., it featured a more complex *mortuary* temple. Tomb art includes depictions of farmers working their fields and tending livestock, fishing, *carpentry*, costumes, religious rituals, and burial practices. Inscriptions and texts also allow research into Egyptian grammar and language. Many wonder how the *ancient* Egyptians were able to build such huge and complex structures using 4,000-year-old technology. The ancient engineering feats at Giza were so impressive that even today scientists can't be sure how the pyramids were built. There are many theories and ideas on who made them, how they were made, and why.

One theory is that they had alien assistance, which would have used advanced technologies to create them. An *infamous* Swiss author, Erich von Däniken, is partly responsible for popularizing the theory of ancient aliens. In his 1968 book, *Chariots of the Gods,* Von Däniken suggested that thousands of years ago life from another planet visited Earth and gave us the knowledge to advance as a civilization. He connects this to many religious texts referring to divine spirits coming from the sky above and claims those spirits must have been aliens. Science-fiction movies such as *2001: A Space Odyssey* and *Prometheus* explore the origins of mankind with links to extraterrestrial influence.

The idea of ancient aliens has become so popular that the theories even feature in a show broadcast and produced by America's History channel titled *Ancient Aliens.* Many historians *decry* these ideas as unscientific and even racist! According to archaeologist and former Secretary General of Egypt's Supreme Council of Antiquities Zahi Hawass: "Many, especially in the USA, believe there are space creatures who came from Mars and built the Pyramids. This is not scientific at all…. the pyramid was Egypt's national project, and that the pyramids have built Egypt."

There is an alternate theory to aliens. Scientists from the University of Liverpool found a ramp which they believe was used to pull huge blocks of stone up the pyramids using a two-way pulley system. This would help explain how such large structures were made without the use of more modern machinery.

There has also been lots of research about the builders themselves. Were they slaves and how were they motivated to work? Many researchers believe the builders were skilled, well-fed Egyptian workers who lived in a nearby temporary city in a highly organized community. It's likely that communities across Egypt contributed workers, as well as food and other essentials, for what became a national symbol to display the wealth and control of the ancient pharaohs. One thing is for sure: the building of the pyramids is an amazing achievement and mystery!

Your Mission

Investigate the making of the periods and discover who made them, how, any why!

References

BBC News. (2020, August 2). *Egypt tells Elon Musk its pyramids were not built by aliens.* https://www.bbc.com/news/world-africa-53627888

CBBC Newsround. (2018, November 6). *How were pyramids built? Discovery of ancient ramps may provide answers.* BBC. https://www.bbc.co.uk/newsround/46113215

Handwerk, B. (2017, March 23). *Pyramids at Giza.* National Geographic. https://www.nationalgeographic.com/history/archaeology/giza-pyramids/

Hawass, Z. (2018, November 8). *Aliens built the pyramids!* Egypt Independent. https://egyptindependent.com/aliens-built-the-pyramids/

History.com Editors. (2009, October 14). *Egyptian pyramids.* HISTORY. https://www.history.com/topics/ancient-history/the-egyptian-pyramid

Who Built the Pyramids History Quiz

1. The pyramids have survived over 4500 years.

    a. True
    b. False

2. Around when were the first pyramids built?

    a. 2430 BCE
    b. 2530 BCE
    c. 2630 BCE
    d. 2730 BCE

3. Who is most likely to believe the theory that aliens were involved in the construction of the pyramids?

    a. Scientists from the University of Liverpool
    b. Swiss author Erich von Däniken.
    c. Secretary General of Egypt's Supreme Council of Antiquities Zahi Hawass.
    d. all of the above

4. What is the name of the first pyramid built in Egypt?

    a. the Great Pyramid of Giza
    b. the Sphinx
    c. the Step Pyramid
    d. We don't know for sure.

5. Which theory on the building of the pyramids is likely most agreed on by scientists?

    a. They are made by humans with a special ramp system.
    b. They are made by aliens from space.
    c. They are made by animals.
    d. They are made by time travelers from the future

Answers at the end of the book

Discussion Questions

1. Describe the quote by Zahi Hawass: "The pyramids built Egypt."

    a. What do you think he means?
    b. Do you agree or disagree with this statement? Why?

2. What are the theories by researchers of how the pyramids were built and who built them?

3. Do you agree or disagree with these theories?

4. If aliens made the pyramids, why do you think they made them?

5. How do you feel about pyramids being built to house the tombs of royalty?

a. Do you feel some people deserve this type of special treatment? Why or why not?

b. How would you feel if people wanted to build a pyramid or special tomb for you?

Projects

1. **Be a Part of History to Complete the Mission:** Now journey to the year 2500 BCE to find out who made the pyramids, how they were made, and what the conditions were like?

2. Research a famous pyramid and answer the following questions:

    a. Who was it built for? Do we know?

    b. Are there any unique aspects about its design?

    c. Are there any mysteries about it we don't know?

3. Design a pyramid! Pyramids have unique maze-like structures inside. Research a famous pyramid and draw a diagram/picture of its structure. Answer the following questions:

    a. Does this pyramid have a special name or location? (Example - The Great Pyramid in Giza)

    b. Who or what is inside the pyramid?

    c. What is special or unique about its design?

4. Find two facts about the pyramids and two opinions (See "Supplement 8: Opinion vs. Facts".)

5. Interview your classmates or friends and family: Who do they believe made the pyramids?

Interview Question: Do you think aliens built the pyramids?		
Name	**Answer**	**Reason**
Taylor	Probably not	No concrete evidence of aliens helping

The "Lost Cosmonauts"

Before You Read

1. Would you be interested in going to space? Why or why not?

2. What do you know about the Space Race of the 1950s and 60s?

   a. Why do you think the Soviets and the US were competing? Were they competing in other ways too?

3. Why do you think governments might not share details about their mistakes or failures? Can you think of any examples?

Vocabulary Definitions

Write the letter of the definition next to the matching word.

1. cosmonaut (n.) ____
2. Soviet Union (n.) ____
3. superpower (n.) ____
4. prove (v.) ____
5. bunker (n.) ____
6. allegedly (adv.) ____
7. ominous (adj.) ____
8. intercept (v.) ____
9. Morse Code (n.) ____
10. propaganda (n.) ____

a. an alliance made up of several communist states (including Russia) that existed from 1922-1991
b. to give facts that support belief
c. to catch or receive something that was not meant for you
d. scary, dark, forbidding
e. a system of communication using electrical pulses to represent letters
f. a Soviet astronaut
g. a very powerful country
h. misleading or biased information used to influence a point of view
i. claiming to be true, not proven
j. a strong underground structure

Answers at the end of the book

Vocab Questions

Discuss with a partner.

1. Have you ever heard of the *Soviet Union* before? What do you know about it?
2. What does *Morse Code* sound like? How/when/why was it used in the past? Do you think it is still used today?
3. Do you think that *propaganda* is a good thing, bad thing, or both? Give examples/reasons.

Your Briefing

723 Words - 1010L - 1200L
Place: Listening station in an abandoned German bunker outside Turin, Italy
Time: May 19, 1961,

During times of conflict and competition between countries, there has always been the idea of holding back information, especially embarrassing information, about failures and setbacks. In the 1950s and 60s, during the Space Race between the United States and the Soviet Union (including Russia), this meant keeping sensitive technology and information about space flights secret. To this day, countries (and companies) will do much to keep secrets, even if sharing the information could help others.

On April 12, 1961, if you could have seen 187 miles (300 km) above you, you would have seen the small spaceship carrying Yuri Gagarin, the first human in space. He circled Earth one time, landing safely 90 minutes later. While many in the Soviet Union and around the world celebrated this achievement, most Americans saw this as yet another loss in the Space Race between the two superpowers. The Soviets had launched the first satellite, Sputnik, just four years earlier. Competition was intense, with both countries racing to be the first to put a man on the moon. And with this competition came great danger as well. Many deadly accidents occurred, especially on the Soviet side. Officially, though, all of these casualties took place within Earth's atmosphere, and no human has ever died or been lost in space. But is this true? Some say radio recordings made by two Italian brothers in the early 1960s prove that up to half a dozen cosmonauts were lost in space, their deaths covered up by an embarrassed and secretive government.

Achille and Gian Battista Judica-Cordiglia were two brothers who lived near the Northern Italian town of Turin. They were interested in radio since they were very young and intrigued by the many space missions that were happening at the time. Because of this, they used scrap metal and parts left by the Americans in World War II to turn an abandoned German bunker into an advanced radio listening post. The brothers had success intercepting transmissions from both American and Soviet space missions, allegedly attracting the attention of NASA, the KGB, and the Italian Secret Service, and became minor celebrities. Aside from their recordings of known missions (such as John Glenn, America's first man in space), the brothers also claimed to have received transmissions from other, unofficial Soviet missions, some of which had deadly outcomes.

"Conditions growing worse, why don't you answer? We are going slower... the world will never know about us." This was the ominous message from space intercepted by the brothers on May 19, 1961, spoken by a woman in Russian. But who was she? The Soviets had only announced the flight of Gagarin a month earlier, and the next official human flight wouldn't come until August. Was this a secret space disaster? Did the Soviets cover up the lonely death of a female cosmonaut in space after the mission became a failure? Another mysterious recording allegedly received by the brothers was of a distress signal in Morse Code: "SOS. SOS. SOS..." Again, at the time, there were not any official Soviet cosmonauts in orbit. Moreover, in the bothers' telling, the signal was moving very fast away from the Earth, into deep space. Perhaps the most chilling recording comes from November 1963 and contains a female voice pleading in Russian,

"5 4 3 2 1. 1 2 3 4 5. Come in. Come in. Come in. Listen! Listen! Come in! Come in! Talk to me! Talk to me! I am hot! I am hot!... I can see a flame!... Am I going to crash?... I will reenter... I feel hot!"

Among nine publicly released recordings made over four years, the brothers claimed to hear multiple spacecraft (and their occupants) going off course, burning up in the atmosphere, and suffering other deadly disasters.

Though the Soviet Union had a long and well-documented history of lies and falsifications concerning its space program, there are reasons to doubt the brothers' findings. For example, some of the recordings have speakers making errors in Russian or using incorrect terminology. Also, the technology to go into deep space, accidentally or purposefully, had not been officially developed yet. Finally, any true failures would likely have been publicized by the Americans for propaganda reasons. What do you think? Are there "lost cosmonauts" out there even today, in the icy darkness of space?

Your Mission

You have been given the most advanced radio equipment available today, along with a device for translating Russian and Italian. Your goal is to prove or disprove the brothers' claims about the Soviet space recordings. How will you proceed? Do you make friends with the brothers, and offer your equipment? Do you make a secret listening post near theirs? Do you contact the Soviets, or the Americans? Be careful!

References

Dark Docs. (2018, July 23). *Lost cosmonauts: did Russia lose the 1st astronauts in space?* [Video]. YouTube. https://www.youtube.com/watch?v=u9dsMELHuTA

Encyclopedia Britannica. (n.d.). Yuri Gagarin. In *Britannica.com*. https://www.britannica.com/biography/Yuri-Gagarin

Hollington, K. (2008, July) Lost in Space.. *The Fortean Times*. Retrieved from https://www.thelivingmoon.com/45jack_files/03files/Lost_Cosmonauts_02.html

Morgans, J. (2020, April 1). *These brothers were eavesdropping on space transmissions when they heard cries for help.* VICE. https://www.vice.com/en_in/article/qjd5dm/judica-cordiglia-brothers-were-eavesdropping-soviet-space-radio-transmissions-cries-for-help-mystery

Ratcliff, J. D. (1965, April 1). Italy's amazing amateur space watchers. *Reader's Digest*. Retrieved from https://www.aerospaceweb.org/question/conspiracy/q0235a.shtml

Scott, J. (2019, March 7). *The mysterious "lost cosmonaut" recording | random Thursday* [Video]. YouTube. https://www.youtube.com/watch?v=RZidFWLrLnU

Veske, M. (2014). *Kosmonauta* [Video]. Vimeo. https://vimeo.com/106216724

Lost Cosmonauts History Quiz

1. The Judica-Cordiglia Brothers listened to ____ transmissions from space flights.

    a. internet

    b. satellite

    c. radio

    d. telescopic

2. The ____ put the first human into space.

    a. Soviets

    b. Americans

    c. Germans

    d. Italians

3. How many recordings did the brothers make public?

    a. 4

    b. 9

    c. 13

    d. none

4. What was the name of the first satellite in space?

    a. Gagarin

    b. Russia

    c. Judica-Cordiglia

    d. Sputnik

5. The brothers built their listening post in an abandoned _____.

    a. radio antenna

    b. bunker

    c. space station

    d. village

Answers at the end of the book

Discussion Questions

1. Imagine you are a cosmonaut about to be sent on a secret mission into space in the early 1960s:

    a. How would you feel?

    b. Do you agree with the secrecy?

    c. Do you trust the scientists, military officers, and politicians who are sending you on the mission?

    d. Do you think it's safe?

    e. Do you think you will return?

2. Why would a country or company want to keep their successes secret?

      a. Can you think of any examples from history?

      b. What was the reason for trying to keep a secret?

      c. Do you think this was the right decision at the time?

3. On the other hand, why would a country or company want to keep their failures secret?

      a. Can you think of any examples from history?

      b. What was the reason for trying to keep a secret?

      c. Do you think this was the right decision at the time?

4. Do you think most countries or companies tell the truth about their technological successes or failures? Why, or why not?

5. Can you think of any examples from the present day where a country or company might be lying, or not telling the whole truth? What would be the leaders' reasons for this? Do you agree, or disagree? Explain.

Projects

1. Search YouTube for "Judica-Cordiglia recordings". Listen to one and read the subtitles. Does it sound real? Could it be fake? See "Supplement 11: Fake News". Leave a comment giving your thoughts/opinions on the recording or reply to another's comment.

2. Research an important satellite. Describe its history and function.

3. Imagine you are the head of your government and create your own secret mission.

      a. What is the mission? Describe it.

      b. What is the goal of your mission?

      c. Why should it be kept secret from the public?

4. Would you like to go to space? For some it sounds like a thrilling idea, while others may find it terrifying. Interview your classmates or friends and family.

Interview Question: Would you ever go on a space flight? Why or why not?		
Name	Answer	Reason
Andrew	Yes	It's one of my dreams!

Project Serpo

Before You Read

1. Do you believe there is life on other planets? Why or why not?
2. Do you believe there have been visitors to Earth from other planets? Why or why not?
3. Why do you think aliens from other planets might visit Earth?
4. If they wanted to bring you to their planet, would you be willing to go?

Vocabulary Definitions

Write the letter of the definition next to the matching word.

1. intergalactic (adj.) ____
2. light-year (n.) ____
3. massive (adj.) ____
4. classified (adj.) ____
5. personnel (n.) ____
6. holograph (n.) ____
7. frightening (adj.) ____
8. extraterrestrial (adj.) ____
9. reverse-engineering (n.) ____
10. innovations (n.) ____

a. secret information not available to the public
b. to learn how to make a product by taking it apart
c. very large
d. staff in an organization or government
e. a 3-D image or video
f. scary
g. from another planet
h. new ideas or inventions.
i. About 6 trillion miles.
j. between multiple planets or universes.

Answers at the end of the book

Your Briefing

341 Words / 1410-1600L
Place: Las Vegas, Nevada.
Time: July 16, 1965

Note: This article describes an unproven theory not commonly regarded as fact by the scientific community.

On July 16, 1965, a *massive* alien spacecraft from the Zeta Reticuli star system landed at the Nevada test site north of Las Vegas. Following a plan set in motion by President Kennedy in 1962, the alien visitors known as the Ebens welcomed 12 astronaut-trained military *personnel* aboard their craft for the 10-month journey to their home planet, Serpo, 39 *light-years* away. The Ebens had technology that was much more advanced than Earth technology. The original crew would spend 13 years on the planet Serpo, learning how to make a host of new inventions such as alternative fuel technologies. In addition, the Ebens presented the US with The Yellow Book, a complete history of the universe recorded *holographically*, allowing the reader to view actual scenes from all history. Following the original trip, an ongoing relationship with the Ebens has led to eight more trips and counting! However, this has been kept secret from the public, possibly to prevent panic or other mysterious reasons!

At the super-secret test site in Las Vegas, Nevada, the most amazing thing has happened - aliens from another planet have landed their spacecraft! Although it seems potentially *frightening*, these aliens have come in peace. Calling themselves the Ebens, they have invited humans to come back to their planet to learn about their technology and ideas which can help advance human progress.

John F. Kennedy, the US President, has agreed to send a team of 12 to the Ebens' planet, Serpo, to live there for several years, and then return to benefit the human race. Now you have a chance to travel to Planet Serpo to witness *extraterrestrial* life and learn secrets that could change the human race forever! By *reverse-engineering* their technology, you should be able to bring new *innovations* back to Earth.

Now it is your responsibility to join this trip to another planet, to discover just what secrets this alien race has. Are they really offering us help and technology or do they have other motives? It is your job to uncover the truth!

Your Mission

What can you learn as a member of Project Serpo? What new technology or ideas can you learn from them?

References

Eisen, J. (2001). *Suppressed Inventions and Other Discoveries: Revealing the World's Greatest Secrets of Science and Medicine*. Penguin.

McMillan, G. (2008, June 24). *Alien abductees tell their own story in Serpo*. Gizmodo. https://io9.gizmodo.com/alien-abductees-tell-their-own-story-in-serpo-5018919

Kasten, L. (2013). *Secret journey to Planet Serpo: A true story of interplanetary travel*. Simon & Schuster.

Project Serpo History Quiz

1. According to the text, the Ebens are an alien race that might have come to Earth in peace and to help humans.

   a. true

   b. false

2. Who was the US President in charge of the original Serpo Project?

   a. Abraham Lincoln

   b. John F. Kennedy

   c. Donald Trump

   d. Lyndon B. Johnson

3. Which type of technology did the Ebens help us create through reverse-engineering, according to the briefing?

   a. Spacecraft

   b. Automobiles

   c. Alternative fuel

   d. Alternative energy

4. What is the name of the book that the Ebens allegedly provided us with historical knowledge?

   a. Yellow Book

   b. Green Book

   c. Red Book

   d. White Book

5. There has only been one mission to Planet Serpo so far.

   a. True

   b. False

Answers at the end of the book

Discussion Questions

1. Do you think this story is true? Why or why not?

2. If this is a true story, why do you think the US government would hide the truth?

3. Would you be willing to go on a mission to Planet Serpo? Why or why not? If you went, what would you be most interested to learn?

4. What do you think aliens might want to learn from us? Make a list of five things you think we might teach them about! These could be inventions, ideas, culture, religion, or anything else!

5. Which planets do you think are most likely to have alien life? Why?

6. Why is *Reverse-Engineering* useful? Can you think of any examples of how it's used?

Projects

1. *Be a Part of History to Complete the Mission.* Write about 1 page on your trip to Serpo. Choose one or more of these questions to consider as you write:

    a. What is the experience like traveling to another planet?

    b. What do the Ebens teach you?

    c. What new ideas or technologies do you bring back to Earth?

2. Research the Planet Serpo Mission and answer the following:

3. Do you believe this mission was real? Why or why not?

    a. What is something important it's claimed that the Ebens taught us?

    b. Why do you think this information is classified?

4. There have been many cases in history of claimed alien encounters or sightings that some believe are real and others think are fake news. Research one claimed alien encounter and decide if it you think it's real or not. See "Supplement 11: Fake News".

5. How do you believe aliens from another planet would be similar or different from us?

6. Draw or find a picture and write a description of how aliens might be similar or different to humans.

7. Interview your classmates or friends and family: do they think aliens visiting us are more likely to help or harm us?

Interview Question: If space aliens came to Earth, do you think they would come to help or harm humans and why?		
Name	**Answer**	**Reason**
Taylor	Help	I believe the movie Close Encounters of the Third Kind is real!

Crop Circles - Real or Hoax?

Before You Read

1. Above is a picture of a *crop circle*.

   a. How do you think it was made? Who made it.

   b. What purpose does it serve?

   c. Could aliens have made them and if so, why?

2. Do you believe there is life on other planets?

   a. If so, do you think aliens have visited Earth? Why or why not?

Vocabulary Definitions

Write the letter of the definition next to the matching word.

1. crop (n.) ____
2. elaborate (adj.) ____
3. geometric (adj.) ____
4. peak (adj.) ____
5. paranormal (adj.) ____
6. genuine (adj.) ____
7. scrutinize (v.) ____
8. symposium (n.) ____

a. A conference or meeting to discuss a subject
b. plants grown on a farm
c. complex or detailed
d. greatest point or amount
e. beyond science, relating to magic or otherworldly things
f. a pattern or design with mathematical shapes
g. to review carefully in detail
h. real, not fake

Vocabulary Questions

Discuss with a partner.

1. Think of at least two examples of *crops*. Have you ever visited a farm yourself?
2. Are or someone you know interested in the *paranormal*? What is the interest?
3. Do you usually *scrutinize* your work carefully before you finish it? Why or why not?

Your Briefing

599 Words - 1210-1400L
Place: Wiltshire, UK.
Time: August 11, 1996

Crop circles are patterns that appear in fields. The pattern is created when certain areas of the crops are stamped down, but others are left intact. The edge is so clean that it looks like it was created with a machine. Even though the stalks are bent, they are not damaged. Most of the time, the crop continues to grow as normal.

Sometimes, the patterns are simple circles. In other instances, they are *elaborate* designs consisting of several interconnecting *geometric* shapes. The earliest versions of crop circles date back to the 1600-1800s but the first real crop circles didn't appear until the 1970s, when simple circles began appearing in the English countryside. The number and complexity of the circles increased dramatically, reaching a *peak* in the 1980s and 1990s when increasingly elaborate circles were produced, including those showing complex mathematical equations.

Crop-circle enthusiasts call themselves *cereologists*, after Ceres, the Roman goddess of agriculture. Most cereologists believe that crop circles are the work of either aliens or creatures naturally through weather. Another theory is that crop circles are messages from future humans that prove that time travel exists! However, in 1991 Doug Bower and David Chorley were filmed showing how they made many of the reported corn field patterns discovered across the UK. The duo said they simply used wooden planks and rope to flatten corn in a circular fashion.

In 1996, a recording was taken near the ancient hill fort of Oliver's Castle, near Devizes, Wiltshire, and has split crop circle researchers as to whether it is an elaborate stunt or *genuine* proof of the *paranormal.*

The story of the video began on August 11, 1996, when a man calling himself John Whaley claimed to have filmed the startling footage that morning. The film shows flashing lights and the formation of one center circle and six smaller surrounding ones. It is just a few seconds long and shows either a very elaborate attempt of fraud or the most incredibly important UFO and crop circle film footage ever.

Suspicions it may not be real were aroused by the "poor quality" of the "snowflake" crop circle that was actually in the field, according to researchers. A private investigator was hired, and John Whaley was discovered to actually be John Wabe, an employee of a Bristol animation studio. Mr. Wabe is even reported to have made a video confession that it was all a hoax, filmed on location at Oliver's Castle.

In spite of this, some crop circle examiners seem to get a kick out of the chance to figure out if it's a genuine film. Video editing experts have analyzed this recording and said that it is either genuine or developed by a group of specialists with a great deal of free time. They additionally noticed that Wabe was playing the video in a bar just hours after the crop circles had shown up in the field. They have additionally *scrutinized* the claimed confession, which is inaccessible on the web.

Finally, the issue of the *Oliver's Castle Crop Circles* was raised during the 27th Glastonbury *Symposium* by cereologist Roeland Beljon, who believes they are not all hoaxes. Referring to the Oliver's Castle video, he told the audience: "It was filmed in 1996, this footage. Look it up on the internet, it is very controversial."

Speaking generally about crop circles, he said: "Is it all a hoax? No, of course it is not a hoax." This is just one of many documented cases of crop circles that is worth investigating. But it's a great place to start. Can you solve the mystery?

Your Mission

Investigate Oliver's Castle Crop Circles! Were they real or a hoax?

Crop Circles History Quiz

1. The first crop circles were discovered in the USA.

    a. true

    b. false

2. When did the first real modern crop circles appear?

    a. 1600s

    b. 1800s

    c. 1970s

    d. 1990s

3. The name cereologists comes from Ceres, the god of agriculture.

    a. True

    b. False

4. The 'Oliver's Castle' crop circle was made by...

    a. John Whaley

    b. an animation team

    c. aliens or UFOs

    d. We don't know for sure

5. Which is NOT a theory on crop circles?

    a. They are made by humans with wood planks.

    b. They are made by UFOs.

    c. They are made by animals.

    d. They are made by time travelers from the future.

Discussion Questions

1. Crop circles began and continue to pop-up all over the world, but especially in the UK. Why do you think this is? Have you ever heard of or seen crop circles in your hometown?

2. Do you agree or disagree with cereologist Roeland Beljon's statement about crop circles: "Is it all a hoax? No, of course it is not a hoax."

3. In 1987, a mysterious crop message was discovered saying "WEARENOTALONE." Skeptics argued that if the message had been from aliens, it would have read "YOUARENOTALONE." Do you agree or disagree with the skeptics? Why?

4. If crop circles are real, why do you think aliens would leave such unique patterns?

5. What is another example of a mystery in your culture that some people think is real or a hoax?

Projects

1. **Be a Part of History to Complete the Mission:** Answer the questions below:

a. Who made the crop circle? Was it John Whaley, or aliens, or time travelers from the future!

b. How was this crop circle made?

c. Why was it made?

2. Watch the video from Oliver's Castle available here https://www.youtube.com/watch?v=AcLcnrpxmUg.

a. Do you think this crop circle was real or a hoax? Why?

b. Design your own crop circle.

c. Draw your own picture or find a picture of an interesting crop circle! Describe if the design has any special meaning.

3. Research and find a picture of an interesting crop circle! Answer the following or see "Supplement 4: Finding Credible Sources".

a. When/where was the crop circle discovered?

b. Who made it? Which of the theories are claimed or proven: *human made, alien made, plasma vortices, time travelers*?

4. Interview your classmates or friends and family:

Interview Question: Do you think crop circles are real or a hoax?		
Name	**Answer**	**Reason**
Taylor	Hoax	Still missing real evidence of aliens or time travelers.

References

Austin, J. (2017, August 17). Mindblowing: Crop circle filmed being formed in seconds by mystery balls of light. *Express.co.uk*. https://www.express.co.uk/news/weird/842579/UFO-crop-circle-made-ball-of-light-aliens

Heberling, K. (2016, March 2) *Plasma vortex theory*. Crop Circles. http://kentheberling.com/projects/CropCircles/Theories/plasmavortex.html

Radford, B. (2017, June 10). *The crop circle mystery: A closer look*. Live Science. https://www.live-science.com/26540-crop-circles.html

Watson, S. (2004, September 29). *How crop circles work*. HowStuffWorks. https://science.howstuff-works.com/science-vs-myth/unexplained-phenomena/crop-circle.htm

Winterson, L. (October 1997). *Inquiring minds need to know: John Whaley (Wheyleigh/Wabe) and the Oliver's Castle video hoax exposed*. Circular Times. http://circulartimes.org/Crop%20Circle%20Video%20Oliver's%20Castle%20Fraud%20LWCMD%20CT.htm

Stephen Hawking's Time Travel Cocktail Party

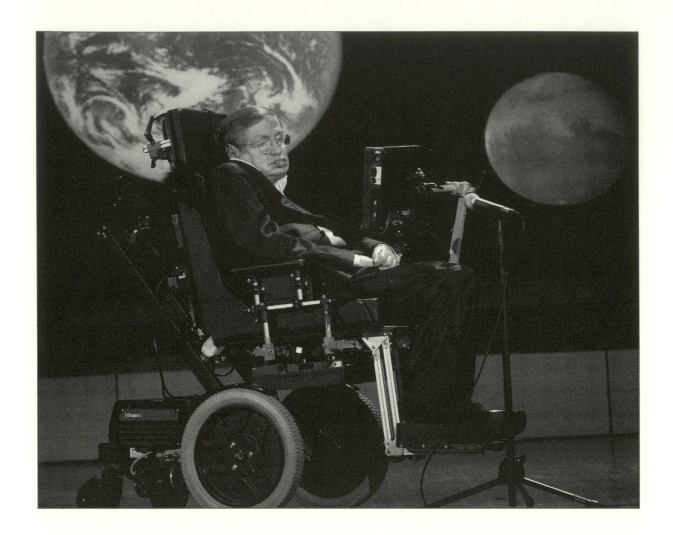

Stephen Hawking was an important figure in theoretical physics, *cosmology*, and pop culture. Though affected by a degenerative disease that had doctors predicting an early death, Hawking instead lived to research the creation of the universe and its possible end, in the form of black holes. Also a popular writer, he published bestsellers including *A Brief History of Time*. Time travel was another topic that fascinated him

Before You Read

1. Look at the picture and description above of Stephen Hawking.

   a. What do you know about him?

   b. Do you share any of his interests? Why or why not?

2. Do you believe time travel is possible?

   a. Why or why not?

Vocabulary Definitions

Write the letter of the definition next to the matching word

1. theoretical physics (n.) ____
2. cosmology (n.) ____
3. invitation (n.) ____
4. pop culture (n.) ____
5. cordially (adv.) ____
6. theory (n.) ____
7. transmit (v.) ____
8. paradox (n.) ____
9. capture (v.) ____
10. coordinates (n.) ____

a. in a warm and friendly way
b. the science of understanding the creation of the universe
c. a branch of physics that uses mathematical models, not experiments
d. an unproven idea
e. modern culture such as fashion, film, and music, often popular with young people.
f. location that can be found on a map using vertical and horizontal
g. to send electronically
h. a contradiction, a series of events that seems impossible
i. a written or verbal request asking someone to join a special event
j. to take a picture or video of something

Answers at the end of the book

Vocabulary Questions

Discuss with a partner.

1. Are you interested in *cosmology*? Why or why not?
2. When did you last receive an *invitation*? What was it for?
3. Do you think time travel could cause a *paradox*? Why or why not?

Your Briefing

376 Words - 810-1000L
Place: Cambridge, England.
Time: June 28, 2009.

What if someone threw a party and told no one about it? Why would they do that?

On June 28, 2009, internationally famous time and space cosmology expert Stephen Hawking prepared a cocktail party with three trays of canapes and flutes filled with Krug champagne. There was a film crew ready to film the guests. No one came and nothing was touched. Why?

Balloons decorated the walls, and a giant banner displayed the words "Welcome, Time Travellers."

Hawking's party was actually an experiment on the possibility of time travel. (Invitations were sent only after the party was over). By only publishing the party invitation in his filmed TV mini-series, Into the Universe with Stephen Hawking, Hawking hoped to attract futuristic time travelers.

"You are cordially invited to a reception for Time Travellers," the invitation read, along with the date, time, and coordinates for the event. The theory, Hawking explained, was that only someone from the future would be able to attend.

Unfortunately, no one showed up from the past, present, or future!

Hawking explained why he came up with the idea: "I like simple experiments ... and champagne." By transmitting the invitation, Hawking thought it might catch the eye of a future time traveler—the brain-breaking paradox being that, if it eventually does, then wouldn't we have seen one or two at the party?

But if time travelers knew about the party, would they want to visit? And if they did, would they want to be captured by a film crew? For Hawking, the event was planned for fun, but also a serious attempt to prove whether time travel is real.

"I'm hoping copies of the invitation, in one form or another, will survive for many thousands of years," Hawking said.

In which case, the party is on June 28, 2009 12:00 UTC, and the coordinates are 52° 12' 21" N, 0° 7' 4.7" E. Any time traveler should easily be able to join, but would they want to?

With a film crew capturing the event, there is evidence that no one seemed to come to the party... or that's what they wanted you to think! Did visitors from another time actually attend secretly? If so, what messages from the future might they have told Hawking?

Your Mission

What really happened at Stephen Hawking's secret time travel party?

Stephen Hawking's Time Travel Party History Quiz

1. Stephen Hawking's time travel party had no attendees.

   a. true
   b. false

2. What evidence did Hawking provide to show who attended the party?

   a. a guest list
   b. his diary
   c. video footage
   d. photographs

3. Invitations were sent for the time travel party

   a. before the event.
   b. after the event.
   c. during the event.
   d. they were never sent.

4. What is NOT one of Stephen Hawking's special interests?

   a. black holes
   b. time travel
   c. life after death
   d. the creation of the universe

5. Copies of the invitation are still open for future time travelers.

   a. true
   b. false

Answers at the end of the book

Discussion Questions

1. Do you think Stephen Hawking's plan to attract time travelers was a good idea? Is there any way his plan could have been improved?

2. If time travel is real, why do you think time travelers didn't attend his party?

3. If you met time travelers from the future, what is the first question you would ask them?

4. Do you think it's possible time travelers could have visited his party secretly?

5. If so, what do you think they might have told him?

6. If you could time-travel to any time in the past…

   a. What time period and place would you visit?
   b. Who would you meet?
   c. What advice would you give them?

Projects

1. **Be a Part of History to Complete the Mission**. Visit Stephen Hawking's time-travel party. Think about the following.

    a. Who do you meet from the future?

    b. What will you discuss about time travel?

    c. Will your visit remain a secret?

2. Research Stephen Hawking and his theories on cosmology or theoretical physics. Cite a source (See "Supplement 4: Finding Credible Sources" for help!)

    a. Do you agree or disagree with his theories?

3. Design your home time machine! Draw a picture or diagram to explain how your machine will work!

4. Interview your classmates or friends and family:

Interview Question: Do you believe time travel is possible?		
Name	**Answer**	**Reason**
Taylor	Yes	But only going to the future, not the past

References

Ewbank, A. (2018, December 24). *When Stephen Hawking threw a cocktail party for time travelers.* Atlas Obscura. https://www.atlasobscura.com/articles/stephen-hawking-time-travelers-party

Hines, N. (2020, April 8). *That time Stephen Hawking threw a champagne party for time travelers.* VinePair. https://vinepair.com/articles/stephen-hawking-time-travel-party/

Kaufman, M. (2018, March 14). *Stephen Hawking hosted a party for time travelers, but no one came.* Mashable. https://mashable.com/2018/03/14/stephen-hawking-time-travel-party/

Laskow, S. (2018, November 2). *For sale: An invitation to Stephen Hawking's cocktail party for time travelers.* Atlas Obscura. https://www.atlasobscura.com/articles/invitation-stephen-hawkings-time-traveller-party

Section VI - Conspiracies and Secrets

Prepared by Agent Peter Lacey

Shakespeare, Marlowe, Spies, and Murder

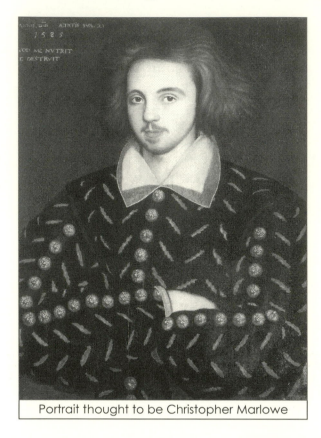

Portrait thought to be Christopher Marlowe

William Shakespeare

Before You Read

1. When you think of famous English authors, who do you think of first?

2. Have you read any Shakespeare or seen any of his plays? If so, what was your opinion?

3. Why would someone try to fake their death?

Vocabulary Definitions

Write the letter of the definition next to the matching word.

1. author (n.) ____
2. scholar (n.) ____
3. attribute (v.) ____
4. conspiracy (n.) ____
5. prolific (adj.) ____
6. basis (n.) ____
7. theory (n.) ____
8. atheism (n.) ____
9. spy (n.) ____
10. speculate (v.) ____
11. coincidence (n.) ____

a. the belief there is no God
b. a person who watches and collects information secretly
c. an explanation or idea that is missing evidence
d. doing something a lot and often
e. a person who writes
f. a secret plan to do something bad
g. a person who studies deeply
h. guess what is possible or likely
i. the foundation, the original factor
j. information or events that appear related without being planned or connection
k. to identify the source or cause

Answers at the end of the book

Vocabulary Questions

Discuss with a partner.

1. Would you like to be an *author*? What would you write?
2. Would you like to be a *scholar*? What would you study?
3. What skills does a *spy* need? Would you be good at *spying*?

Your Briefing

478 Words - 1010-1200L
Place: London, England
Time: May 30, 1593

Is the most famous English *author* actually a fake? Some historians and literary *scholars* believe that William Shakespeare did not actually write the plays and poetry that are *attributed* to him. They believe there was a *conspiracy* to hide the true author of *Romeo and Juliet*, *Macbeth*, and all his other famous plays. But what is their evidence?

Not much is known about Shakespeare's personal life, but some scholars believe he did not have the background to become such a *prolific* and highly successful author. They believe that someone who became the most famous author in the English language would have gone to the best schools and lived an upper-class lifestyle. However, Shakespeare was not upper-class. Even though many of his plays are about *royal* life and high society, he was from a small town called Stratford, which is in the countryside far from London. Furthermore, there is no record of his education. In fact, Shakespeare signed and even spelled his name several different ways. All of this is the *basis* for the conspiracy *theories*.

There are many theories about who was the real Shakespeare, but one of the most popular is that it was Christopher Marlowe. Marlowe was a well-known and successful author in England who wrote the same kind of plays as Shakespeare, and many scholars think Shakespeare was influenced by Marlowe because of similarities in their work. But are they only similarities? One of Marlowe's most famous plays is *Doctor Faustus*, which is about a man who makes a deal with the devil. The devil gives Faustus great power on earth, but he is sent to hell forever as a result. Some people think Marlowe made a similar deal to sell his soul in order to be a great author.

Marlowe was not alive when Shakespeare became popular because he was murdered at Deptford, London in 1593. At least, that is the official story. Marlowe had been accused of *atheism*, which was a serious crime at that time in England, and some scholars *speculate* he faked his death to avoid punishment. Additionally, some historians think he was likely working as a *spy*. The men who were with him when he died all had connections to Queen Elizabeth's spymaster. These men had to be experts at keeping secrets, and it is likely they knew how to fake a murder.

The final piece of evidence that supports the conspiracy theory is that all of Shakespeare's work was published after Marlowe's death. Although they were the same age, their public careers did not overlap. Is it only a *coincidence* that Shakespeare's name first appeared just a few weeks after Marlowe's murder?

There are many people who don't believe there was any conspiracy. They believe that William Shakespeare was the real author of all the famous work, but there is only one way to know the truth for sure. You must go back in time to meet the real men. Can William Shakespeare show you proof he is the author? Will you find a conspiracy at the house in Deptford where Marlowe was meeting three other men on May 30, 1593?

Your Mission

Travel to England in 1593 to find William Shakespeare and investigate Christopher Marlowe's death. Discover who is the true author of the most famous English literature.

References

Barber, R. (2009). Shakespeare authorship doubt in 1593. *Critical Survey, 21*(2). https://doi.org/10.3167/cs.2009.210205

The Marlowe Society. (2018, December 30). *Our policy.* https://www.marlowe-society.org/about-the-society/our-policy/

The Marlowe Society. (2020, May 12). *Death in deptford.* https://www.marlowe-society.org/christopher-marlowe/life/death-in-deptford/

Pruitt, S. (2015, July 15). *Did Shakespeare really write his own plays?* HISTORY. https://www.history.com/news/did-shakespeare-really-write-his-own-plays

Shakespeare History Quiz

1. Who was William Shakespeare?

    a. a conspiracy theorist

    b. a famous English author

    c. a king of England

    d. a spy

2. Where was Shakespeare born?

    a. Stratford

    b. London

    c. Marlowe

3. Manchester

4. When was Christopher Marlowe murdered?

    a. 1616

    b. 1600

    c. 1593

    d. 1539

5. Why was Christopher Marlowe in trouble with the law?

    a. He faked his own death

    b. He was accused of atheism

    c. He murdered his friend

    d. His dramas were not popular

6. Which is one of Shakespeare's famous plays?

    a. *Doctor Faustus*

    b. *Romeo and Juliet*

    c. *Christopher Marlowe*

    d. *Royal Life and High Society*

Answers at the end of the book

Discussion Questions

1. Does it matter if Shakespeare is fake? Why do you think people like to investigate conspiracies about Shakespeare?

2. Do you think it is possible Christopher Marlowe successfully faked his death? How could he have accomplished it?

3. Can you imagine a situation where you would try to fake your death? Explain.

4. Why do you think Shakespeare became the most famous English author? What makes his work so popular?

Projects

1. **Be a Part of History to Complete the Mission**: Discover the truth about Shakespeare.

    a. Describe what you witness in Deptford. Are the spies part of a conspiracy? Is Christopher Marlowe actually murdered or does he escape? Does he live to write as Shakespeare?

    OR

    b. Can you find William Shakespeare and prove he is the real author? Describe your meeting with him. What does he show you that proves he is the real author?

2. Watch a movie based on one of Shakespeare's plays and write a review.

    a. Give a summary of the story and your opinion of the movie.

    b. What details were interesting to you?

3. Choose one of Shakespeare's poems for a class presentation.

    a. Explain the theme and give your opinion.

    b. Read it aloud or challenge yourself to recite it all from memory.

4. Create a presentation on the life and death of a famous author from your home country.

    a. Make a visual presentation that shares the major events of their life.

    b. Give examples of the literature they are famous for.

    c. Are there any mysteries about their life?

    d. Add an interactive activity where your classmates guess what is true and false about the author. See "Supplement 10: Fact or Fiction".

5. Interview your classmates or friends and family:

Interview Question: Who is your favorite author, and what have they written that you enjoy?		
Name	**Answer**	**Reason**
Peter	Ernest Hemingway, <u>A Farewell to Arms</u> and <u>The Sun Also Rises</u>	I like novels about travel and expatriate life, and Hemingway has a straightforward style and relatable characters.

The Illuminati: Secret Societies and Conspiracy

(left) Portrait of Adam Weishaupt, founder of the Illuminati. In Bavaria on 1 May 1776.

(right) part of the reverse side of the US one-dollar bill designed in 1935. The pyramid symbol is an adaptation of The Great Seal of the United States, designed by Charles Thomas. Some people say that that this symbol was influenced by secret societies, such as the Illuminati.

Before You Read

1. Have you ever been a member of a club?
    a. What activities did you do?
    b. How often did you meet?
    c. Was it difficult to join?
    d. Are you good at keeping secrets? Explain.
2. What do you know about secret societies?
3. Do you believe secret organizations have power over our lives?

Vocabulary Definitions

Write the letter of the definition next to the matching word

1. exclusive (adj.) ____
2. controversial (adj.) ____
3. manipulate (v.) ____
4. domination (n.) ____
5. notorious (adj.) ____
6. suspect (v.) ____
7. conspiracy theory (n.) ____
8. philosopher (n.) ____
9. superstition (n.) ____
10. subtly (adv.) ____
11. alias (n.) ____
12. initiation (n.) ____
13. rituals (n.) ____
14. outlaw (v.) ____
15. mastermind (v.) ____
16. occult (n.) ____
17. satanic (adj.) ____

a. causing strong disagreement
b. to control secretly or unfairly
c. total control
d. carefully to avoid attention
e. only for a special group, not everyone
f. to believe or doubt without proof
g. belief in secret plans and hidden truth behind real events
h. famous for something bad
i. to make a law against something
j. someone who studies knowledge and ideas of life
k. a belief that is unscientific
l. a magical belief system
m. a fake name
n. to plan and control an event
o. formal, traditional activities with special meaning
p. event or activities to join a special group
q. from or supporting enemies of God

Answers at the end of the book

Vocabulary Questions

Discuss with a partner.

1. Are you a member of any *exclusive* groups? If so, what are the rules for joining?
2. What is an example of a common *superstition*? Do you believe it? Explain.
3. Are there any common activities you think should be *outlawed*? Explain.

Your Briefing

591 Words - 1010-1200L
Place: Bavarian Germany
Time: 1784

Joining a club is a good way to meet people. Usually, we just think of clubs as a way to share hobbies and have fun, but throughout history there have been more serious clubs organized with much bigger goals. Some of these groups are *exclusive*, secretive, and *controversial*, and they are often called secret societies. Although it's actually not unusual to join a secret society at your university or in connection to your work life, some people believe there are a few secret societies that try to influence or *manipulate* world events by controlling banking, entertainment, and government. Some people even fear that secret societies are planning world *domination*.

The most *notorious* secret society is called the Illuminati. Although there have not been any known members for hundreds of years, people often *suspect* the Illuminati is still active and controlling major world events. Many celebrities, business leaders, and politicians are believed to be secret Illuminati members. It seems any major news leads to more Illuminati *conspiracy theories*. They are blamed for the 1963 assassination of US President John F. Kennedy and are also accused of using famous musicians and Hollywood stars to send secret messages in movies and music.

Even though these conspiracy theories are often ridiculous and cannot be proved, we know that the Illuminati was a real secret society. It was started by a *philosopher* named Adam Weishaupt in Germany in 1776. This was during The Enlightenment, a period in Europe when there was a shift away from religious leadership and toward scientific thinking. Like many philosophers during The Enlightenment, Weishaupt was upset with the Catholic Church. He believed they were against freedom and knowledge, that religion was harmful *superstition*. He wanted science and philosophy to have more power in society.

However, Weishaupt did not want to start a public fight with the church, so his solution was to form a secret society of powerful men who could *subtly* influence political decisions. He named it The Order of The Illuminati. To maintain secrecy, the Illuminati used symbols for identification and its members chose *aliases*. They held secret meetings where they discussed their goals and had formal *initiations* for new members. Some people believe the gatherings included *occult* activities, but the truth about that is still a mystery.

After a few years, there were between 1,000 and 3,000 members in Europe. As more people joined, though, there were disagreements within the group. They argued over *rituals* and whether to join other secret societies. The group became too large to stay secret, and the Catholic Church found out about their activities and tried to stop them. As a result, the Bavarian government *outlawed* all secret societies in 1784, and Weishaupt was forced to move and take a new job. Historians think that the Illuminati probably ended at that time, but some people think otherwise.

Only a few years after being outlawed, the Illuminati were accused of *masterminding* the French Revolution of 1789-1799. Later in the 1800s, churches across Europe and America started to preach against the Illuminati and warned of a connection between the Illuminati and the occult. Over time, the conspiracy theories continued: The Illuminati puts *satanic* messages in music, the Illuminati planned the September 11 attack on New York, the Illuminati controls political elections—could any of these theories be true? Is it possible that the Illuminati still exist and control governments around the world? The only way to know what happens in a secret society is to join it. Do you think you are up to the task?

Your Mission

Travel to Bavarian Germany in 1784 and join The Order of The Illuminati. Find out their plans for the future and decide if they are dangerous for the world. If it is necessary, help religious leaders stop all secret societies.

Illuminati History Quiz

1. Who founded the Illuminati?

    a. French revolutionaries
    b. John F. Kennedy
    c. Adam Weishaupt
    d. The Catholic Church

2. Where was the Illuminati started?

    a. Germany
    b. France
    c. New York
    d. Hollywood

3. What was The Enlightenment?

    a. a secret society in Germany
    b. a shift away from religion and toward science
    c. a conspiracy theory
    d. an important Catholic church

4. When did the Bavarian government outlaw secret societies?

    a. 1776
    b. 1784
    c. 1789
    d. Never

5. Which events have been blamed on the Illuminati?

    a. The French Revolution
    b. The assassination of John F. Kennedy
    c. The September 11 attacks on New York
    d. All of the above

Answers at the end of the book

Discussion Questions

1. If you had the chance to join a secret society, would you do it? Explain. Discuss the pros and cons of being a secret society member.

2. Is it possible that news media or governments sometimes lie to the public or withhold information? Why might they? Does anything that governments do need to remain secret? Explain.

3. Do you believe celebrities' connection to the Illuminati could be true?

    a. What other celebrity conspiracy have you heard about? Do you believe it?

4. Why do people believe in conspiracies when there is no good evidence?

a. Have you ever argued with someone about a conspiracy theory? What happened?

b. Is it possible to know the truth about the Illuminati and other secret societies? How?

5. Do you think it is possible for religion and science to share power in our cultures? Why do religious leaders and scientific leaders often argue against each other?

6. Which is more dangerous: a society that does not allow any religion or a society controlled by one religion? Explain

Projects

1. **Be a Part of History to Complete the Mission**: Visit Bavarian Germany in 1784 and join the Illuminati. Describe your initiation experience and the truth about the Illuminati.

   a. What do you have to do to join the group?

   b. What are the details of their plans?

   c. Do they survive being outlawed by the government?

   d. Decide whether you must help end all secret societies.

2. Start an ESL secret society. Invite friends or classmates to start a special English club.

   a. Create an initiation ceremony for new members. What must people do before they can join?

   b. Design a symbol for your club and give all members a special alias.

   c. What will you discuss at your meetings? Will they be secret?

3. Create an Illuminati presentation. Use a slideshow or other visual aid to present about a conspiracy theory.

   a. Explain the historical background and what is officially true. Who, what, where, when, and why?

   b. Explain what the conspiracy theory is and why people believe it.

   c. What is your opinion? Try to convince your classmates that the conspiracy is true OR false.

4. Conduct a survey. Find out your friends' opinions of conspiracy theories.

   a. Search for famous conspiracy theories and choose three or more that are interesting to you.

   b. Talk to 10-20 people and find out how many believe each conspiracy. Ask them to explain why. Evaluate their answers as subjective or objective. (See "Supplement 8: Opinions vs. Facts.")

   c. Record yes/no answers and report the survey results. Which conspiracy is the most believed?

5. Create an alias. Choose a new name to use for secret purposes or special occasions.

   a. Decide what kind of name it is—historical, international, invented, or common?

   b. Does your alias have a special meaning, or is it just fun to say?

   c. Try using your alias at a cafe—nobody will know who *really* ordered the coffee!
6.   Interview your classmates or friends and family:

Interview Question: Do you have an alias?		
Name	**Answer**	**Reason**
Peter	No	My nicknames are all just versions of my real name.

References

Contexts -- Societies -- Illuminati. (n.d.). Frankenstein: The Pennsylvania Electronic Edition. knarf.english.upenn.edu/Contexts/i`llumin.html

Edwards, P. (2016, January 19). *9 questions about the Illuminati you were too afraid to ask.* Vox. https://www.vox.com/2015/5/19/8624675/what-is-illuminati-meaning-conspiracy-beyonce

Hernandez, I. (2019, September 3). Meet the man who started the illuminati. *National Geographic.* https://www.nationalgeographic.com/history/magazine/2016/07-08/profile-adam-weishaupt-illuminati-secret-society/

Bessie Coleman

Before You Read

1. What is Bessie Coleman wearing in the picture? Why?
2. What could she be thinking about?
3. Could she be in danger? Why?
4. When were you in danger?

Vocabulary Definitions

Write the letter of the definition next to the matching word.

1. aviatrix (n.) ____
2. shoddy (adj.) ____
3. small-mindedness (n.) ____
4. to found (v.) ____
5. daredevil (n.) ____
6. shortcut (n.) ____
7. run-down (adj.) ____
8. downtrodden (adj.) ____
9. perpetuate (v.) ____
10. stereotypes (n.) ____
11. dismantle (v.) ____
12. backers (n.) ____
13. sabotage (v.) ____

a. badly made or done
b. rigid thinking
c. poor, depressed
d. to continue
e. to start or begin
f. a risk-taker
g. a female pilot
h. a quicker way to get somewhere
i. worn out
j. oversimplified images of a group of people
k. break down
l. financial supporters
m. deliberately destroy

Answers at the end of the book

Vocabulary Questions

Discuss with a partner.

1. What can you do to improve a shoddy building?
2. Why is it exciting to be a daredevil?
3. Which stereotypes about your culture are true?

Your Briefing

499 words - 1010-1200L
Place: Jacksonville, Florida
Time: May 1, 1926

On May 1, 1926, 34-year-old aviatrix Bessie Coleman was riding behind William D. Wills, who was her mechanic, publicity agent and friend, when the badly maintained, shoddy aircraft took an unexpected dive. Bessie was ejected from the plane and fell 2000 feet. She died instantly. Wills went down with the plane which exploded on impact; he did not survive. Later, investigators checked the burned wreckage and found an out-of-place wrench stuck in the controls of the engine.

Bessie Coleman's death deprived the world of an ambitious, adventurous, generous spirit dedicated to aviation. Although women had been flying planes since the beginning of the 19th century, flight instructors were all men. Unfortunately, those men had a narrow view of who they would accept as a potential pilot. Bessie, of mixed racial heritage, did not allow other people's *small-mindedness* to interfere with her reaching her goals. She found sponsors among the African American business community in Chicago, learned French, and moved to France to attend flight school. When she returned to the US, after earning an international pilot's license, Bessie reached out to women of color, both African Americans and Native Americans, with a sense of adventure who wanted to learn to fly. Her dream was *to found* a school for young black aviators.

In order to prove herself and draw more attention to her abilities as a pilot, Bessie performed *daredevil* stunts. In 1923, she broke a leg and three ribs when her plane crashed in Los Angeles, California. After spending three months in the hospital, she needed to raise money to buy a new plane to replace the one destroyed in the crash. After 18 months she was back in the air. Her skills included figure eights, loops, and near-ground dips. Her shows also featured other Black pilots and Black parachutists. She toured the country spreading a message of racial equality. If an airshow refused to allow blacks to attend, Bessie wouldn't fly. Although she was admired by blacks and whites alike, some journalists criticized her style and personality.

A Curtiss JN-4 biplane, the same kind that Bessie Coleman flew.

Coleman had more training than most pilots of her day. She was daring and capable, but her lack of money may have caused her to take shortcuts with safety. Since planes were expensive, her planes were usually older, run-down, and worn-out. She may not have had the time nor money for proper mechanical maintenance. Furthermore, her desire to be the best, most popular flyer may have caused her to take unnecessary risks, such as flying without her seat belt in an open cockpit plane. At the same time, Bessie Coleman's fearlessness extended to her politics. Scheduled to star in a movie, she quit rather than play a poor, downtrodden woman. She refused to perpetuate racial stereotypes that she wanted to dismantle even though the film company was black-owned. Putting her beliefs above profits may have led Bessie to anger some of her backers or others who felt threatened by Bessie's popularity. But would someone resort to sabotage? Was Bessie murdered?

Your Mission

Determine the true cause of Bessie Coleman's accident and prevent her death.

Bessie Coleman History Quiz

1. Bessie Coleman died when she was:

    a. hit by a plane

    b. thrown out of a plane

    c. killed in a plane

    d. killed by flying debris

2. Bessie Coleman is famous because she:

    a. started a school for Black aviators

    b. built unusual airplanes for rich people

    c. entertained by doing stunts

    d. was a movie star

3. Why did Bessie Coleman go to France?

    a. to take flying lessons

    b. to learn French

    c. to work as a pilot

    d. to travel in Europe

4. What is NOT listed as one of her accomplishments?

    a. speaking French

    b. surviving a plane crash

    c. directing a movie

    d. speaking to crowds

5. Many people looked up to Bessie Coleman

    a. true

    b. false

Answers at the end of the book

Discussion Questions

1. How would you save Bessie Coleman from crashing? What would you tell her? Remember she is fearless, so you have to have a good argument for anything you propose.

    a. To help you create a good argument, look at "Supplement 9: Logic and Logical Fallacies" to first practice creating bad arguments to try to keep Coleman from flying.

2. Do you think the plane crash was mechanical failure, pilot failure, or sabotage?

3. What other plane crashes have you heard about? What happened?

4. How do you think people survive plane crashes?

    a. What are some points that are important to remember?

    b. Discuss with a partner or in a small group.

Projects

1. **Be a Part of History to Complete the Mission**: Write a 1-page report to Bessie Coleman to persuade her to be more careful. Choose to write from the position of a mechanic, a safety advisor, another pilot who admires Bessie, or someone who is jealous of Bessie. How would the report of someone who is jealous of Bessie be different than someone who sincerely wants Bessie to succeed?

2. Make a list of all of the problems facing Bessie on the day of her death. What changes do you need her to make? How can you convince her to make those changes? What tone should you use? What style of delivery: lecture, Q and A, scientific approach or conversational would be the most effective?

3. Research flight. How do airplanes fly? How have they changed over the years? What is the most important change? Write 1 page. (Here's a video that can start your research: www.grc.nasa.gov/www/k-12/UEET/StudentSite/dynamicsofflight.html)

4. Amelia Earhart and Beryl Markham are both historical females who piloted planes. Research their background and prepare a presentation for a small group or your class. Or choose Beverley Bass, the first woman to become a captain at American Airlines.

5. Does your city have an aviation museum? Research and report back to the class. Would it be worthwhile to go visit.

6. Interview your classmates or friends and family. Afterward, compare their answers. How are they the same or different? What do you think about the results?

Interview Question: Why do you think most airplanes crash?		
Name	**Answer**	**Reason**
Catherine	Pilot error	Pilots are human. They can become overwhelmed and make mistakes.

References

Borden, L., & Kroeger, M. K. (2004). *Fly High!: The story of Bessie Coleman,* Perfection Learning.

PBS. (2017, September 7). *Bessie Coleman | American experience.* https://www.pbs.org/wgbh/americanexperience/features/flygirls-bessie-coleman/

Plantz, C. (2014). *The life of Bessie Coleman: First African-American woman pilot.* Enslow Publishers.

Save JFK

John Fitzgerald "Jack" Kennedy (May 29, 1917 – November 22, 1963), commonly referred to by his initials JFK, was an American politician who served as the 35th president of the United States from January 1961 until his assassination in November 1963.

"Ask not what your country can do for you, ask what you can do for your country." — John F. Kennedy's Inaugural Address, January 20, 1961

Before You Read

1. Read the famous quote by former US President John Fitzgerald Kennedy)above. What does this quote mean? Do you agree or disagree with this statement? Why?

2. What else do you know about JFK? Can you think of anything important he did?

3. What do you know about any other US Presidents? What is one important thing they did?

Vocabulary Definitions

Write the letter of the definition next to the matching word

1. achievements (n.) ____
2. assassinated (n.) ____
3. convertible (n.) ____
4. motorcade (n.) ____
5. fatally (adv.) ____
6. disputed (v.) ____
7. comprehensive (adj.) ____
8. escalate (v.) ____
9. immensely (adv.) ____
10. influential (adj.) ____

a. to increase or make stronger
b. something that many disagree about
c. a car with an open top
d. causing death
e. complete
f. murdered
g. a parade of cars
h. successful things done with skill; accomplishments
i. greatly listened to and followed to by others
j. a large amount; very

Answers at the end of the book

Vocabulary Questions

Discuss with a partner.

1. What is one of your best achievements? Describe it.
2. Do you know anyone famous who has been assassinated? Describe who it was and what you know about the situation.
3. Who is someone influential in your life and why? They could be family, friend, or someone famous!

Your Briefing

485 Words - 1410-1600L
Place: Dallas, Texas - USA
Time: November 22, 1963

John Fitzgerald Kennedy was the 35th president of the United States. He was one of the youngest ever presidents who made great *achievements* both domestically (His "New Frontier programs which emphasized economic and civil rights) and abroad (setting up the Peace-Corps and avoiding war with Russia). JFK was *assassinated* while traveling through Dallas, Texas, in an open-top *convertible*. First Lady Jacqueline Kennedy was beside him, along with Texas Governor John Connally and his wife, in a *motorcade* on a 10-mile route through the streets of downtown Dallas on November 22.

Sitting in an open Lincoln convertible, the Kennedys and Connallys drove along the parade route waving and smiling at what appeared to be a friendly crowd. But at 12:30pm, tragedy struck: As their vehicle passed the Texas School Book Depository Building, Lee Harvey Oswald allegedly fired three shots from the sixth floor, *fatally* wounding

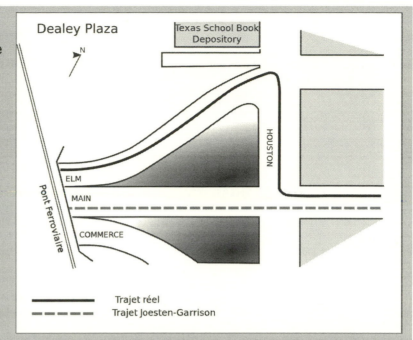

A map of President Kennedy's route through Dallas including the Texas Schoolbook Depository where Oswald was waiting.

President Kennedy and seriously injuring Governor Connally. Kennedy was pronounced dead 30 minutes later at Dallas' Parkland Hospital. He was 46.

Lyndon B. Johnson, the vice-president at the time, would be sworn in and serve as the president of the US from 1963-1969, winning his own election in 1964.

Oswald was captured and killed shortly thereafter in what some believe to be a *conspiracy.* Witnesses of the shooting made claims of gunfire originating from multiple locations and even the number of shots fired has been *disputed,* with claims of 5 to 11. But who would want to kill JFK and why?

There are many conspiracy theories. Some of them include:

- *The Mob* - They had him killed because Kennedy was unsuccessful in overthrowing Fidel Castro in Cuba. That meant the Mafia-run casinos in Cuba remained shut down. Also, JFK's brother, Robert Kennedy, was cracking down on the mob in his role as attorney general.

- *The Government* - Some rogue element in the CIA was angry over the unsuccessful Bay of Pigs invasion in Cuba. Or they were concerned about Kennedy pulling out of the Vietnam War.

● *The Vice-President* - Lyndon B. Johnson has even been named in some conspiracy theories. Maybe the vice-president wanted power. Or perhaps some elements of the government (see above) thought he would be more willing to work with them on important issues like escalating the Vietnam War.

JFK was an immensely popular president and many theories have been debated about what he would have done if he had lived. In 2009, filmmaker and scholar Koji Masutani took on the subject of Kennedy and Vietnam in Virtual JFK: Vietnam If Kennedy Had Lived.

Masutani and the researchers concluded that Kennedy would have sought a more diplomatic solution than Johnson, who committed more troops to the Vietnam War in 1964, and that Kennedy wanted to be out of Vietnam entirely by 1966.

But what would this immensely popular and *influential* world leader have done if he had survived? Only you can help!

Your Mission

Save the President's life and solve the mystery!

Save JFK History Quiz

1. John F. Kennedy was the ____ .president of the United States.

    a. 1st

    b. 10th

    c. 35th

    d. 50th

2. John F. Kennedy was assassinated while riding in a_____.

    a. motorcycle

    b. airplane

    c. limousine

    d. convertible

3. All experts agree that the assassin who killed JFK was Lee Harvey Oswald.

    a. True

    b. False

4. What is NOT listed as one of JFK's accomplishments?

    a. helping the Civil Rights Movement

    b. avoiding war with The Soviet Union

    c. ending Slavery

    d. setting up the Peace Corps.

5. JFK was one of the youngest presidents in US history.

    a. true

    b. false

Answers at the end of the book

Discussion Questions

1. Why do you think a *lone gunman* like Lee Harvey Oswald would want to kill JFK?

2. Why do lone killers sometimes want to kill famous or important people?

3. Compare the conspiracy theories about JFK's assassination.

4. Which seems the most likely? Which seems the most unlikely?

5. Do you think JFK was an important American president?

    a. What other American presidents do you think were important? Why?

6. Do you know of any other political assassinations in history? In your own country or area?

7. How can leaders be protected from assassination?

    a. Has it become easier or more difficult to protect leaders in the modern age? Why?

Projects

1. **Be a Part of History to Complete the Mission:** Write about 1 page. Here are some questions to consider as you write:

   a. Can you save the president?

   b. Who are the real assassins? Is it just Oswald or are there other conspirators?

2. Find one source that claims the JFK assassination was a conspiracy, and one that claims it wasn't. Compare the biases in each one. Which is more believable? See "Supplement 4: Finding Credible Sources".

3. Research about JFK: Write about 1 page and answer 1 or both questions below

   a. What were his greatest achievements?

   b. Do you believe in one shooter (Oswald) or a conspiracy?

4. What if JFK had lived? Research at least one theory or idea on what he might have done.

5. Interview your classmates or friends and family. Afterward, compare their answers. How are they the same or different? What do you think about the results?

Interview Question: Do you think JFK was assassinated by Lee Harvey Oswald alone or was it a conspiracy?		
Name	**Answer**	**Reason**
Taylor	The mob did it.	The mob was after Bobby Kennedy.

References

Bomboy, S. (n.d.). *What if JFK had survived his assassination? - National Constitution Center.* National Constitution Center. https://constitutioncenter.org/blog/what-if-jfk-had-survived-his-assassination/

Hallemann, C. (2017, October 26). *The Kennedy conspiracy theories that still endure 50 years after JFK's death.* Town & Country. https://www.townandcountrymag.com/society/politics/a13093037/jfk-assassination-conspiracy-theories/

History.com Editors. (2009, November 24). *President John F. Kennedy is assassinated.* HISTORY. https://www.history.com/this-day-in-history/john-f-kennedy-assassinated

Selverstone, M. (2020, May 27). *John F. Kennedy: Domestic affairs.* Miller Center, University of Virginia. https://millercenter.org/president/kennedy/domestic-affairs

The First Lady's Lover

First Lady Eleanor Roosevelt (second from the left side of the photo) and Lorena Hickock (far right)

Before You Read

1. Have you ever been in love?
2. Have you ever written a love letter?
3. Why do some people keep their love a secret?

Vocabulary Definitions

Write the letter of the definition next to the matching word.

1. byline (n.) _____
2. devastated (adj.) _____
3. status (n.) _____
4. stock market crash (n.) _____
5. back on (its) feet (adj.) _____
6. basically (adv.) _____
7. adjoining (adj.) _____
8. ordeal (n.) _____
9. lesbian (n.) _____
10. dwindled (v.)
11. a crush (n.) _____

a. social standing
b. an idiom meaning recovered
c. next to
d. a painful experience
e. a woman who is attracted to other women
f. a sudden collapse in the price of stocks
g. the writer's name on a published article
h. fundamentally
i. become smaller, down to zero
j. romantic feelings
k. destroyed

Vocabulary Questions

Discuss with a partner.

1. When was the last *stock market crash*?
2. Who is in the *adjoining* room?
3. Is it a good idea to tell your *crush* your feelings?

Your Briefing

452 Words - 1010-1200L
Place: Hyde Park New York, USA
Time: May 1, 1968

Lorena Alice Hickock (Hick) went from an unhappy, abused, abandoned child to becoming the first woman to have her *byline* on the front page of the *New York Times*. Although lucky in her career, she was unlucky in love. Her first long-term girlfriend left her for a man, and Lorena was *devastated*. Her heartbreak was balanced by her *status* as the best female reporter in the country.

The United States at that time was recovering from the Great Depression of 1929. The Great Depression began on October 29, 1929 with a *stock market crash*. People were afraid to spend money and businesses failed. Because of this, the unemployment rate in 1932 was 23.6%, which is three times the September 2020 rate of 8.4%. Franklin Delano Roosevelt, a wealthy New Yorker and the governor of New York State, proposed a New Deal to get the country *back on its feet*.

During Franklin Roosevelt's presidential campaign in 1931-32, Hick interviewed the candidate's wife, Eleanor, and soon developed *a crush*. Eleanor was intelligent, elegant, and compassionate. Eleanor had feelings for Hick. Six months after the election, Hick and Eleanor headed off on a 3-week road trip. Afterwards, Hick *basically* lived at the White House in a bedroom *adjoining* Eleanor's for almost 12 years, which newspapers did not report.

Eleanor and Hick admitted their romantic feelings for each other in letters. They confessed to each other their love; they spoke of adoring each other in French, a language of romance. Hick wrote, "I want to put my arms around you and kiss you at the corner of your mouth."

Eleanor loved her husband too, but she did not like kissing him. She told her daughter that sex was an *ordeal*. Her husband fell in love with another woman, and Eleanor was very unhappy about his affairs. She turned to her friend Hick.

Over the course of Eleanor's lifetime, the two women exchanged thousands of letters. The letters are love letters. Although Hick was a *lesbian*, and many of her friends were lesbians, Eleanor did not identify as a lesbian. She was married to the president of the United States, and same-sex relationships were unsupported at that time.

After President Roosevelt died, the romance between Hick and Eleanor *dwindled*. Eleanor fell in love with a much younger man. Hick remained her friend. After Eleanor died on November 7, 1962, Hick lived alone, preferring the company of books and dogs to people. She was not mentioned in Eleanor Roosevelt's obituary as a lover. She was always considered a friend. President Franklin Delano Roosevelt never commented on the relationship of his wife and her "friend." Only the thousands of letters show that Hick and Eleanor were more than friends.

Your Mission

Decide what to do with the love letters

References

Frank, R. H., Jennings, S., & Bernanke, B. (2012). *Principles of microeconomics* (3rd ed.). McGraw-Hill.

Goodwin, D. K. (2013). *No ordinary time: Franklin & Eleanor Roosevelt: The home front in World War II.* Simon & Schuster.

Hauser, B. (2016, October 24). Eleanor Roosevelt's 'mistress' died heartbroken and alone. *New York Post.* https://nypost.com/2016/10/22/eleanor-roosevelts-mistress-died-heartbroken-and-alone/

Schiff, S. (2016, September 22). The woman in Eleanor Roosevelt's life. *The Washington Post.* https://www.washingtonpost.com/opinions/the-woman-in-eleanor-roosevelts-life/2016/09/22/30a

Wong-shing, K. (2020, April 1). Eleanor Roosevelt allegedly had an intense lesbian affair — Here's the tea. *GO Magazine.* http://gomag.com/article/eleanor-roosevelt-allegedly-had-an-intense-lesbian-affair-heres-the-tea/

Eleanor Roosevelt's Love Letters History Quiz

1. Lorena Hickock was the first woman to....

   a. write an article for the New York Times newspaper.

   b. marry another woman.

   c. have a byline on the front page of the *New York Times* newspaper.

   d. marry another woman.

2. In 1932, almost a quarter of the people in the US were.......

   a. without a job

   b. working for the government

   c. investing in the stock market

   d. cheating on their spouse

3. How many people were president of the United States before Franklin Delano Roosevelt?

   a. 32

   b. 31

   c. 30

   d. none

4. One sign of an unusually close relationship between Hick and Eleanor was

   a. Hick had a bedroom at the White House.

   b. Eleanor never went anywhere without Hick.

   c. Hick was appointed to a high government position.

   d. Eleanor came out as a lesbian

5. Franklin Delano Roosevelt _____ talked about his wife's relationship with Hick.

   a. always

   b. seldom

   c. often

   d. never

Answers at the end of the book

Discussion Questions

1. Use the Internet to explain the letters (and + sign) in LGBTQ+? What does it mean to be an "ally"?

2. Research the laws concerning homosexual behavior in the past. Choose to research laws in the US, your country, or both. What are they now? How have the laws changed? Refer to "Supplement 4: Finding Credible Sources".

3. Complete the checklist to identify bias in *one* of the sources you use in your research.

4. Search for the connection between rainbows and the LGBTQ+ community.

5. *Empathy* is the ability to feel what another person is experiencing. Discuss with your classmates how "empathy" is important in understanding members of your own, or another, community.

Projects

1. **Be a Part of History to Complete the Mission**: Imagine you are standing at Hick's deathbed. With her last breaths, she asks you what she should do with the letters. Burn them? Share them? If yes, how? Work with a partner or a small group to decide what to do with the love letters. Discuss these different options and decide which option would be the best for Hick, Mrs. Roosevelt, history, and society.

    a. Burn all the letters.

    b. Donate the letters to a library. People can read them the day after Hick's death in 1968.

    c. Donate the letters to a library. Ask that no one read them for 10 years.

    d. Bury the letters in the backyard.

2. Search what really happened to the letters. Do you agree or disagree with this decision? Why?

3. By yourself, with a partner or in a small group, write a list of words that you might see in a love letter. Discuss love letters in your culture. Are they common?

4. Learn the history of Pride Month. Without writing anything down, what are five things you remember from your research? Share with a partner, group, or the class. Discuss how to become an ally to the LGBTQ+ community.

5. Interview your classmates or friends and family:

Interview Question: Why is it dangerous to "out" gay people?		
Name	**Answer**	**Reason**
Catherine	Coming "out" as gay is incredibly personal.	LGBTQ+ individuals want to feel safe. Certain cultures and religions are intolerant of same-sex romantic relationships and may insult or injure LGBTQ+ members.

Section VII - Screams, Murderers, Witches and Ghosts

Prepared by Agent Mina Gavell

The Salem Witch Trials

An artist's depiction of a witch trial, created around 1892. In this scene, a bolt of lightning breaks the accused witch's handcuffs and knocks down the accuser.

Before You Read

1. What is your definition of a witch? Are they always evil? Do they always have magical powers?

2. Witches appear in the legends and stories of many cultures. What witches or other supernatural beings are part of your culture?

3. When someone is accused of a crime, what kind of proof is necessary to show guilt or innocence?

4. False confessions (when people say they committed a crime they actually did not do) are not uncommon. Why do you think innocent people sometimes claim to be criminals?

Vocabulary Questions
Discuss with a partner.

1. Talk about a bizarre experience you have had or heard about.

2. What are some different ways that criminals were executed in the past?

3. What are some common things people experience paranoia about? Why do you think this happens?

Vocabulary Definitions

Write the letter of the definition next to the matching word

1. contorted (v.) ____
2. bizarre (n.) ____
3. witchcraft (n.) ____
4. charged (v.) ____
5. confessed (v.) ____
6. frail (adj.) ____
7. testified (v.) ____
8. accuse (v.) ____
9. executed (v.) ____
10. hysteria (n.) ____
11. fungus (n.) ____
12. spasms (n.) ____
13. delusions (n.) ____
14. paranoia (n.) ____

a. formally said to have done something illegal
b. twisted and bent into a strange shape
c. the practice of using magic and spells, usually for evil purposes
d. to claim another has done wrong
e. very strange
f. spoke as a witness or gave evidence in court
g. unreasonable fear
h. uncontrolled movements of muscles
i. admitted to doing something wrong or illegal
j. put to death as a punishment
k. weak and easily injured or broken
l. uncontrolled emotion often in a group of people
m. a kind of organism such as molds, yeast, and mushrooms
n. untrue beliefs or ideas

Answers at the end of the book

Your Briefing

504 words - 810-1000L
Place: Salem, Massachusetts
Time: 1692

In the winter of 1692, one of the coldest on record, two girls aged 9 and 11 began to act very strangely. They complained of feeling pinches and screamed and threw things as their bodies *contorted* themselves. As the news of this behavior spread, so did the behavior itself, and other girls in the American village of Salem began to also act in *bizarre* ways. The local doctor blamed *witchcraft*.

Soon, three women were *charged* with being witches. The first woman, Tituba, was a slave from the Caribbean. The second was Sarah Good, a pregnant and homeless woman. The third was a poor, elderly woman named Sarah Osborne. Though all three women denied being witches at first, eventually Tituba *confessed*. She said it was true she was a witch but had been forced into it by Sarah Good and Sarah Osborne. Though Sarah Good and Sarah Osborne still claimed to be innocent, all three women were put in jail.

Once in jail, the situation for the women and the community became worse. Sarah Osborne, already *frail*, could not survive the difficult conditions and died. Rather than defending his wife, Sarah Good's husband said it was true that she was a witch. Good's four-year old daughter was also put in prison until she also *testified* against her mother who was later hanged for her crime. Tituba was allowed to go free.

Meanwhile, the people of Salem started to believe everyone in their community was a witch and began to *accuse* one another. Once people, mostly women, were arrested, they were given a choice: confess to being a witch and go free or be executed for being a witch. A confession always involved accusing others as well, and so the cycle continued. Moreover, those who spoke out about the accusations and arrests were often charged with witchcraft as well. By the spring of 1693, over 200 hundred people had been accused, more than 100 were jailed, 20 were *executed*, and five others died while in jail. Salem and the surrounding area were living in total fear, not only of witches but of the accusations of one another.

The *hysteria* finally came to an end when the wife of the governor of Massachusetts was accused of being a witch. Governor Phipps then put an end to the accusations and trials and released those still in prison.

So why did this happen? Were there really witches in Salem casting spells and putting curses on the village people? It seems unlikely. A study published in 1976 suggested that a *fungus* commonly found in the food of that time could have acted as a poison, causing the girls to have *spasms* and *delusions*. Most likely, we will never know what caused the original symptoms that led to the accusations of witchcraft. However, we do know that the people of Salem were too quick to turn on one another, and some even used the situation to harm enemies and benefit themselves. Innocent people died as a result of fear and *paranoia*.

Your Mission

Find the source of the hysteria and put an end to it.

Salem Witch Trials History Quiz

1. The Salem Witch Trials began because some ___ were acting in a strange way.

    a. girls

    b. women

    c. men

    d. animals

2. ____ confessed to being a witch.

    a. Tituba

    b. Sarah Good

    c. Sarah Osborne

    d. Governor Phipps

3. Why didn't someone stop the Salem Witch Trials sooner?

    a. Witchcraft was a serious problem in Salem.

    b. People were scared to speak up.

    c. They were finding so many witches.

    d. The witches prevented it.

4. How many people died as a result of the trials?

    a. 200

    b. 100

    c. 25

    d. 5

5. What happened when Mrs. Phipps, the wife of the governor, was accused of witchcraft?

    a. She was hanged.

    b. She confessed.

    c. She accused her husband of being a witch.

    d. Her husband ended the trials.

Answers at the end of the book

Discussion Questions

1. Why do you think Tituba, Sarah Good, and Sarah Osborne were accused of witchcraft?

2. How do you think the difficult conditions of living at that time contributed to people's enthusiasm for the witch trials?

3. What do you think caused the girls to experience the strange symptoms in the first place?

4. Have you heard of similar accusations of witchcraft in other countries?

5. What would you do if you were accused of being a witch?

Projects

1. **Be a Part of History to Complete the Mission**: Consider the viewpoint of someone living at that time. Write a journal entry about what your community is experiencing and how you feel about it.

2. Re-enact a trial: What are the accusations? How do the accused defend themselves? What do the witnesses say? What does the judge and/or jury decide?

3. Compare and contrast: Witches are present in many cultures and stories around the world. Choose two cultures and compare and contrast how they think of witches. Consider their appearance, their powers, and whether they are helpful or harmful. Present your findings in a poster. Consider using Wikipedia and the guidelines in "Supplement 12: Using Wikipedia" to guide your research.

4. Interview your classmates or friends and family:

Interview Question: Do you believe in witches or other supernatural beings? Why or why not?		
Name	**Answer**	**Reason**
Mina	Yes	My friend saw a ghost once.

References

Blumberg, J. (2007, October 23). A brief history of the Salem witch trials. *Smithsonian Magazine*. https://www.smithsonianmag.com/history/a-brief-history-of-the-salem-witch-trials-175162489/

History.com Editors. (2011, November 4). *Salem witch trials*. HISTORY. https://www.history.com/topics/colonial-america/salem-witch-trials

Pavlac, B. (2020, May 4). *What really happened during the Salem Witch Trials - Ted-Ed* [Video]. YouTube. https://www.youtube.com/watch?v=NVd8kuUfBhM

Murder at the World's Fair

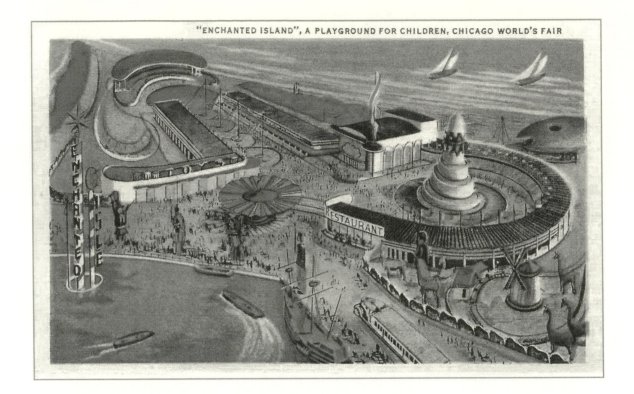

"ENCHANTED ISLAND", A PLAYGROUND FOR CHILDREN, CHICAGO WORLD'S FAIR

Before You Read

1. What is a World's Fair?
2. Do you know of a world's fair in your country?
3. What can you see/hear/eat at a world's fair?
4. Have you ever been to a World's Fair?

Vocabulary Definitions

Write the letter of the definition next to the matching word.

1. in common (n.) ____
2. spectacle (n.) ____
3. surgical instruments (n.) ____
4. inhale (v.) ____
5. aroma (n.) ____
6. offensive (adj.) ____
7. serial killer ____
8. innovations (n.) ____
9. setting (n.) ____
10. boast (v.) ____
11. persuade (v.) ____
12. maze (n.) ____

a. tools that doctors use
b. hurts someone's feelings
c. breathe in
d. new examples of technology
e. the place where something happens
f. motivate
g. a labyrinth
h. a person who murders people repeatedly
i. fragrance, smell
j. a great thing to see
k. similarity
l. brag, make a big deal of

Answers at the end of the book

Vocabulary Questions

Discuss with a partner.

1. What do you have *in common* with your best friend?
2. What parts of your body do you use to *inhale*?
3. When do people in your culture *boast*?

Your Briefing

173 words - 1010-1200L
Place: Chicago, Illinois
Time: May 1, 1893

What do the Ferris Wheel, peanut butter and the hot dog have *in common*? All three were invented for world fairs, which were a *spectacle* for all the senses.

The first world fair, officially called the French Industrial Exposition of 1844, attracted tourists from all over. It was a *spectacle* for all the senses. Visitors could see socially useful products (such as a roller player piano and *surgical instruments*), hear the *Hymne à la France*, a new work by the famous composer Hector Berlioz, shake hands with King Louis Philippe I (if you won an award for your exhibit), *inhale* the *aroma* of decorative roses, and taste hot crepes with jam. Soon, people in other cities wanted to have a world fair to show off their products, art, and culture.

Sometimes the exhibits were insensitive; for example, the 1905 Lewis and Clark Centennial Exposition in Portland, Oregon, had exhibits of living people: individuals in traditional dress from communities in the Philippines and Native Americans from the US, a decision that might seem *offensive* today.

One of the most well-known of these world fairs was the 1893 World's Columbian Exposition in Chicago, Illinois. Here were technological *innovations* such as the first gas-powered motorcar and a 1,500-pound statue of the Venus de Milo made of chocolate.

Igorot (Ipugaw) women weaving fabric at the Lewis and Clark Exposition, Portland, Oregon, 1905

Not everything at the world's fair was entertaining. This world fair is also the *setting* for H. H. Holmes, a *serial killer* who *boasted* of killing over 200 people. Visitors came to see the architectural wonders of the world's fair and were *persuaded* by the charming Mr. Holmes to visit his home. Holmes's home was also an architectural wonder. The house had trapdoors, soundproof rooms, and *mazes* of hallways and staircases. Holmes was finally caught and hanged in May of 1896. He wrote in his autobiography: "I could not help the fact that I was a murderer, no more than the poet can help the inspiration to sing."

Your Mission

Stop H.H. Holmes before he kills again.

The World's Columbian Exposition History Quiz

1. Why are world fairs popular?

    a. People can learn how to build new technology.

    b. There is a lot of alcohol.

    c. People can see new products.

    d. There are many opportunities for exercise.

2. Why was the World's Columbian Exposition called "The White City?"

    a. There were many white people who attended.

    b. The buildings were painted white.

    c. The ground was covered with snow.

    d. Cocaine was legal and many bought it.

3. What could you experience at a world's fair?

    a. A car made out of chocolate

    b. A rock and roll concert

    c. An exhibit of bankers and politicians

    d. Food that you had not tasted in your hometown.

4. What is insensitive about exhibiting living people?

    a. It is rude to stare at people.

    b. It is not insensitive.

    c. People's cultures are not entertainment.

    d. The people in the exhibit could get cold and hungry.

5. Why was H.H. Holmes hanged?

    a. He was a serial killer.

    b. He didn't buy a ticket.

    c. He protested against the exhibits of living people.

    d. Lynching was a popular entertainment at that time.

Answers at the end of the book

Discussion Questions

1. H.H. Holmes visited the exposition and killed people he persuaded to come to his home. How do you think he persuaded them?

    a. What behaviors should you be on the lookout for in your search for the killer?

2. What can you say to the police to convince them to investigate H.H.?

    a. What would be the difference in the reaction of the police if H.H. were a dentist or other professional compared to a janitor or other service worker?

    b. How would H.H.'s ethnicity affect the willingness of the police to investigate your accusations?

3. How can you convince the sponsors of the exposition that it is in their best interest to warn people that a serial killer is at the fair?

4. You break into H.H. Holmes's house to try to find evidence. You are worried that you might get lost in the house. You do not have a flashlight nor do you have a weapon. You do, however, have a ball of string. How can you use the ball of string to get you through the house safely?

5. H. H. Holmes wrote in his autobiography: "I could not help the fact that I was a murderer, no more than the poet can help the inspiration to sing." Read "Supplement 8: Opinions vs. Facts" to discuss this quote. Which part is fact and which part is opinion?

Projects

1. **Be a Part of History to Complete the Mission**: How would you catch serial killer H.H. Holmes? Remember he is intelligent. He is evil. His house is a maze. Write a 1-page plan.

2. Organize a world's fair for your city. What technological innovations, local dishes, or cultural examples, would you include?

3. The fair sponsors will allow you (and your team) to make a poster to warn visitors not to leave the fair with a stranger. However, the sponsors don't want fairgoers to get too scared. Can you create a poster that alerts visitors to the danger without making them run from the fair?

4. Interview your classmates or friends and family:

Interview Question: Why do people become serial killers?		
Name	**Answer**	**Reason**
Catherine	The frontal cortex is damaged, limiting empathy.	Their brains could be damaged as they were being made or the damage could be a result of their genes.

References

Crighton, J., & Mudgett, H. W. (2016). *Holmes' own story: Confessed 27 murders, lied then died*. Aerobear Classics.

Field Museum. (2018, May 14). *Fun facts about the world's Columbian exposition*. https://www.fieldmuseum.org/fun-facts-about-worlds-columbian-exposition

Larsen, E. (2010). *The devil in the white city*. Random House.

Rydell, R. W. (n.d.). World's Columbian exposition. In *Encyclopedia of Chicago*. Retrieved 18 May 2021. https://www.encyclopedia.chicagohistory.org/pages/1386.html

The Phantom Barber

Before You Read

1. What was your best haircut experience? Your worst haircut experience?
2. What do you think a Phantom Barber is?
   a. What can you infer about this situation?
   b. Why do you think this is happening?

Vocabulary Definitions

Write the letter of the definition next to the matching word.

1. phantom (n.) _____
2. barber (n.) _____
3. boom (n.) _____
4. stalked (v.) _____
5. lock (n.) _____
6. shearing (v.) _____
7. convent (n.) _____
8. baffled (adj.) _____
9. intruder (n.) _____
10. grudge (n.) _____

a. someone who cuts hair
b. clueless, having no idea
c. similar to a ghost, something that barely is seen
d. cutting
e. a Christian community where nuns usually live
f. (here) a large increase
g. anger or resentment toward someone related to a bad experience in the past
h. to follow or approach sneakily
i. (here) a piece of a person's hair
j. a person entering a place where they are unwelcome or secretly

Answers at the end of the book

Vocabulary Questions

Discuss with a partner.

1. When was the last time you visited a *barber*? Was it a good experience? What was your best or worst experience getting a haircut?
2. What would you do if an *intruder* entered your house?
3. Have you ever had a *grudge* against someone? Has anyone ever had a *grudge* against you?

Your Briefing

478 Words - 1010-1200L
Time: June 1942
Location: Pascagoula, Mississippi

In June 1942, after a population *boom* brought about by the increased manufacturing of warships in the area, the citizens of Pascagoula, Mississippi were *stalked* by a hair-cutting *phantom* who terrorized the night. These attacks began and ended in 1942 with no culprit ever being formally charged for this very mysterious and creepy crime.

The man nicknamed the *Phantom Barber* by newspapers worked in the darkness made more profound by the army's blackout regulations. These blackout regulations required that besides streetlights, all windows and doors should be covered at night with heavy curtains, cardboard, or paint to prevent the escape of any glimmer of light that might aid enemy aircraft. As a result, with streetlights off nightly, it made it easy for the phantom to sneak around. On Monday or Friday evenings, he slit a window screen to gain access to a house, crept inside, and cut the hair of sleeping occupants, particularly blonde girls. Sometimes he would take one *lock* or two, but sometimes he *sheared* as much as a full head of hair. He took nothing else from the home except his unusual prize.

He began with two young girls in the *convent* of Our Lady of Victories, followed by a six-year-old female child visiting another family. That time, he left a clue—the print of a man's bare foot in sand on an unoccupied bed in the room. The police were *baffled* and offered a $300 reward for information. The public was in a panic.

Women refused to go outside at night. Men applied for pistol permits. Bloodhounds were brought in to track the bizarre intruder, but the efforts failed. The Phantom Barber continued his hair cutting incursions.

Finally, the phantom broke his pattern, or so it seemed. A window screen was slit in the home of Mr. and Mrs. Terrell Heidelberg, and the *intruder* came inside their bedroom. However, rather than cutting hair, he brutally assaulted the couple. Mrs. Heidelberg lost her front teeth and was knocked unconscious, while her husband was beaten with a metal bar. Both survived the attack. Two months later, the police chief announced the arrest of a suspect, William A. Dolan, a chemist, who was charged with attempted murder.

A connection between Dolan and the Phantom Barber came with the discovery of human hair *allegedly* found near his residence. He was convicted of the attack on the Heidelberg; he had borne a *grudge* against Terrell's father, a judge. — But he continued to deny he was the phantom and he was never charged with the phantom's acts. Since the Phantom Barber never touched his victims other than their hair, it would seem no meaningful tie exists between Dolan and the Phantom Barber, whose break-ins ended as mysteriously as they began. Was the Phantom Barber caught? Did he (or she) stop for some unknown reason? This mystery remains very much unsolved.

Your Mission

You are dropped into the police station in Pascagoula, Mississippi. Using the clues above can you catch the Phantom Barber?

Phantom Barber - History Quiz

1. Which days of the week did the Phantom Barber usually strike?

    a. Mondays and Fridays

    b. Tuesdays and Thursdays

    c. Saturday and Sunday

    d. Wednesday

2. How much was the reward for information on the Phantom Barber?

    a. $100

    b. $300

    c. $500

    d. $1000

3. The Phantom Barber made his attacks in Pascagoula which is located in the state of...

    a. California

    b. New York

    c. Minnesota

    d. Mississippi

4. What kind of person was the Phantom Barber's favorite target?

    a. blonde men

    b. blonde women

    c. dark-haired men

    d. dark-haired women

5. The Phantom Barber only touched the hair of his victims

    a. true

    b. false

Answers at the end of the book

Discussion Questions

1. What do you think the Phantom Barber's motivation was? What kind of person do you think they were? Do you think there are other types of people with similar interests or obsessions?

2. How did the Phantom Barber sneak into people's houses undetected?

3. What do you think about the army's blackout regulations? How would that affect you if you had to have blackout regulations in your neighborhood?

4. How would you feel if the Phantom Barber visited you?

5. How would you react if you saw them cutting someone else's hair?

6. Has anything strange ever happened to you while you were sleeping? If so, what was it?

Projects

1. **Be a Part of History to Complete the Mission:** Write the story! Write about 1 page. Here are some questions to consider as you write:

    a. What is your plan to catch the Phantom Barber?

    b. Who is the Phantom Barber? What is their motivation?

    c. What is the punishment for their crimes?

2. Draw a picture! What do you imagine the Phantom Barber looks like? Are they: Male or female? Old or young? Large or small? What kind of clothes do they wear?

3. Write a short essay about William Dolan. Why do you think he was a suspect but never convicted? Examine the *logical* reasons he may or may not be the Phantom Barber. See "Supplement 9: Logic and Logical Fallacies".

4. Interview your classmates or friends and family.

Interview Question: What do you think the punishment of the Phantom Barber should be?		
Think about what crimes should he be charged with		
Name	Answer	Reason
Taylor	Pay for new haircuts.	The victims weren't hurt but they probably need their hair fixed.

References

Adams, N. (2014, July 31). *10 strange little-known unsolved mysteries*. Listverse. https://listverse.com/2013/02/05/10-strange-little-known-unsolved-mysteries/

Lammle, R. (2014, August 18). *Mississippi's Phantom Barber of Pascagoula*. Mental Floss. https://mentalfloss.com/article/55316/strange-states-mississippis-phantom-barber-pascagoula

United Press International. (1942, June 18). 'Phantom barber' creates mystery. *The Telegraph-Herald*, 21. Retrieved from https://news.google.com/newspapers?id=PAxeAAAAIBAJ&sjid=_F8NAAAAIBA-J&dq=phantom%20barber%20pascagoula&pg=3193%2C5396580

The Haunting of The Geiser Grand Hotel

Before You Read

1. Do you believe in ghosts? Why or why not?
2. Have you ever seen a ghost before? How about someone else you know?
3. What kinds of places are most common for people to see ghosts? Why do you think this

Vocabulary Definitions

Write the letter of the definition next to the matching word.

existence/exist (n/adj) _____   a. common or found everywhere

sordid (adj.) _____   b. facts to show something is true

elegant (adj.) _____   c. strange or secretive actions

shenanigans (n.) _____   d. graceful and stylish in appearance or behavior

ubiquitous (adj.) _____   e. To be real.

Prohibition (n.) _____   f. ghost or spirit

apparition (n.) _____   g. lacking respect, sleazy, dark

bohemian (adj.) _____   h. a period in the US when the manufacture and sale of alcohol was illegal, between 1920 and 1933

proof (n.) _____   i. short for disguise, to take another appearance or identity

guise (n.) _____

j. a socially unconventional in an artistic way

Answers at the end of the book

Vocabulary Questions

Discuss with a partner.

1. Describe one thing that you think *exists* and one thing that doesn't.
2. What is something *ubiquitous* in daily life? Do you use it much?
3. Who is someone you know that is *bohemian*? Why do you think so?

Your Briefing

581 Words - 1210-1400L
Place: Baker City Oregon
Time: January 2011

The *existence* of ghosts is one of our greatest mysteries. Many people claim to have seen them in many places, and many experts and shows are dedicated to looking for them. Various hotels around the world even have claimed to be haunted, perhaps reflecting their *sordid* or unusual histories and guests. One example is the Geiser Grand Hotel in Baker City, Oregon.

When the Geiser Grand Hotel opened in 1889 its customers were primarily drawn to the Gold Rush happening in the area. Still, it was an *elegant* and modern building with a four-story clock tower and a stained-glass ceiling. A second-floor balcony overlooked the dining room's marble floors, crystal chandeliers, and Honduran mahogany paneling. Finally, the hotel included only the third elevator ever built west of the Mississippi River.

So why does the hotel have a reputation for being haunted? Part of it is connected to the mysterious *shenanigans* reported to go on in the hotel. For example, in the hotel's basement, subterranean windows open to underground tunnels dating back to the gold frenzy. Those tunnels allegedly led to brothels, which were so *ubiquitous* that Baker City had a related tax that paid for its streetlights! They were also used during heavy snow and good for hiding alcohol during *prohibition*.

Several ghostly *apparitions* have allegedly been spotted over the years. The most famous of those is *The Lady in Blue*, also known as "Granny" Annabelle. This elegant lady, a former resident of room 302, presided over the hotel from her permanently reserved chair in the bar while she was alive, and maybe still today as a ghost! In fact, modern guests claim to have seen a beautiful Victorian woman dressed in a blue gown, descending the staircase and disappearing into the wall. In addition, Annabelle is suspected of moving guests' jewelry and eating their snacks while they were sleeping, but her presence is most often felt in the bar—as a pinch on the rear end of anyone who dares sit in her chair.

In addition to Annabelle, a host of other ghostly presences have apparently been spotted at the hotel including:

- A saloon girl laced into a red bustier who leans over the balcony railing
- A long-gone cowboy who chats up patrons in the bar
- A little girl who wanders the third floor
- Flappers, young *bohemian* women from the 1920s

The reputation of the hotel is so famous that even international ghost hunters have come to visit the Grand Geiser! 'Ghost Hunters' describe teams of people who go to haunted locations to investigate the presence of ghosts. These teams bring a variety of audiovisual and recording equipment, to try to record *proof* of ghosts. For example in 2011, *Unbelievable*, a highly rated TV show from Japan chose the Geiser Grand Hotel as one of the ten most interesting spots on the planet! The director of the program, Takayama Nakayama, had visited the hotel more than ten years earlier and said about the hotel that "it's authentic, you feel the real history everywhere, and it's so beautiful." Nakayama has searched for ghosts all over the world in over 13 years of filming. The Geiser Grand is the only place in which he has had a personal experience.

The whole crew is hoping to investigate the hotel and encounter more ghosts! A special member - you - will join the crew under the *guise* of hotel staff to help with the ghost hunt! Do ghosts really *exist?*

Your Mission

Investigate whether the Geiser Grand Hotel is haunted.
What do you think you will find?

The Haunting History Quiz

1. The guests of the Geiser Grand Hotel originally mostly came looking for gold.

    a. true

    b. false

2. What advanced technology of the time did the Geiser Grand Hotel feature when it opened?

    a. Wi-Fi

    b. an elevator

    c. marble floors

    d. crystal chandeliers

3. Who is NOT one of the ghostly figures claimed to be at the Geiser Grand Hotel?

    a. Annabelle

    b. the Cowboy

    c. Director Nakayama

    d. flappers

4. Which is claimed about Anabelle?

    a. People have chatted her up at the bar.

    b. People have felt her pinching them if they sit in her chair.

    c. She has been seen learning over the balcony railing.

    d. She has been seen walking around on the third floor.

5. Nakayama has seen ghosts at many of the other places he has investigated before the Geiser Grand Hotel.

    a. True

    b. False

Answers at the end of the book

Discussion Questions

1. What do you think of the history of the Geiser Grand Hotel? Why do you think it could be haunted?

2. Many hotels claim to be haunted. Why do you think hotels would be a common place for ghosts?

3. Which other types of places do you think are likely to be haunted? Why?

4. Have you (or someone you know) ever seen a ghost? If so, describe the experience.

5. Do you think ghosts are more likely to be harmless or dangerous? Why?

Projects

1. Be a Part of History to Complete the Mission!:Go look for evidence that the hotel is haunted. Write about 1 page. Choose one or more of these questions to consider as you write:

a. Do you encounter any ghosts at the Geiser Grand Hotel?

b. How will you document what you do or don't encounter?

2. Watch the video online from the TV show *Unbelievable* (http://www.geisergrand.com/unbelievablemov2.html). Did the ghost hunters find any evidence of ghosts?

3. Research another famous haunted place and answer the following:

a. What is the history of the place? Why do people think it's haunted?

b. What types of ghost sightings have been claimed?

c. Do you think the place is really haunted? Why or why not?

4. Research methods on real life 'ghost hunters' methods for finding ghosts. See "Supplements 4 and 5: Finding Sources for Help".

a. ○ What methods do they use to find or contact ghosts?

b. ○ Which methods do you think are most effective?

c. ○ Would you be willing to join a ghost-hunting team? Why or why not?

5. Interview your classmates or friends and family

Interview Question: Do you believe ghosts exist?		
Name	**Answer**	**Reason**
Taylor	Pay for new haircuts.	The victims weren't hurt but they probably need their hair fixed.

References

Geiser Grand. (2011, Jan 17). *Japanese New Years Eve Segment.mp4* [Video]. YouTube. https://www.youtube.com/watch?v=Vhx2k0ly4XU

Helderman, J. (2016, October 20). Guests are frightened and intrigued by what they've seen at this 1889 hotel. *Country Living.* https://www.countryliving.com/life/a40229/geiser-grand-baker-city-oregon/

Moore, W. (1906, December 23). Baker City has no poor. *The Reading Eagle*, 5. Retrieved from https://news.google.com/newspapers?id=wHgtAAAAIBAJ&sjid=ApgFAAAAIBAJ&dq=geiser%20grand%20hotel%20baker&pg=3617%2C2123717

Sidway, B.G. (n.d.) *Unbelievable as seen on FUJI TV in Japan.* Geiser Grand Hotel. http://www.geiser-grand.com/unbelievable.html

Slender Man is not Real!

Before You Read

1. What is strange about the photograph?
2. Are they friends?
3. Are friends sometimes dangerous?
4. Do you know about Slender Man?

Vocabulary Definitions

Write the letter of the definition next to the matching word.

1. bicyclist (n.) ____
2. stabbed (v, past participle) ____
3. blood vessel (n.) ____
4. skinny (adj.) ____
5. octopus (n.) ____
6. castle (n.) ____
7. worthy (adj.) ____
8. lose consciousness (v.) ____
9. prove (v.) ____
10. major organs (n.) ___

a. very narrow
b. your mind goes black
c. an eight-legged sea animal
d. to give facts that support belief
e. the house of a king or queen
f. the parts inside your body that keep you alive
g. has value
h. stick with a knife
i. network inside your body that carries blood
j. someone who rides a bike

Answers at the end of the book

Vocabulary Questions

Discuss with a partner.

1. What is a *skinny* animal?
2. Who in the world lives in a *castle*?
3. When can someone *lose consciousness*?

Your Briefing

493 words - 410-600L
Place: Waukesha, Wisconsin, USA
Time: May 30, 2014

On May 30, 2014, Peyton Leutner walked to a road in a state park in Waukesha, Wisconsin. When she got to the road, she fell down. She could not walk any more. A *bicyclist* stopped and called 9-1-1, the emergency number. "There is a girl here. She's been *stabbed*."

Peyton Leutner had been stabbed 19 times. One of the stab wounds was one millimeter away from a major *blood vessel* in her heart. As the emergency medical technicians (EMTs) were putting her on the stretcher, they asked her who had hurt her. She named her best friends: Anissa Weier and Morgan Geyser.

Anissa Weier and Morgan Geyser were 12 years old. They liked to read. They liked to go for walks. They also liked scary stories on www.creepypasta.com, a website where readers can post horror stories. One of these stories was about Slender Man. Slender Man was very tall and very *skinny*. He had long arms like an *octopus*. He had no face. He lived in a *castle* five hours away from where the girls lived. Anissa and Morgan read that if you killed someone, you could work for Slender Man. You could live in his castle. Peyton did not like these stories. It scared her that Morgan liked Slender Man so much.

Anissa and Morgan decided to kill Peyton. After they killed her, they wanted to walk to Slender Man's castle. They wanted to tell him that they were *worthy* to be his friend because they had killed their other friend, Peyton.

The day Anissa and Morgan stabbed Peyton, they packed a bag with snacks and one long knife. They invited Peyton to go into the woods with them for a walk. On the walk, Anissa and Morgan decided that it might be difficult to kill Peyton if she was looking at them. They took her to a rest room and told her to go to sleep. Anissa hit Peyton very hard in her head. She hoped Peyton would *lose consciousness*. Peyton did not.

Peyton continued to walk with Anissa and Morgan. She did not hear them arguing about who should kill Peyton. Morgan was supposed to kill her, but she couldn't. Anissa didn't want to either. However, they decided they must do it. They had to kill Peyton to prove that Slender Man was real.

Morgan jumped on Peyton. She began stabbing her. "It was like air," she explained to the policeman later. After the stabbing, Anissa and Morgan turned Peyton away from the road. They told her to lie down and go to sleep. Peyton lay down on the ground. Anissa and Morgan walked away. They had to find Slender Man's castle.

After they left, Peyton stood up. Her heart was cut. Her liver was cut. Her spleen, her pancreas, and many of her other *major organs* were injured. Peyton could not breathe, but she could not lie down. She wanted to live.

She stood up and began to walk.

Your Mission

Encourage Peyton's friends to feel empathy to stop them from doing harm to Peyton.

Slender Man History Quiz

True or False?

1. Slender Man lives in Wisconsin.

2. Slender Man has no nose.

3. Anissa and Morgan were bad friends.

4. Peyton was stabbed 18 times.

5. Anissa and Morgan were sad they tried to kill Peyton.

Answers at the end of the book

Discussion Questions

1. The friendship between Peyton, Anissa and Morgan was not good; it was toxic. A toxic relationship is one that makes you feel bad. Discuss with your classmates how to find and keep good friends.

2. Empathy is the ability to understand someone else's experience. One way of thinking about empathy is that you are "walking in someone else's shoes." It is very difficult to do, but important for helping in situations. Morgan and Anissa were not able to feel empathy for Peyton. What about you? To build empathy, it is important to listen and understand. Try this activity:

   a. Partner A: Tell a story about when you felt attacked or disappointed by a friend.

   b. Partner B: Listen to the story, then paraphrase what you heard.

   c. Partner A: What did Partner B get right? How can you help Partner B understand your story better?

3. Sometimes empathy is difficult because we need more information and experiences. For example, you see a homeless person and you want to practice empathy. With a group or a partner, make a list of ways that you can begin to empathize with a homeless person.

4. A bicyclist stopped to help Peyton. Listen to the 9-11 call. https://www.youtube.com/watch?v=FDJk-yXc2FQ What are some problems for the bicyclist? Make a list by yourself or with a partner.

Projects

1. **Be a Part of History to Complete the Mission**: Write a 1-page conversation with Anissa and Morgan. You are (choose one):

    a. a 12-year-old friend

    b. a parent

    c. a teacher

    d. a police officer

2. What do you say to help Anissa and Morgan understand that they are wrong about Slender Man and that it is important to be agents of care (good people)?

3. To build empathy, it is important to make suggestions if a person is in danger. With your partner, make a list of clues that showed that Anissa and Morgan were dangerous. In a group, with a partner or by yourself, make a list of clues that show a person or people are dangerous.

4. Read about Fake News in "Supplement 11: Fake News". Why is the Slender Man

Interview Question: What is an example of empathy?		
Name	**Answer**	**Reason**
Catherine	Understanding why someone might vote differently than you.	It is easy to be upset when a friend disagrees with you, but you have to remember that even friends might have different opinions.

story an example of fake news? Why is this story dangerous?

5. Do you know any monsters? Are they real? Try this activity.

    a. Partner A: Draw a 5-page graphic novel about a monster. Do not write any words. Then give your graphic novel to Partner B.

b. Partner B: Write the words to the graphic novel. Ask Partner A for suggestions about changes.

6. Watch one of the many YouTube videos about this case. You can search for "Slender Man stabbing". What happened to Peyton? What happened to Anissa? What happened to Morgan? Write a paragraph.

7. Interview your classmates or friends and family:

8. BONUS: Peyton knew that her friends Anissa and Morgan were not always kind. Weeks before they tried to kill Peyton, Anissa hit her, and Morgan told her scary stories about Slender Man to make her uncomfortable. Why did Peyton stay friends with Anissa and Morgan? Maybe Peyton remained friends with the two girls because she needed friendship. Anissa and Morgan were unkind, but, possibly, Peyton's need for the friendship made her not see her friends' negativity.

Everyone needs food, water, and oxygen, but people have other needs that make them blind to toxic friends. What are your basic needs? Do you need people to smile at you? Do you need people to do things with? Do you need a hug? Do you need to make 100% on your tests?

Make a list of five things that are important to you. Do not tell people your list. Remember your list, and, if someone makes you feel bad, think about your basic needs. What does this person give you that makes it hard to walk away? And remember, you can walk away. Remember Peyton. She walked to the road, and her walk saved her life. (You might want to research Maslow's hierarchy of needs to learn more.)

References

Dewey, C. (2016, July 27). The Complete History of 'Slender Man,' a meme that convinced two girls to kill their friend, *The Washington Post*. https://www.washingtonpost.com/news/the-intersect/wp/2014/06/03/the-complete-terrifying-history-of-slender-man-the-internet-meme-that-compelled-two-12-year-olds-to-stab-their-friend/

Harlowe, S. (2019, October 9). *Slender man made me do it* [Video]. YouTube. https://www.youtube.com/watch?v=RuAaFEcQfVA&t=2921s

Heston, K. (2018, February 12). *How to teach empathy to adults*. wikiHow. Retrieved December 15, 2020, from https://www.wikihow.com/Teach-Empathy-to-Adults

Section VIII - A Miscellany

Tsodilo Botswana and Ancient Art

Before You Read

1. How many different kinds of art do you know?

    a. Where can people find examples of each kind of art?

2. Have you ever created your own art?

    a. What kind of art was it?

    b. What tools and colors did you use?

    c. Why did you make it?

3. What examples of ancient art from your culture do you know?

    a. How old is the art?

    b. Why was it created?

Vocabulary Definitions

Write the letter of the definition next to the matching word

1. chances are (phrase.) ____
2. decorate (v.) ____
3. ancient (adj.) ____
4. archaeologist (n.) ____
5. carving (n.) ____
6. random (adj.) ____
7. graffiti (n.) ____
8. cave (n.) ____
9. mural (n.) ____
10. sculpture (n.) ____

a. person who studies ancient sites
b. design created in a hard surface like wood or rock
c. painting or writing in a public place, usually illegally
d. expression that shows something is very likely
e. a natural room or space under the ground
f. very old
g. to add artwork to a place or thing
h. 3D art that is usually made from stone or clay
i. a large painting on a wall
j. without a plan or organization

Answers at the end of the book

Vocabulary Questions

Discuss with a partner.

1. What is the difference between a mural and graffiti? Do either of these art forms exist in your neighborhood?
2. How do you decorate your room? What about your house?
3. What do you think you would find if you explored a big cave?

Your Briefing

457 Words - 1010-1200L
Place: Tsodilo Botswana
Time: ~24,000-10,000 BCE

There are many places in the world with special meaning, and *chances are* that you have participated in some traditional or modern gatherings at special locations before. Perhaps it was at a religious site, a concert hall, or a sports stadium. You also probably have noticed that people like to *decorate* the places that are special to them. This is something that people have done since *ancient* times, and *archaeologists* and historians study examples of ancient art to learn about human history.

Tsodilo is the name of one place that people decorated in ancient times. It is a rocky natural area in the northwest corner of Botswana in Africa. The large rocks have thousands of paintings and *carvings*. Archaeologists believe this art was done by different groups of people over many, many years. The paintings are different colors and different styles, and they often show animals and people. Historians are not sure why these paintings were made or why the rocks were an important place for such a long time. However, they do believe that humans have been returning to these rocks for nearly 100,000 years. In addition to the paintings and carvings, they have found very old pieces of tools and other evidence of ancient human activity.

Was Tsodilo important for religion, business, entertainment, or some other reason? It is not the only site with ancient rock paintings, so the thousands of paintings cannot be just *random*. In fact, the art at Tsodilo follows a pattern in ancient human behavior. You can find examples of ancient animal art in *caves* around the world. The most famous cave paintings are in France, but there are many other famous sites in places like Indonesia and North America. The oldest evidence of human artwork from South Africa is 164,000 years old, and historians think Tsodilo's oldest art is probably more than 10,000 years old.

Most things about human life have changed since cave paintings and rock art were made, but one thing is the same: Humans still like to make art in public places and for special events. You can find *murals* and *graffiti* on city walls, holiday decorations inside and outside businesses, and *sculptures* in parks and on campuses. Sometimes the art has a message or meaning, but sometimes it is simply for beauty.

But what about Tsodilo? Why did ancient people of Botswana return again and again to make carvings and paintings on this special group of rocks? Historians want to understand the reasons for the art and the importance of the rocks to ancient people, but they can only guess based on small pieces of evidence. What would they learn if they could travel back in time and speak with the people who created the art?

Your Mission

Travel to ancient Botswana to discover the meanings of ancient art and the people who made it. Talk with the people to understand their culture and the importance of the Tsodilo site.

Tsodilo and Ancient Art History Quiz

1. Where is Tsodilo?

    a. many places in the world

    b. Botswana

    c. France

    d. Indonesia

2. What is Tsodilo?

    a. a place with many ancient rock paintings

    b. an ancient sports stadium

    c. a kind of artwork

    d. a holiday decoration

3. Where can you find cave paintings?

    a. France

    b. Indonesia

    c. North America

    d. all of the above

4. How old is the oldest human art?

    a. 10,000 years

    b. 100,000 years

    c. 164,000 years

    d. 2.5 million years

5. Who made Tsodilo's art?

    a. mural artists from France

    b. archaeologists digging in the area recently

    c. many people over a long period of time

    d. tourists in the 20th century

Answers at the end of the book

Discussion Questions

1. What do you think was the main reason for ancient cave paintings? Why do they often show animals?

2. Have you ever visited an ancient cultural site?

    a. Where was it and how old is it?

    b. Was there any artwork? Describe what you saw.

3. What kind of art exists in your city or neighborhood?

    a. What does it show and what is its purpose?

    b. Do you like it? Explain.

4. Have you ever visited an art museum?

    a. If so, what kind of art did you see there?

    b. What was your opinion of the experience?

5. If you had the chance, what would you paint on the rocks or walls in your community? Explain your thinking.

Projects

1. **Be a Part of History to Complete the Mission:** Travel to ancient Botswana and discover the reasons Tsodilo was a special place to the people living there. Join the people at the rocks and write about your experience and what you learn.

    a. Why are they painting the rocks and what do they tell you about their culture?

    b. Is there any ceremony or tradition involved with the painting?

    c. What tools do they use to paint? Describe everything you see.

2. Create a slideshow to present about one example of cave paintings from around the world. Find and cite a reliable source for information on your chosen cave art. (See Supplements 4 and 5 on research skills.)

    a. Give the general details—Where are the paintings? Who made them? When?

    b. Describe the colors and style.

    c. Describe your reaction to seeing and learning about the paintings.

3. Report on examples of murals and graffit0i in your community. Search for and photograph as many different examples as you can find and write a short paper.

    a. Describe what you find and where.

    b. Tell who you think made it and why?

    c. Give your opinion about what you saw.

4. Create your own artwork in a public space. Plan the design by yourself or with friends. Will you include a message about a social issue or something else that's important to you?

a. With permission, draw or write with colored chalk on the street or sidewalk outside your home or school. If you cannot use chalk, draw or paint on a poster and hang it in a window or other area where it will be easily seen.

b. Invite neighbors or classmates to see your art and explain your creation to them. Why did you choose the colors/designs/message?

5. Interview your classmates or friends and family:

Interview Question: What is your favorite kind of art?		
Name	**Answer**	**Reason**
Peter	Impressionist paintings	I like the use of color and attention to natural light and movement

References

The British Museum. (n.d.). *Tsodilo Hills, Botswana.* https://africanrockart.britishmuseum.org/country/botswana/tsodilo/

Ehrenreich, B. (2020, January 10). 'Humans were not centre stage': How ancient cave art puts us in our place. *The Guardian.* https://www.theguardian.com/artanddesign/2019/dec/12/humans-were-not-centre-stage-ancient-cave-art-painting-lascaux-chauvet-altamira

Marchant, J., & Mott, J. (2016, January 6). A journey to the oldest cave paintings in the world. *Smithsonian Magazine.* https://www.smithsonianmag.com/history/journey-oldest-cave-paintings-world-180957685/

Sample, I. (2018, September 13). Earliest known drawing found on rock in South African cave. *The Guardian.* https://www.theguardian.com/science/2018/sep/12/earliest-known-drawing-found-on-rock-in-south-african-cave

UNESCO World Heritage Centre. (n.d.). *Tsodilo.* https://whc.unesco.org/en/list/1021/

"Fire!"

Before You Read

1. Have you ever built a fire? How did you build it? Did you cook in the fire?
2. Have you ever told stories around a campfire?
3. Have you been to a party with a bonfire?
4. Have you ever gotten a burn? What happened?
5. What is the first thing (not a person or pet) you would save if your house caught fire?

Vocabulary Definitions

Write the letter of the definition next to the matching word.

1. raged (v.) ____	a. uneducated
2. forceful (adj.) ____	b. broken
3. extinguish (v.) ____	c. cause
4. subdued (adj.) ____	d. evil person
5. ruptured (adj.) ____	e. old-school
6. margarine (n.) ____	f. strong
7. origin (n.) ____	g. butter substitute
8. villain (n.) ____	h. put out
9. ignorant (adj.) ____	i. controlled
10. old-fashioned (adj.) ____	j. burned strongly

Answers at the end of the book

Vocab Questions

1. Discuss with a partner.
2. 1. Which is the most *forceful* natural event: a hurricane or an earthquake?
3. 2. Which is most delicious: *margarine* or butter?
4. 3. Who is your favorite *villain* from a book or movie?

Your Briefing

470 words - 1010-1200L
Place: Chicago, Tokyo, France/Italy
Time: 1871, 1923, 1999

On the night of October 8th, 1871, a fire raged through Chicago, the second largest city in the United States at that time. The fire killed three hundred people, destroyed $200 million of property, and left one-third of the city's population homeless. The fire's average temperature of 329o Fahrenheit (165o Celsius) melted hats on firemen's heads. The blaze's average height was as tall as a 10-story building, and the wind the heat created felt as forceful as a hurricane. Chicago had only 17 fire engines, and all 17 rushed to extinguish the huge fire. More help arrived, on Tuesday, October 10th, when rain subdued what the firemen could not, but Chicago lay in ashes.

On September 1, 1923, 50 years after the Great Chicago Fire and a half world away, Tokyo burned in the aftermath of The Great Kanto Earthquake. In that blaze, 144,000 people died. They were victims of ruptured gas mains and overturned cooking stoves that ignited wooden houses like so many matchsticks.

Sometimes it is not houses that burn. On March 24, 1999, a truck loaded with margarine and flour caught fire in the Mont Blanc Tunnel connecting Italy and France. Some cars were able to turn around to escape the tunnel, but many were trapped. The 1,830o Fahrenheit (1,000o Celsius) furnace incinerated the tunnel's wires, which shut off power. For 53 hours, trapped firefighters and drivers prayed as tires and other trucks' loads around them exploded. Unfortunately, authorities pumped air into the tunnel to clear the smoke. This air fed the fire, making it grow.

There are many reasons fires burn. Sometimes we know the

causes; sometimes we don't. For example, the origin of the Great Chicago Fire remains unknown. Popular stories and songs accuse a cow of kicking over a lantern. Catherine O'Leary, the owner of the cow, became a villain in this story. Because Mrs. O'Leary was Irish and the Irish were new immigrants, ignorant people connected her Irish heritage to this tragedy. People thought she might have set the fire in anger. Religious people warned that the fire was God's way of punishing sinners. They wanted the society to return to old-fashioned traditions.

What we do know is that some materials are more flammable than others. In Chicago, the barn where the fire started was filled with dry hay which burned quickly. The city was crowded with wooden structures, which were cheap, but easily burned. Like Chicago, Tokyo's neighborhoods of wooden buildings could not stand up to the heat of the flames. In the Mont Blanc Tunnel, the margarine in the truck acted as gasoline and fed the fire. In each fire, there were few safe places for people to hide.

After each of these fires, local governments made changes. What changes could have been made to prevent the fires before they started?

Your Mission

Who is to blame for the Chicago fire? You decide!

References

Bailey, C. (2003). *Case studies: Historical fires: Mont Blanc Tunnel fire, Italy/France*. The University of Manchester, Department of Mechanical, Aerospace and Civil Engineering. Retrieved from https://web.archive.org/web/20181029052004/www.mace.manchester.ac.uk/project/research/structures/strucfire/CaseStudy/HistoricFires/InfrastructuralFires/mont.htm

Hammer, J. (2011, April 30). The great Japan earthquake of 1923. *Smithsonian Magazine*. https://www.smithsonianmag.com/history/the-great-japan-earthquake-of-1923-1764539/

Smith, C (n.d.) *The O'Leary legend*. The Great Chicago Fire & The Web of Memory. Chicago https://www.greatchicagofire.org/oleary-legend/

Fire! History Quiz

1. A cow is perhaps the villain in which fire?

    a. the fire after The Great Kanto Earthquake

    b. the Great Chicago Fire

    c. the Mont Blanc Tunnel Fire

    d. the family bonfire

2. What is one reason the Great Chicago Fire spread so quickly?

    a. lots of flammable wooden houses

    b. lots of stores full of margarine

    c. lots of trucks full of gasoline

    d. lots of barns full of hay

3. What happened when they pumped air into the Mount Blanc tunnel during the fire?

    a. the fire was extinguished

    b. the fire was moved

    c. The fire was subdued

    d. The fire grew

4. Which choice is correct?

    a. The Great Chicago Fire: cow, trucks, tunnel

    b. The Tokyo Fire: wooden houses, margarine, cooking stoves

    c. The Great Chicago Fire: cow, hay, melted hats

    d. The Mont Blanc Tunnel Fire: trucks, cows, margarine

5. In these fires, why were people sometimes the problem?

    a. They made errors which made the situation worse

    b. They stand around looking at the fire

    c. They set the fire

    d. They like fires

Answers at the end of the book

Discussion Questions

1. Please work in a group, with a partner, or alone to find all the words connected to the word "fire" in the briefing:

Noun (12 words)	Verb (7 words)	Adjective (4 words)
1.	1.	1.
2.	2.	2.
3.	3.	3.
4.	4.	4.
5.	5.	
6.	6.	
7.	7.	
8.		
9.		
10.		
11.		
12.		

2. Discuss the meanings of these words with members of other groups. Can you use the words in sentences?

3. Choose one of the fires. Learn the events for the fire you've chosen. Tell the story of the fire you chose without looking at notes. Can they guess which fire you've chosen?

4. Which fire, Chicago, Tokyo, or Mont Blanc, was the most dangerous? The least dangerous? Discuss with your classmates. How would you have gotten out alive?

5. Some people believed that Mrs. O'Leary's Irish heritage may have made her angry and this was the reason why she started the fire. What are some reasons why an immigrant, from any country, might be angry in America?

Projects

1. **Be a Part of History to Complete the Mission:** Catherine O'Leary (The Great Chicago Fire) and Gilbert Degrave (The Mont Blanc Tunnel Fire) were considered villains. Here are articles that explain their role in the fires.

   • O'Leary: https://www.irishtimes.com/life-and-style/abroad/catherine-o-leary-the-irishwoman-blamed-for-starting-the-great-chicago-fire-1.2983646

   • Degrave: https://www.independent.co.uk/news/world/sixteen-accused-of-manslaughter-in-mont-blanc-inferno-5384917.html

Are they guilty? Choose one "villain" and prepare an argument to explain why they are guilty or innocent. Present your argument to a partner, group, or class. Check "Supplement 9: Logic and Logical Fallacies "to make sure that your arguments are not logical fallacies.

2. In each of the three fires, how could people have stopped the fires before they began and/or spread? Think about:

    a. Accelerants: hay, wood, cooking stoves, lanterns, margarine

    b. Building materials: wood, bricks, metal

    c. Cost, appearance, advantages, and disadvantages of these materials

    d. Devices for safety: smoke detectors, fire extinguishers

3. What were the changes made to keep people safe after these fires? Choose one of the fires, list the sources you used for research and write a list of three new safety improvements.

4. Visit the fire safety checklist from San Francisco's fire department. https://sf-fire.org/home-fire-safety-checklist

    a. Which step is written twice?

    b. Using the fire safety checklist, make a poster *without* words to explain fire safety. Explain your poster, using words, to a partner, a group, or the class.

    c. Write a story using 5-10 of the fire vocabulary words in #1 of Discussion Questions, above. Write 1 page if possible. Write a story where you are the hero, one that takes place in your hometown, or one that takes place 100 years ago., or use one of your own ideas.

5. Interview your classmates or friends and family:

Interview Question: How do you safeguard your residence in case of fire?		
Name	**Answer**	**Reason**
Catherine	I have a fire extinguisher and smoke alarms.	I need to have these things to get insurance for my home.

The 27 Club

Before You Read

1. Above is a picture of Kurt Cobain from the rock band Nirvana who died at the age of 27. How do you think he died?

2. Why do you think some celebrities die young?

3. Can you think of any other musicians or celebrities who died young? Who are they and how did they die?

Vocabulary Definitions

Write the letter of the definition next to the matching word.

1. variable (adj.) ____

2. curse (n.) ____

3. legacy (n.) ____

4. noteworthy (adj.) ____

5. beat the odds (idiom) ____

6. suspect (v.) ____

7. freak accident (n.) ____

8. visionary (adj.) ____

9. grunge (n.) ____

a. important, in the news
b. to succeed at something unexpectedly
c. bad luck, sometimes considered supernatural
d. leaving something for future generations
e. a type of rock music popular in the 1990s
f. changeable
g. ahead of their time
h. an unexpected and unusual accident
i. believe something is true

Answers at the end of the book

Your Briefing

202 Words - 800 -1010L

Are some ages more unlucky than others? For years, it seems that the age of 27 has been a *curse* for many musicians and celebrities who've passed away at that age.

The 27 Club is made up of primarily musicians, but also other celebrities, who died at the age of 27. All of the members of this club died while they were famous and left a *legacy*, but what more could they have done?

Iconic musicians Jim Morrison, Janis Joplin, and Jimi Hendrix all died within a 2-year period at the age of 27 which was *noteworthy* at the time, but the 27 Club was not given a name until Kurt Cobain committed suicide in April of 1994. As journalists began to notice a connection, it was claimed that if a rock star made it to age 28, he or she *beat the odds*.

Studies did find that the risk of death by suicide or *accident* did increase slightly for the general population between the ages of 25 and 32, but there was no greater risk for musicians. However, musicians may lead more reckless lives than most people.

The deaths of members of the 27 Club have many causes including murder, suicide, and *freak accidents* but the most common is drug abuse.

Jimi Hendrix was known for taking many pills all at once, even if he didn't know what pills he was taking. On the night he died, Hendrix took a sleeping pill called Vesparax. Half of a Vesparax pill has the power to cause a man to sleep for eight hours, and that night Hendrix was *suspected* to have taken at least nine pills.

Whatever caused influential and *visionary* musicians to die at the age of 27, we know that was too young for all of them to die. Nirvana founder Kurt Cobain's tragic suicide in particular ended a revolution in rock music known as *grunge*. If he hadn't died, how might music be different today?

Partial List of Members of the 27 Club

Kim Jong-hyun (April 8, 1990-December 18, 2017), lead vocalist and lyricist for Shinee, death by suicide (carbon monoxide poisoning)

Amy Winehouse (September 14, 1983-July 23, 2011), singer-songwriter, death by alcohol poisoning.r

Stretch (April 8, 1968-November 30, 1995), rapper, murdered

Richey Edwards (December 22,1967-February 1, 1995), lyricist and guitarist for Manic Street Preachers, disappeared. Officially presumed dead November 23, 2008

Kurt Cobain (February 20, 1967-April 5, 1994), leader of Nirvana. death by suicide (gunshot)

Jim Morrison (December 8, 1943-July 3, 1971), leader of the Doors, death by heart failure

Janis Joplin (January 19, 1943-October 4, 1970), singer-songwriter, death by drug overdose

Jimi Hendrix (November 27, 1942-September 18, 1970), guitarist, singer and songwriter, death by asphyxiation due to drug overdose

Brian Jones (February 28, 1942-July 3, 1969), founder of the Rolling Stones, death by drowning

Robert Johnson (May 8, 1911- August 16, 1938) blues singer and musician, death by strychnine poisoning

Your Mission

Can you save a member of the 27 Club

The 27 Club History Quiz

1. All of the members of the 27-Club died at the age of 27.

    a. true

    b. false

2. The 27-Club is made-up of primarily...

    a. actors

    b. musicians

    c. politicians

    d. doctors

3. Which age is considered to have a higher chance of dying from an accident?

    a. 15

    b. 20

    c. 25

    d. 35

4. Which musician's death led to the naming of the 27-Club?

    a. Kurt Cobain

    b. Janis Joplin

    c. Jim Morrison

    d. Amy Winehouse

5. What statement about the 27 Club is true, according to the passage?

    a. Many musicians kill themselves at age 27 to be part of the club.

    b. No one knows how Kurt Cobain or Jimi Hendrix died.

    c. Drug abuse is the most common cause of death of members.

    d. The club only includes people who died before 1969.

Answers at the end of the book

Discussion Questions

1. Why do you think 27 would be a common age where many musicians or celebrities have died? Do you think it's just a coincidence?

2. Do you think the number 27 has any significance?

3. Are there any ages in your culture that are considered lucky or unlucky? Why?

4. If you could choose any age to be, which would you choose? Why?

5. Which of the people described in the 27-Club do you most wish had survived longer? Why?

Projects

1. **Be a Part of History to Complete the Mission**: Go back and save 1 musician! Think about the following:

      a. Who do you choose to save? Why?

      b. How would you help them?

      c. What is the result? Can you save this person?

2. Research a member of the 27 Club. Choose someone from the list above or another of your choice. Answer the following questions:

      a. How did they die?

      b. What was the impact of their death?

      c. What do you think their impact would be if they were still alive today?

3. A lot of members of the 27-Club died under mysterious circumstances. Research one of the members' deaths that was most unusual or strange. (See "Supplement 4" Finding Credible Sources" and "Supplement 5: In-Text Citations of Sources" for help)

4. Interview your classmates or friends and family:

Interview Question: How do you safeguard your residence in case of fire?		
Name	**Answer**	**Reason**
Taylor	Drazen Petrovic NBA shooting guard	He was my favorite player for the Blazers and Nets!

References

27 Club. (2020, Sept. 28). In Wikipedia. https://en.wikipedia.org/w/index.php?title=27_Club&oldid=980756253

Baker, C. (2012, July 7). List of members of the forever 27 club. Spinditty. https://spinditty.com/artists-bands/The-dead-at-27-Club

Shamsian, J. (2019, April 5). 12 great artists who died at the age of 27. Insider. https://www.insider.com/27-club-celebrities-musicians-died-27-years-old-2017-9

Stone, R. (2019, December 8). The 27 club: A brief history. Rolling Stone. https://www.rollingstone.com/culture/culture-lists/the-27-club-a-brief-history-17853/robert-johnson-26971/

The Number 23 Enigma

Before You Read

1. Are any numbers considered lucky in your culture? Do you know why?
2. Are any numbers considered unlucky in your culture? Do you know why?
3. Do any numbers have any special meanings to you? Why or why not?

Vocabulary Definitions

Write the letter of the definition next to the matching word.

1. enigma (n.) ＿＿
2. betrayal (n.) ＿＿
3. inherent (adj.) ＿＿
4. chromosomes (n.) ＿＿
5. obsessed (adj.) ＿＿
6. significance (n.) ＿＿
7. incident (n.) ＿＿
8. aspect (n.) ＿＿
9. tragic (adj.) ＿＿
10. preventable (adj.) ＿＿

a. importance
b. something difficult to understand
c. existing in something permanently from the beginning
d. overly focused on something, often to the point of ignoring almost anything else
e. going against one's own people or country
f. genetic information in the form of genes. humans have two pairs of 23
g. describing a terrible or unfortunate situation
h. can be stopped
i. an event, often used in a negative sense
j. a part or feature of something

Answers at the end of the book

Vocabulary Questions

Discuss with a partner.

1. What is something you are or have been *obsessed* with? Describe your obsession.
2. What is a mistake you or someone you know made that was *preventable*? Describe it?
3. What is one *aspect* of yourself that you like? What is an *aspect* you'd like to change?

Your Briefing

487 Words - 1010-1200L

There are lots of numbers that are considered either lucky or unlucky in history. For example, the number 7 is often considered lucky in Western culture. It goes back to the story of the creation of the world in 7 days from the Bible, (the 7th day being the day of rest and completion). At the same time, the number 13 is often regarded as unlucky in Western culture. This is also related to the Bible and the *betrayal* of Jesus Christ by Judas Iscariot, the 13th apostle. In many Asian cultures, the number 4 is unlucky because its Kanji/Chinese character translates to 'death.' As a result, you may be surprised to find buildings in the East or West missing a 4th or 13th floor!

Besides 7 and 13, many other numbers have special *significance* around the world. One of those with a unique history and supposed magical properties is the number 23. Some believe the number 23 is *inherent* to human nature because in humans, each cell normally contains 23 pairs of *chromosomes*. 22 of these pairs look the same in both men and women, the 23rd pair is the sex chromosome and that is different for men and women. Women have two X chromosomes while men have one X and one Y chromosome.

The number has been the subject of not one, but two films: the 1998 German movie, *23*, and *The Number 23*, starring Jim Carrey, released in 2007. Each has a main character *obsessed* with the number. In addition, many famous athletes including Michael Jordan, David Beckham, Brian Bellows, LeBron James, Don Mattingly have worn the number. Jordan believed the number 23 was special, took it everywhere, and even ate a 23-oz steak as his pregame preparation meal.

The 23 *Enigma* is the belief that the number 23 has special significant powers and meanings. While 7 is considered lucky and 13 unlucky, 23 is often cited as the number of *incidents*. What this means is that many important moments in history contain some aspect of the number 23, which could relate to the date or many other *variables*. In particular, the number is connected to many *tragic* situations:

Here are a few examples of The Number 23 Incidents:

1. Julius Caesar was stabbed to death by numerous enemies in the Roman Senate. His stab wounds were said to number 23!

2. William Shakespeare is believed to have been born on 23 April 1564 and he died on 23 April in 1616, aged 52. The number 23 was the constant in these two dates. It is believed a brief illness or overdrinking led to what could have been a *preventable* death!

3. One of many conspiracy theories about the terrorist attacks known as 9/11 is that the numbers involved in the date (9+11+2+0+0+1) add up to the number 23!

The number 23 has been connected to many mysterious situations. Which others can you investigate?

Your Mission

Find and **prevent** a tragic situation connected to the 23 Enigma

The Number 23 History Quiz

1. Which number is considered lucky in Western culture?

    a. 4

    b. 7

    c. 13

    d. 23

2. Which number is considered unlucky in Asian culture?

    a. 4

    b. 7

    c. 13

    d. 23

3. The 23rd chromosome is important in humans because it determines sex?

    a. true

    b. false

4. Which is NOT a country that made a movie about the number 23?

    a. Germany

    b. the USA

    c. France

5. Which is NOT cited as an example of a Number 23 Incident?

    a. 9/11

    b. Julius Caesar's murder

    c. Shakespeare's death

    d. 23 Chromosomes

Answers at the end of the book

Discussion Questions

1. Do you agree with the idea that some numbers are lucky or unlucky?

2. Have you ever made any decisions or changed your behavior because of a certain number?

3. Many athletes (like basketball player Michael Jordan who also wore 23) are superstitious about wearing certain numbers. Did you ever have this experience?

4. Do you agree with the explanations about the number 23? Do you think the connection to human chromosomes make sense? Can you think of any other reasons this number might be important?

5. Which of the incidents described above would you most want to prevent? Why?

6. Are there any words with lucky/unlucky or mysterious meanings in your culture?

Projects

1. **Be a Part of History to Complete the Mission**: Research a number 23 coincidence.

    a. What was the situation? Who was involved? Where did it happen?

    b. Do you believe it's a true coincidence?

    c. How could you experience it firsthand?

2. Research another number that has special meaning in your or any culture (See "Supplement 12: Using Wikipedia" for help)

    a. Describe the number and its special meaning.

    b. Do you agree or disagree? Why?

3. Numerology is the study of numbers. Research one belief in numerology. What do you think about it?

4. Interview your classmates or friends and family.

Interview Question: Which number do you consider lucky or unlucky and why?		
Name	**Answer**	**Reason**
Taylor	7	The age I started my new favorite school.

References

Hutyra, H. (2020, March 24). *102 Michael Jordan quotes that show strength and dedication*. KeepInspiring.me. https://www.keepinspiring.me/michael-jordan-quotes/

Kiger, P. (2019, January 4). *What's the fascination with number 23?* HowStuffWorks. https://science.howstuffworks.com/science-vs-myth/everyday-myths/whats-fascination-with-number-23.htm

Milmo, C. (2011, November 15). *23 fascinating facts about the number twenty-three*. *The Independent*. https://www.independent.co.uk/news/uk/this-britain/23-fascinating-facts-about-the-number-twenty-three-6262624.html

A New US Holiday

Before You Read

1. What is the 4th of July in the US?
2. Is there an Independence Day in your country?
3. What is your favorite holiday?
4. Do you want to make a new holiday? What about?

Vocabulary Definitions

Write the letter of the definition next to the matching word.

1. Congress (n.) ____
2. Federal (adj.) ____
3. "American Dream" (n.) ____
4. unity (n.) ____
5. indigenous people (n.) ____
6. commemorate (v.) ____
7. unjust (adj.) ____
8. recognition (n.) ____
9. Latinx (adj.) ____
10. civil-rights activist (n.) ____
11. admire (v.) ____

a. to get what you want in life
b. coming together
c. a part of government that makes laws
d. First Peoples
e. not morally right
f. a person of Latin-American origin
g. to think well of
h. of the central government
i. recall and show respect for
j. appreciation of or for someone/something
k. someone fighting for equal rights

Answers at the end of the book

Vocabulary Questions

Discuss with a partner.

1. Who are the indigenous people in your culture?
2. What kind of people get recognition in your culture?
3. Who do you admire? Why?

Holidays

Match the holiday to when it is celebrated.

1. New Year's Day___
2. Martin Luther King, Jr. Day___
3. George Washington's Birthday___
4. Memorial Day___
5. Juneteenth
6. Independence Day___
7. Labor Day___
8. Columbus Day___
9. Veterans Day___
10. Thanksgiving Day___
11. Christmas Day___

a. the 1st Monday in September
b. the last Monday in May
c. November 11th
d. July 4th
e. the 2nd Monday in October
f. December 25th
g. the 4th Thursday in November
h. January 1st
i. the 3rd Monday in February
j. the 3rd Monday in January
k. June 19th

Answers at the end of the book

Your Briefing

593 words - 1010-1200L
Place: Washington, D.C.
Time: The Future

Federal holidays in the United States are, by law, for employees of the government, but banks and other companies usually take the day off too. There are ten federal holidays in all 50 states of the US. (An eleventh federal holiday, Inauguration Day, is not celebrated in all states.) These holidays celebrate religion (Christmas), history (Martin Luther King Jr's Day, George Washington's birthday, Memorial Day, Independence Day, Columbus Day, Veterans Day, and Thanksgiving), workers (Labor Day) and the new year (New Year's Day). These holidays often, but not always, celebrate a moment in history.

Martin Luther King, Jr Day in January celebrates the birthday of a great American leader who fought against unjust laws. These laws prevented Black people from riding the bus in the front, attending the schools of their choice, or even drinking from the same water fountain as whites. Dr. Martin Luther King, Jr. is famous for working to change these laws. He gave hope to Americans that everyone had a chance at the *"American Dream."*

Martin Luther King, Jr. Day reminds us of a time in our country when people fought for *unity*. His day became a holiday on November 3, 1983, when US President Ronald Reagan signed a bill calling for a celebration of Dr. King on the third Monday of every January. On this day, Americans think about Dr. Martin Luther King, Jr's message, from his "I Have a Dream" speech, that all people deserve a seat at "the table of brotherhood."

On the other hand, there are some American holidays that do not seem good. Some Americans question the message of these other holidays. For example, Columbus Day celebrates the coming of Christopher Columbus to the New World, but for many *indigenous people*, the arrival of Christopher Columbus began a period of slavery and violence that resulted in the death of many communities of Native Americans. Memorial Day and Veterans Day *commemorate* the service of soldiers in wars, wars that some Americans believe were *unjust*.

Some Americans suggest new holidays. One new holiday was just added in 2021, Juneteenth, a day celebrating June 19th, 1865. This day is important because it refers to the freeing of slaves. Although indigenous people and whites could be made to work without pay, it is the experience of Black men and women brought from Africa to work on farms in the American South. These men and women were treated as property and their children also became slaves. Their experience is what we usually think of when we hear the word "slavery." After the George Floyd protests in the summer of 2020, and the rise of the Black Lives Matter movement, people began to question why Juneteenth, a celebration of African American freedom, wasn't a holiday. So on June 17th, 2021, US President Joe Biden signed a bill to make Juneteenth the first federal holiday since Martin Luther King Day was created in 1983.

But there are still many more opportunities for new holidays! There have been other important Americans who deserve *recognition*. Another idea for a federal holiday is Susan B. Anthony Day. Susan B. Anthony fought for women to get the right to vote at the beginning of the twentieth century. *Latinx* Americans want to see a holiday for Cesar E. Chavez, a *civil rights activist* who co-founded the United Farm Workers. These ideas have not become federal holidays. One reason is that a holiday can cost businesses hundreds of millions of dollars.

The current question is, however, what part of American history is important for us to *admire*?

Your Mission

Choose or create a new holiday for the US.

Holiday History Quiz

1. The law says that federal holidays are for...

    a. students

    b. everyone

    c. government employees

    d. bank employees

2. Dr. Martin Luther King Jr. is known as a great man for...

    a. all Americans

    b. Latinx Americans

    c. Black Americans

    d. LGBTQ+ Americans

3. Who made Martin Luther King Jr. Day a holiday?

    a. Cesar E. Chavez

    b. Christopher Columbus

    c. Ronald Reagan

    d. Susan B. Anthony

4. June 19th, 1865 is the day...

    a. President Ronald Reagan signed a bill

    b. Black people were told they were no longer slaves

    c. Latinx farmers gained the vote

    d. American women gained the vote

5. How many federal holidays are there in the US?

    a. 11, with Inauguration Day in some states every four years

    b. 11, with Inauguration Day

    c. 10, with Inauguration Day

    d. 10, with Inauguration Day in some states every four years

Answers at the end of the book

Discussion Questions

1. Choose one of the federal holidays. Find five things that are done on this holiday that make it special:

1.

2.

3.

4.

5.

2. Write five important facts about one of the following (circle one): Susan B. Anthony, Juneteenth, Cesar E. Chavez.

Use a credible source. Check "Supplement 4: Finding Credible Sources" to be sure.

1.

2.

3.

4.

5.

3. In your opinion, what are three important things that every holiday should have?

1.

2.

3.

4. What is the most important holiday in your culture? Why?

5. Why are holidays important?

Projects

1. **Be a Part of History to Complete the Mission**: choose or create a new holiday for the US. You can choose Cesar E. Chavez Day, Susan B. Anthony Day, Christmas Eve, Black Friday or Pride Day or make one up. If you create a holiday, pick a name and a date for the holiday. Explain to Congress, the part of the US government that makes laws, why the chosen/created holiday is important to celebrate. Start your argument with:

   _____ is a new holiday. It will celebrate _____.

   This holiday is important because _____

2. What songs will be sung? Choose a song that you know or write one. If you do not want to write one, think of the style of the song. Listen to songs for holidays; for example: "Happy Birthday to You" by Stevie Wonder for Martin Luther King Jr. Day, "We Wish You a Merry Christmas" for Christmas, and "Auld Lang Syne" for New Year's. What kind of song will people sing on the holiday?

3. What food will be eaten? Choose three of the following to discuss/write a recipe (circle three): appetizer, soup, bread, salad, entree, pasta, dessert, cheese plate, beverage. The dish should be special for your day.

4. Explain why this new holiday is important to (choose one): European Americans, African Americans, Muslim Americans, LGBTQ+ Americans, Asian Americans, Jewish Americans, Christian Americans, or another group.

5. Interview your classmates or friends and family.

Interview Questions: 1. What is your favorite holiday? 2. If you could choose/create a new holiday for the US, what would it be?		
Name	**Answer**	**Reason**
Catherine	1. Christmas 2. Native American Recognition Day July 7th	1. Christmas combines the beauty of lights, music, and delicious food with the emotions of family reunions and Bible stories. 2. This is a new holiday commemorating the July 2020 classification of much of Oklahoma as Indian land..

References

The Editorial Board of USA Today. (2020, July 8).Make Juneteenth a national holiday for the American dream of liberty and justice for all. USA TODAY. https://www.usatoday.com/story/opinion/to-daysdebate/2020/07/08/why-juneteenth-should-national-holiday-all-americans-editorials-de-bate/5385438002/

NCC Staff. (2016, October 10). Five other days that could be proposed as federal holidays - National Constitution Center. National Constitution Center. https://constitutioncenter.org/blog/five-other-days-that-could-be-proposed-as-federal-holidays/

Strauss, J. (2014, May 9) Federal holidays: Evolution and current practices. Congressional Research Service. https://fas.org/sgp/crs/misc/R41990.pdf

Supplementary Activities

1. Summary

Choose one of the articles in this collection and fill out the details on it below!

Name of Topic: _____

Time: _____

Location: _____

1. Summary: In a short paragraph (30-50 words) describe this historical period:

_____

_____

_____

_____

_____

2. Vocab: Write 3 New Vocabulary words you learned and their definitions:

Words	Definitions

1. After You Read Reaction: Choose one of the After You Read questions, and write a short answer below:

Question _____

_____

Response _____

_____

2. Project: Choose one of the Projects from the article. Answer below or on another page.

Project _____

Response _____

_____

_____

2. Create Your Own Mystery

Research a historical mystery from your country or another!

Name of Topic: _____

Time: _____

Location: _____

1. Description (what is the situation and why is it still a mystery?)

_____

_____

_____

_____

2. Solution: (How will you solve this mystery? If you were going back to this time, what would you do and what would you see?)

_____

_____

_____

_____

_____

3. Vocab: Write 2 new vocab you learned related to this topic

Words	Definitions

4. Source to support your research:

_____

_____

_____

PHOTOCOPIABLE - *History's Mysteries*

3. Mini Mysteries

Choose one of the mini-mysteries below and research to answer the questions below.

1. Why do dogs have cold noses?

2. When did humans discover...

    a. Fire

    b. The wheel

    c. How to make bread

3. Why do hot dog *buns* usually come in packs of eight while hot dogs usually come in packs of 10?

4. Which are smarter, cats or dogs?

5. Why do we say that cats have nine lives?

6. Investigate the expression! Discover the origin of one of the two expressions:

    a. The greatest thing since sliced bread.

    b. The early bird gets the worm.

7. What animal has the longest lifespan?

8. What makes hair curly?

9. What is the meaning of life?

10. Why is the *middle c* in Connecticut silent? (We say CO-*NET*-I-CUT not CON - *NECT* - I CUT)

11. Which came first, the chicken or the egg?

12. Why are there more right-handed people than left-handed people?

13. Why is there an S in Illinois?

Answers at the end of the book

1. Which mini-mystery did you choose and why?

2. What is the answer or explanation?

3. List your website or source below (use APA or MLA format if possible)

4. Finding Credible Sources

In the age of the internet, a great amount of good information is available, but also false information and lies. Sometimes people post biased information and sometimes sources appear official but are in fact fake. So how do you know if a source is credible, which means believable and reliable? The key is a good source should be RELIABLE. This means the source is one that we can trust versus an UNRELIABLE source that we're unsure provides trustworthy information.

So roughly we can consider reliable:

- Anything that is a primary source – statistics, professional speeches from conferences or TED Talks, research on the ground, interviews etc.
- Peer reviewed journals as they go through the process of peer review
- Books as they get edited and the author usually has done a lot of research to write them
- Papers written by experts.

Examples of less reliable/unreliable sources:

- Newspaper articles (except that which is primary) as they often have both bias and have very little time to check facts.
- Forums, blogs etc.
- Social Media of public figures or others promoting an agenda.
- Wikipedia and other user generated content – however Wikipedia will often give links to find more reliable information.

Criteria for Evaluating Sources:

There will be exceptions; a blog by a professor on his specialist subject is as likely to be as reliable as any papers he writes. Use the checklist below to evaluate your source before using it.

- ☐ Is this a primary source or secondary?
- ☐ If secondary, does it link to the primary source so you can verify?
- ☐ Is the source falsified or disguised?
- ☐ Is the source well-known and authoritative (a university or well-known publication) or a random blog or unknown organization?
- ☐ Has the information been verified or edited (peer-reviewed journal, book,)?
- ☐ Is the source known to have a bias?
- ☐ Is the article internally consistent?

Sources

Evaluating news resources: Steps and tools for evaluating the news. Research Guides. (n.d.). https://libguides.rutgers.edu/fake_news.

Purdue Writing Lab. (n.d.). General guidelines. Purdue Writing Lab. https://owl.purdue.edu/owl/research_and_citation/conducting_research/evaluating_sources_of_information/general_guidelines.html.

5. In-Text Citations of Sources

Generally, when citing a source or reference in research, there are four primary methods:

1. Direct Quotation in-text
2. Direct Quotation end-of-text
3. Paraphrase in-text
4. Paraphrase end-of-text

All references in your paper must include **author** and **year.**

All direct quotations must include **page** or **paragraph** number.

A period (full-stop) always comes at the end of parentheses ().

If the author of a website or article is unknown: use **article title** in quotations: "Types of Microbiology."

If the year is unknown, write **n.d.**

Below are examples of each type of citation in APA style.

Direct Quotation:

A direct quotation is a word-for-word quote from a source. One of the important things to remember in quoting directly from a source is to note the page or paragraph number. This is important so that any reader can quickly find the quotation if they want to review its accuracy.

An in-text quotation has two main variations: Both have similar meaning and use and effective writing uses variety to avoid repetition.

Using 'according to' with no reporting verb. Using a reporting verb such as claims/ states/argues/believes/etc....

In-text citation: (Author or Group name) "quotation...." (page or paragraph).

> According to Dollahite (2013) "A good source refers to the original" (p.81).
>
> Dollahite (2013) states that "A good source refers to the original" (p.81).
>
> "Good leadership types" (n.d.) states that "a good leader must have empathy" (par. 1).

End of text: (Author or "Title"/Year, page or paragraph)

> "A good source refers to the original" (Dollahite, 2013, p.81).

Paraphrase:

A paraphrase describes when you are citing the ideas from a source but writing in your own words. Unlike direct quotations, although both variations can be used in most situations, your choice of paraphrase can have a difference in meaning:

In-text - use especially when you want to clearly introduce an idea from another source

End-of-text - use when you are making a claim and want to use a source to support or backup your claim.

Generally the formatting and rules are the same as a direct quotation, just simpler!

Remember, any time you are using another source's idea you need to give paraphrase credit!

3. **In-text**: (author or "title"/ year).

> According to Dollahite (2013) a good source comes from the first paper.
>
> Dollahite (2013) claims that having effective sources are necessary to write a good paper.
>
> According to "Good leadership tips" (n.d.) being a leader, he or she should have empathy.

4. **End of text:** (Author or "title"/ year)

> A good source comes from the first paper (Dollahite, 2013).

Methods of Paraphrasing:

1. Change *synonyms* in citation.

2. Change *active to passive* or *passive to active*.

3. *Tell-A-Friend Method*: Look away from the source, then write. Read the text you want to paraphrase several times until you feel that you understand it and can use your own words to restate it to someone else.

4. *Chunking Method*: Chunking is a method of presenting information which splits concepts into small pieces or "chunks" of information to make reading and understanding faster and easier.

More useful links to avoid plagiarism:

Purdue Writing Lab. (n.d.). *Avoiding plagiarism / Purdue Writing Lab.* https://owl.purdue.edu/owl/teacher_and_tutor_resources/preventing_plagiarism/avoiding_plagiarism/index.html

The Writing Center. (n.d.). *Quoting and paraphrasing.* https://writing.wisc.edu/Handbook/QPA_paraphrase.html

PHOTOCOPIABLE - *History's Mysteries*

6. List of Sources or References

When using academic sources for research, it's important to cite the FULL source at the end of your writing. Academic References should be listed in an academic format. APA and MLA are the two most common. The best website with the most current rules on academic format, which are constantly changing, is Purdue OWL. There are lots of free websites like Citation Maker or Citefast to help make a reference. It is important to check carefully when using these, as they are prone to making mistakes!

General Notes

1. Alphabetize (A-Z) source lists using LAST Name (or group/article title if no name).

2. List all authors for a source, not just the first one!

3. *Italicize* book and journal titles.

4. Rules about article or webpage titles vary depending on the source and style.

5. Capitalization rules vary from style to style.

6. Use HANGING INDENT. Indent all lines after the first of each source. It makes them much easier to see on the list!

References – APA

Andrews, C. (2013, Sept. 16). Nikola Tesla - The man and his legacy. *E & T Magazine*. Retrieved from https://eandt.theiet.org/content/articles/2013/09/nikola-tesla-the-man-and-his-legacy/

Cheney, M. (1981). *Tesla, the man out of time*. Prentice-Hall.

Ebert, Roger. (2006, June 1) *An Inconvenient Truth movie review*. Roger Ebert.com. www.rogerebert.com/reviews/an-inconvenient-truth-2006

- Single-spaced
- Author's first name is initial
- Article not in quotes or italicized
- Web page name is italicized
- Date comes after author, in parentheses
- Only first word and proper nouns capitalized in titles

Works Cited – MLA

Andrews, Crispin. "Nikola Tesla - The Man and His Legacy." *E & T Magazine*, 16 Sept. 2013, eandt.theiet.org/content/articles/2013/09/nikola-tesla-the-man-and-his-legacy/.

Cheney, Margaret. *Tesla: Man out of Time*. Prentice-Hall, 1981.

Ebert, Roger. "An Inconvenient Truth Movie Review (2006): Roger Ebert." *Roger Ebert.com*, 1 June 2006, www.rogerebert.com/reviews/an-inconvenient-truth-2006.

- Double-spaced
- Author's first name is spelled out
- Article and web page names in quotes
- Website name italicized
- Date comes after name of source
- Important words in titles capitalized

For more examples see Purdue's Online Writing Center website: https://owl.purdue.edu/owl/research_and_citation/resources.html

7. In-Text and Citation Practice Activities

Research an interesting source online and write an in-text citation and a full reference. Don't forget to choose a *reliable* sources (See "Supplement 4: Finding Credible Sources" for more info)

Use an academic format approved by your teacher, for example APA or MLA. Find and write an example of each type of source below:

Use online resources like Purdue Owl, Citation Machine, or Citefast if you need help!

1. Format (choose one)

    a. APA
    b. MLA
    c. Other (Harvard/Chicago/_____)

2. Author:

3. Title of article, web page, or chapter (optional):

4. Title of longer work such as book, journal (optional):

5. Date the source was created (if given):

6. Publisher of book or website (optional):

7. In text citation (use in or end-of-text style)

8. Reference

8. Opinions vs Facts

One important skill when making any claim is understanding the difference between opinions or *subjective* statements and facts or *objective* claims.

Subjective Statements

Based on or influenced by personal feelings, tastes, or opinions. They are neither true nor false. They are one person's view about a topic or issue.

> *Example: My phone payment is very expensive.*

Words to Identify Opinions:

Biased Words (bad, worse, worst, good, better, best, worthwhile, worthless, etc.)

Qualifiers (all, always, likely, never, might, seem, possibly, probably, should, etc.)

Types of Opinions:

Positions on controversial issues

> *Example: I think the death penalty should be legal/illegal.*

Predictions about things in the future

> *Example: I think robots will do most of the teaching.*

Evaluations of people, places, and things

> *Example: The leader of my country is a good decision maker.*

Objective Claims

Not influenced by personal feelings or opinions in considering and representing facts. Objective statements can be verified and proven true or false. They contain information but do not tell what the writer thinks or believes about the topic

> *Example: My phone payment is $50 per month.*

Questions to Identify Objective Statements or Facts:

Can the statement be proved or demonstrated to be true?

> *Example: The USA has 500 million people (FALSE - The USA has about 328 million as of 2020)*

Can the statement be observed in practice or operation? Can you see it happen?

> *Example: Today is a sunny day (can be checked by looking outside!)*

Can the statement be verified by witnesses, manuscripts, or documents?

Example: Using a source to support a claim

Practice Activities: Objectivity and Subjectivity Practice

1.   Identify Facts and Opinions

When doing research or writing a paper, it's always key to differentiate fact from opinion. Look at the statements below and decide whether they are OPINION (subjective) or FACTS (objective). Circle your answer.

Example:

The USA has over 300 million people.   **F**   O

The USA has lots of very smart people.   F   **O**

1. Alligators provide no physical care for their young.   F   O
2. About 250 babies are born every minute.   F   O
3. All babies are cute.   F   O
4. Solar power is the only solution as a future power source.   F   O
5. The average efficiency of a solar panel is 15-25%   F   O

Answers at the end of this section

2. Locate Judgment Words

Another way to spot bias or opinion is the use of judgment words. Underline or circle the words that show bias or judgment.

Example: Purchasing a brand-new car is a terrible waste of money.

1. Many fantastic diet pills are available for purchase online.

2. Spider-Man is the most likable of all Marvel superheroes.

3. The English grammar textbook comes with an amazing poster with charts.

4. Volunteers for Habitat for Humanity are engaged in a worthwhile activity.

5. Donald Trump is the smartest leader and most stable genius in world history.

Answers at the end of this section

PHOTOCOPIABLE - *History's Mysteries*

3. Distinguish Between Fact and Opinion in a Paragraph

Read the paragraph and note below if each sentence is a Fact (F) or Opinion (O)

[1] There are over 3,500 species of mosquitoes in the world currently. [2] In the view of most people, mosquitoes are considered a pest and annoyance. [3] And not only are mosquitoes a pest, but mosquito bites are responsible for over 1 million deaths from the spread of malaria yearly. [4] In addition, their appearance and color is not attractive so many people may wish we could eradicate them all! [5] However, if mosquitoes were extinct, their absence on the food chain would result in the loss of many species of birds and fish and even plants, as they are also pollinators of 100s of types of plants.

1. _____   2. _____   3 _____   4 _____   5 _____

Answers at the end of this section

4. Recognize Informed Opinion

Informed Opinions: The opinions of experts are known as informed opinions. As experts in their field, they may make observations and offer comments that are not strictly factual. Instead, they are based on years of study, research, and experience.

> Example: Chimps are in massive danger of extinction from dwindling habitats. (Jane Goodall, primate expert and ethologist)

Questions to Identify Informed Speakers:

1. Does the speaker have a current and relevant background to the topic under discussion?

2. Is the speaker generally respected within the field?

3. Does the speaker carefully signal, via judgment words, to identify when they are presenting opinions vs. facts?

Read the sentences and underline or circle the phrase that acts as a clue.

> Example: **It seems clear** that parents who would bring a young child to an R-rated movie are putting their own interests ahead of what's best for the child.

1. Voters rejected the proposed rapid transit system connecting the southern and northern suburbs, possibly because of racial issues.

2. According to the city superintendent of schools, school uniforms lead to improved behavior and fewer disruptions in the classroom.

3. The destruction of our planet and resources may prompt humanity to move to Mars or another planet, some prominent researchers claim.

5. Write Your Own Facts and Opinions

Write 2 statements below, one using objective facts, and the other subjective opinion. Underline or circle key phrases.

Example:

1.   I think most dogs are smarter than cats.

2.   The data suggests dogs may know 100 words, but they can only vocalize about 15 different sounds. Cats may only understand 25 to 35 words, but they can make about 100 different vocalizations.

1. _____

_____

2. _____

_____

Answers

1. Identify Facts and Opinions
1. F
2. O
3. F
4. O
5. F

2.   Locate Judgment Words
1. Many fantastic
2. Most likable
3. Amazing
4. Worthwhile
5. smartest

3.   Distinguish Between Fact and Opinion in a Paragraph
1. F
2. O
3. F
4. O
5. O

4.   Recognizing Informed Opinion
1. possibly because of
2. According to the city superintendent of schools
3. some prominent researchers claim

5.   Write Your Own Facts and Opinions
Answers will vary

References

Dubec, R. (2019). *Fact vs opinion resource*. Teaching Commons | Teaching Commons. https://teachingcommons.lakeheadu.ca/fact-vs-opinion-resource

Facts vs. Opinion. (n.d.). Montgomery College, Maryland. https://www.montgomerycollege.edu/_documents/academics/support/learning-centers/writing-reading-learning-ctr-rockville/student-resources-tech/fact-vs-opinion.pdf

Rosenthal, Cathy M. (2012, July 16). *The intelligence of dogs and cats*. Animals Matter. https://blog.mysanantonio.com/animals/2012/07/the-intelligence-of-dogs-and-cats/.

9. Logic and Logical Fallacies

Noticing and Avoiding Weak Arguments

Key Vocabulary	Definition
logic (n.)	A system of rules for thinking clearly
logical (adj.)	About logic or following the rules of thinking clearly
fallacy (n.)	A mistake, something false, a wrong belief

You will have a very hard time convincing people if you argue with fallacies.

Understanding logical fallacies is also helpful when you are not sure what is true. Listening for logical fallacies in arguments will help you decide who is thinking clearly about the topic and who you can trust.

However, it is very easy to use fallacies—they are a kind of mental laziness, so people may use them even when strong logic is possible. Avoid this mistake. If you want to change someone's mind, make sure your logic is strong no matter how sure you are of the truth

Common Fallacies to Avoid:

1. Ad Hominem - You argue using insults or character attacks instead of supporting your opinion.

   | Example: Crazy Andy who has purple hair says we should legalize marijuana.

2. Appeal to Authority - You support your opinion with a powerful or famous person's opinion instead of evidence.

   | Example: I believe the earth is flat because Kyrie Irving said it's true.

3. Appeal to Popular Opinion - You support your opinion without evidence by saying it is popular or common.

   | Example: Everybody knows aliens are not real.

4. Begging the Question - You support your opinion using the same idea.

   | Example: I believe Taylor is honest because I know he never lies.

5. Cherry Picking - You choose one example that supports your opinion but ignore others.

   | Example: Exercising is dangerous. After all, my friend broke his arm skateboarding.

6. Slippery Slope - You predict an extreme series of causes and effects to argue against an opinion.

> Example: If we legalize marijuana, it's only a matter of time before children are addicted to heroin."

7. Straw Man - You try to connect the topic to another idea that is easier to argue.

> Example: How can you believe aliens are not real? Don't you know that the government lied about the war and the economy? You can't trust what they say!"

8. Whataboutism - You change your attack instead of defending your argument.

> Example: Scientists are wrong about climate change, and also what about the coronavirus? Why were they not ready for that?"

Note that there are more fallacies than are listed here, and these have been simplified to show the way you could hear them in casual conversation rather than in academic contexts.

Activities:

A.   Read the paragraphs for logical fallacies.

Underline the sentences that contain obvious fallacies. (There is more than one per paragraph.) Explain to a partner why you think there is a fallacy in the argument.

1. John F. Kennedy was assassinated by the Mafia. It would have been very difficult for Lee Harvey Oswald to plan and complete the shooting alone, and several witnesses think they saw another shooter. Furthermore, everybody knows the Mafia hated JFK They had a good reason to kill him. Mafia members have gone to jail for murdering people on many occasions. They have a history of violent crime, and John Gotti and Whitey Bulger went to jail for murder. So it is obvious they would help kill the president.

2.   The moon landing was a hoax. The US government faked it in order to intimidate the Soviets during the Cold War. You cannot trust the liars who say it was real. Even though NASA says the photos and video of the landing are real,

PHOTOCOPIABLE - *History's Mysteries*

they are fake. It is easy to fake photos. After all, the photo of the Loch Ness

Monster and the video of Bigfoot were both fake.

Answers at the end of section

B.   Read the following sentences for fallacies.

Mark clear logic with an **L** and logical fallacies with an **F**. Compare your answers with a partner and explain the fallacies that you see.

1. ___ All of my friends support President Jones, so you can be sure he is a good president.

2. ___ The people who want to legalize marijuana are dirty hippies that smell bad and waste time on video games.

3. ___ I do not trust Bob because I saw him cheat on the test and lie to his friends about it.

4. ___ Bob was not really cheating, and what about the time that you didn't help with the group project?

5. ___ If I have class at 8 a.m., I will have to go to bed early and miss the party and I will not have any friends.

6. ___ My Saudi neighbor has a great job and many friends, so I am sure there is no racism in my city.

7. ___ Research shows marijuana is less addictive than alcohol and cigarettes.

8. ___ It is unlikely Bigfoot is real because there is no visual record or scientific studies that show evidence.

C.   Share your experience:

1. Write an example of a *logical fallacy* you have heard repeated about a topic you are familiar with.

2. What kind of *logical fallacy* is it?

3. What would be a strong logical argument for *or* against the topic?

Answers at the end of section

Topic: _____

Common Fallacy You Have Heard: _____

_____

_____

_____

_____

Strong Logic: _____

_____

_____

_____

_____

Answers at the end of section

D.   Advanced Listening Project

1. Watch a political discussion show and listen for examples of logical fallacies in the speakers' statements. Take notes.

2. Do you hear any logical fallacies? Which ones?

3. Did any guests avoid using fallacies?

4. How does the host of the show respond to different opinions of the guests?

5. Who do you agree with and why?

Answers:

A: Paragraph 1, "Everybody knows the Mafia hated JFK" - appeal to popular opinion; "They have a history of violent crime, and John Gotti and Whitey Bulger went to jail for murder" - straw man and/or ad hominem

Paragraph 2, "You cannot trust the liars who say it was real." - Ad hominem and/or begging the question; "It is easy to fake photos. After all, the photo of the Loch Ness Monster and the video of Bigfoot were both fake." - Cherry picking and/or straw man.

B: 1, 2, 4, 5, 6 are Fallacies, 3, 7, 8; Fallacy are Logical

C: Answers will vary.

D: Answers will vary

References

Hansen, H. (2020, April 2). Fallacies (Stanford encyclopedia of philosophy). *Stanford Encyclopedia of Philosophy.* https://plato.stanford.edu/entries/fallacies/

PHOTOCOPIABLE - *History's Mysteries*

10. Fact or Fiction

Half of the following facts about famous people are true and half are false. Guess and then research to find which ones are true or false! Underline and Correct the false mistakes!

Examples

> Elizabeth I of England suffered from anthophobia, a fear of roses. **-** *TRUE*
> Walt Disney was afraid of cats **-** *FALSE, he was afraid of mice.*

A. Strange Facts about Famous People - True or False

Circle the correct answer

1.	Napoleon constructed his battle plans in a sandbox.	T	F
2.	Michael Jordan makes more money from Nike annually than all of the Nike factory workers in Malaysia combined.	T	F
3.	Barbie's full name is Barbara Jo Lewis.		T
4.	Titan is one of the moons of Jupiter.	T	F
5.	Kermit the Frog is left-handed.	T	F
6.	Robert Ladlow, the world's tallest person, was 10ft/305cm.	T	F
7.	A man named Charles Osborne had the hiccups for 50 years!	T	F
8.	Virginia Woolf wrote all her books standing.	T	F
9.	Ernest Vincent Wright wrote a novel, "Gadsby", which contains over 50,000 words, none of them with the letter T!	T	F
10.	Jimi Hendrix and William Shakespeare died on their birthdays.	T	F
11.	President Abraham Lincoln is in the Boxing Hall of Fame	T	F
12.	George Washington had wooden teeth.	T	F

B. Make Your Own - Interesting Historical Facts

Try your own: Write pieces of information below on another piece of paper about famous historical people or places, one that is TRUE and one that is FALSE (it should have a clear mistake). Find a source to support both claims.

Share both your examples with the class (without showing the answers!) See if you can find out which one is true!

Examples

> Madagascar is the largest island in the world by area - *FALSE, Greenland is the largest island by area. Source: https://www.infoplease.com/world/geography/large-islands-world*

Jeanne Louise Calment from France, is currently verified as the longest living human, having reached 122 years - *TRUE* Source: *https://www.cbsnews.com/ news/worlds-longest-living-person-jeanne-calment-fraud-russian-researcher- guinness-record*

Answers

A. Strange Facts about Famous People - True or False

1. True.

2. True.

3. False - Barbie's full name is Barbara Millicent Roberts.

4. False - Titan is a moon of Saturn.

5. True.

6. False - Ladlow is the world's tallest person, but he was really 8ft 11in or 272cm.

7. False - A man named Charles Osborne had the hiccups for 69 years.

8. True.

9. False - he wrote the book with none of them with the letter E.

10. False William Shakespeare died on his birthday, but Jimi Hendrix did not.

11. False - he is in the Wrestling Hall of Fame.

12. False - he had many types of false teeth including ivory and gold, but never wood.

B. Make Your Own - Interesting Historical Facts:

Answers will vary

11. Fake News

Fake news — stories that seem real but aren't — is not new. In one famous case, radio host Orson Welles, told his listeners on October 30, 1938, that Martians had invaded the state of New Jersey. Welles had explained at the beginning of the show that this story was fiction, but many people believed that the Earth was under attack.

Or did they?

In 2008, Michael Sokolow in an article in *The Chronicles of Higher Learning* cited four other researchers who claim that few people heard the original radio broadcast, and that the people who did tune in, knew they were listening to fiction. So, how was it that history remembers the radio show as causing wide-spread panic, even suicides? Seems that other media sources, such as newspapers at the time, reported a panic, and their exaggeration is now remembered as fact.

Distinguishing fact from fiction, being able to tell what is real and what is fake, is the foundation of critical thinking. In order to be sure, as history investigators, that we are telling the truth, we have to be able to trust our sources. This is difficult.

Artificial intelligence and new technology allow liars to post frequently to social media or to manipulate video images to say whatever whenever. In other words, it's important to remain skeptical and use common sense when exposed to surprising claims online or in the media. So, what can you do to ensure credibility?

According to, one way to check credibility is to use the CRAP test: Is your source Current? Reputable? Who is your source's author? What are the author's credentials? Can you verify them? Finally, what is the purpose of the article/video? Do you feel someone is trying to sell you something?

In 1938, believing a radio show, or thinking that other people believed the radio show may not have been important, but is it important now?

Kerry Tomlinson, a veteran KATU and KPTV news reporter in Portland, Oregon and anchor on Archer News Network, gave us her take on fake news. (Her comments have been edited for length and clarity.)

Kerry, would you go so far as to call "fake news" dangerous?

I do think fake news is very dangerous. It can hurt you, hurt others, cause people to lose their jobs and even their lives. If you use social media, you are soaked in a world of misinformation spread by people, countries, political groups, companies and activists to make money off of you and influence your vote, your life, your money and turn your happiness to anger.

What is an example of "fake news" that shocked you?

I am rarely shocked by fake news. After 30 years in broadcast journalism, most in television news, I have seen and heard misinformation of many kinds, often ugly and destructive. Often, you absorb and spread the fake news and misinformation to others.

A current example of fake news now is the claim that people with the anti-fascist group Antifa are deliberately setting fires in Oregon.

Another example of misinformation/fake news can be found in comedian Amy Schumer's Instagram post the day after the 2016 presidential election. She posted what appeared to be a quote from Donald Trump in People in 1988 that said, "If I were to run, I'd run as a Republican. They're the dumbest group of voters in the country." Schumer acknowledged that the quote was false. "Yes, this quote is fake but it doesn't matter."

That hits at the heart of the problem. People want to believe, and therefore embrace and share fake news/misinformation because it supports their world view.

It's important to be able to corroborate information. How many sources should I have before I can be certain that what I'm seeing or hearing is the real deal?

Here are steps you can take to help you evaluate a news story:

Be skeptical of headlines
Investigate the author/site
Check the sources cited in the article
Check the domain name
Check the actual date of the story or event
Look at other reports
Check your biases

Before you research the information, the most important step is to confront the bias in your own mind. What do you want to believe? Which tactics are the influencers using on you, and what are you susceptible to? One of the key strategies of misinformers is to make you angry. You turn to more people and sources that support your anger. You turn away from people who may not look, think or act like you. With anger, the influencers can persuade you to vote, spend or act a certain way. They want you to be angry. They want you to hate.

The truth may be a moving target. You are more likely to find out a prevailing understanding of truth if you look at many mainstream news sources across many biases, instead of just relying on one or two sources that could be influenced by fake news and a unique bias.

Remind me why I shouldn't spread "fake news?"

You can kill people with fake news. As we see in the example of the Oregon fires, an angry neighbor may shoot a 'stranger' in the neighborhood because they read that people who disagree with their political views are setting fires. You can destroy lives. If you spread fake news, then you are adding to hatred and anger in the world, and it may ultimately foment violence against you as well. You share a potentially fake news story about a politician you love to hate? You increase the likelihood that someone will counter that with fake news about you and people in your political group. And the back-and-forth will continue, damaging lives, causing distrust in all humans and institutions, adding to societal instability. In addition, you are playing into the hands of the influencers, the governments, political parties who want to control you and manipulate you.

And you are generating more fear and anger in your own heart and mind.

So, "fake news" isn't new, and the media has always tried to persuade its audience, but technological advances increase the spread, frequency and power of artificial journalism to manipulate emotions. Unscrupulous authors weaponize readers' hatred against one person, a class of people, a company or a government. Imagine this angry audience transforming into a swarm of biting gnats in attack mode with one goal: destruction.

As the 90s television show *The X-Files* says, "The truth is out there." We just have to find it, and spread it, by committing to checking our feelings, as well as our sources. Recognizing "fake news" is the first step. Caring about the effect "fake news" has on others is the second. In order to protect ourselves and fight back, we must raise our awareness by asking one simple question: Am I working from what I know or from what I feel?

Try it out in practice:

1. Did you hear that Joe Biden fell asleep during a live interview? Before you spread the information as proof then-2020 presidential candidate Biden is too old to be president, do some checking.

   Here is a list of fact-checking websites, again from www.cyberwise.org, that might help. A fact-checking website verifies information and sources by linking to primary sources, finding independent verification, avoiding biased interpretations and using basic logic. What did you find?

   Snopes.com

   Factcheck.org

   Politifact.org

   Opensecrets.org

   Truthorfiction.com

2. How about a story that is less current, and not about politics. Did you know that reptile people exist? According to David Ickes' book, *The Biggest Secret: The Book That Will Change the World,* lizard people use technology to appear human, but are really from another dimension where they retain their reptile appearance. People who believe this think that many famous people are, actually, lizards. How can you check whether this is "fake" news?

One last thing

Finally, look back at the chapter "Slender Man is Not Real" in Section VIII. How is the information online about Slender Man fake news? Why were these stories problems? What could be done to keep people safe from stories about Slender Man?

Answers

Try it out in practice

1. Snopes.com says that the video was manipulated. Factcheck.org says that the story is false. Check the Ask Factcheck archives. Politifact.org presents quotes from the media and shows whether they are true or false; there's no place to ask questions. When the question was typed into the search bar, Opersecrets.org linked to an article that explained why the video had been manipulated. Truthorfiction.com did not have information regarding this story.

2. It's difficult to find out whether this is true. Searching "How can David Ickes be debunked?" pulls up loads of YouTube videos purporting to debunk the lizard theory and Ickes's new theory that Covid-19 results from 5G bandwidth technology. This goes to show you that the crazier a theory, the more likely it is to continue because scientists are not going to waste their time proving the theory false.

References

Spencer, J. (2016, Dec 7). *Helping students identify fake news.* [Video]. YouTube. www.youtube.com/watch?v=xf8mjbVRqao

CyberWise. (2019, August 10) *What is Fake News?* [Video]. YouTube. https://www.youtube.com/watch?v=V4o0B6IDo50

History.com editors. (2020, October 28) Orson Welles's "War of the Worlds" is broadcast. *HISTORY.* https://www.history.com/this-day-in-history/welles-scares-nation.

Novak, M. (2013, October 29). Did the 'War of the worlds' radio broadcast really cause mass panic?. *Paleofuture.* https://paleofuture.gizmodo.com/did-the-war-of-the-worlds-radio-broadcast-really-cause-1453582944

Ovadya, A. (2018, September 11). *Fake news is about to get much worse. Here's a solution.* [Video]. YouTube. http://www.youtube.com/watch?v=Z1WtNJmz3c0

12. Using Wikipedia

Introduction/Warm-up

topic

hyperlink

references

table of contents

sub-topics

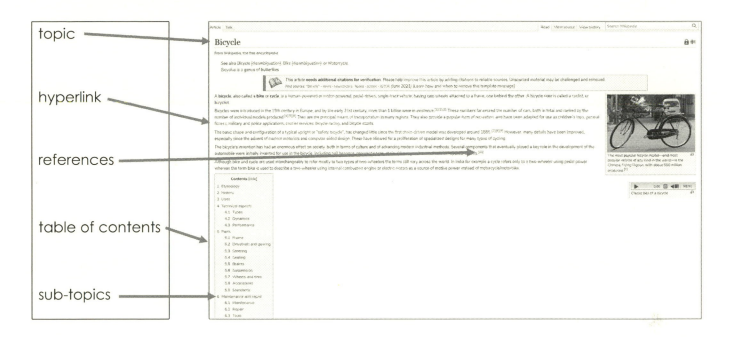

1. Where do people go for information? Name some common sources.

   a. Now, put these sources in order from "most trustworthy" to "least trustworthy". Why did you choose this order? Does your partner agree? Why or why not?

2. What is an encyclopedia? What is Wikipedia? Tell your partner.

   a. Have you used either of these before? What did you research? Why?

   b. How much do you trust the information in a "traditional" encyclopedia? Why, or why not?

   c. What about Wikipedia? Do you trust it more, less, or the same? Why?

Wikipedia is a free, online, crowd-sourced encyclopedia, with over 6.2 million articles in English and 54 million articles overall. It is one of the most popular sites on the internet, with more than 1.5 billion different visitors per month, and relies on donations, not ads, to operate. Crowdsourcing is a great advantage of the site, since anybody can add to or edit articles, giving the site great reach. There is also a talk feature for each entry, where people can debate and discuss what information should be included. However, this same factor can also cause problems, since those who edit the articles may have bias, prejudices, agendas, or just lack enough knowledge. These are the two main ways that Wikipedia differs from a traditional encyclopedia. How can we use this amazing tool while making sure we get the truth?

Activity One - How to Read a Wikipedia Entry

Vocabulary Definitions

Write the letter of the definition next to the matching word.

1. topic _____
2. sub-topic _____
3. table of contents _____
4. hyperlink _____
5. references _____

a. a guide, or map, which helps you find how information is organized on the page
b. the main idea
c. sources, proof that the information comes from somewhere
d. an idea under the main idea
e. something you click on to go to another page

Answers at the end of the section

1. All Wikipedia *topic* pages start with a summary, followed by a *table of contents* listing the *sub-topics*. They also contain *hyperlinks*, media (such as pictures, audio, or video), and *references* at the end.

    a. Go to wikipedia.org and search for a topic that interests you. How quickly can you find these five features?

    b. Search for a couple more topics. Is the organization similar? Can you find the same five features quickly and easily?

    c. Alone or with a partner, compare and contrast two Wikipedia entries:

Activity Two - References in a Wikipedia Entry

1. Look for the small numbers in blue, above the last word in some sentences. These are called *footnotes*. What are these? What do they mean? Ask a partner.

    a. Follow one of the footnotes to the *references* section. Find out whether it is a *primary source*, *secondary source*, or *tertiary source* (you can use Wikipedia to find the definitions of these three terms).

Source Number	Primary, Secondary, or Tertiary Source?	How Do You Know?

    b. What are some of the different types of sources in the references section? Make a list here:

    c. Some of the sources are hyperlinks. Click on a few. Where do they take you?

PHOTOCOPIABLE - *History's Mysteries*

d. If you can't access the source online (or find it elsewhere), is it still OK to use the citation? Why, or why not?

e. Which is better, the primary (original) source, or the secondary/tertiary source (such as the Wikipedia entry). Why?

Activity Three - How Use Wikipedia as a "Source" (advanced)

1. Starting in junior high, most American students are required to write research papers on a variety of topics and must use sources.

a. Have you ever written a research paper? What was the topic? What types of sources did you use? How did you find them?

b. A Wikipedia article is generally *not* considered a source? Why is this?

c. However, Wikipedia is a great starting place, and a great place to find sources. Explain why this is.

d. Choose a topic and imagine you are writing a research paper on it. Go to the Wikipedia entry on the topic and find at least three facts you could include in your paper.

Find the references that go with each fact and find the original sources online (if possible).

Along with "Supplement 5: In-Text Citations of Sources", practice how to include these facts in your research paper.

13. Critical Questions for Media Literacy

It's easy to believe everything we read, especially when it looks and sounds professional. We may see or hear something really amazing and share it without looking further into where it comes from or why it was created. This is often the case with social media, but it can also happen with traditional print media and even with history. Anyone who writes and publishes has a purpose. Sometimes the purpose is merely to share information, but sometimes the writer wants to persuade the reader to believe something. Therefore, whenever we read, we should read critically. We can do this by asking some important questions.

1. Who is the author? (Not just the name but where are they from? Who do they work for?)
2. Who benefits from this text? (Who looks good?)
3. Who is disadvantaged by this text? (Who looks bad?)
4. Whose viewpoint is missing from this text?
5. What does the writer want you to think or do after reading this text?

1. Inauguration Photo

Let's try it with an image. Go to https://www.voanews.com/usa/factcheck-trump-and-spicers-statements-inaugural-crowd-size or scan the QR code at right, and look at the first image (don't scroll down yet). Try to answer the questions above (For images, we'll change question #1).

Below are some example answers.

1. *It's a picture of Donald Trump's inauguration in 2016.*
2. *Donald Trump and his supporters*
3. *People who don't support Trump.*
4. *People watching from other sides or above.*
5. *Trump is very popular.*

Now read the rest of the article. How did the photographer's viewpoint affect the photo and how others feel when they look at the photo?

2. Stanford Study

Let's try it with this image right. For now, skip question number one. After answering questions 2-5, use the link (https://news.stanford.edu/news/2015/january/emissions-social-costs-011215.html) or scan the QR code to check your answers.

1. What is this a picture of?
2. Who benefits from this image?
3. Who is disadvantaged by this image?
4. Whose viewpoint is missing from the image?
5. What does the publisher want you to think after viewing this image?

3. Headlines

Headlines are an easy way to grab a reader's attention. Sometimes people don't even read the rest of the article, so a headline can have a great effect on what someone thinks. Let's try using our five critical questions on these headlines. For headlines, we'll change question #1.

1. What is the article generally about?
2. Who benefits from this headline?
3. Who is disadvantaged by this headline?
4. Whose viewpoint is missing from this headline?
5. What does the writer want you to think or do after reading this headline (other than read the article)?

1. Rioters run wild in Los Angeles but reason for latest unrest is unknown

https://www.foxnews.com/us/lapd-issues-tactical-alert-protests-gather-outside-police-headquarters-smash-window-local-business

2. War in the Caucasus Will Draw in Russia and Turkey

https://www.bloombergquint.com/gadfly/armenia-azerbaijan-war-will-draw-in-russia-turkey-u-s

3. What can US do to stop migrant caravans?

https://www.foxnews.com/transcript/what-can-us-do-to-stop-mi-grant-caravans

4. Don't blame global warming for killer wildfires

https://trib.com/opinion/columns/reagan-dont-blame-global-warming-for-killer-wildfires/article_42691740-39fc-546e-96d3-bd0f5375de70.html

5. Full Articles

These five critical thinking questions are useful when reading full text articles as well. While articles are meant to be mostly informative, some may also try to persuade the reader to believe a certain viewpoint. Asking these five questions when reading any article is a good idea, but they're especially important when we come across articles on social media. People often share such articles when they want to convince others to share their viewpoints. Next time you read news shared on social media, take a moment to ask and answer these questions.

Let's try it with the following article from *The California Globe*. Go to https://californiaglobe.com/section-2/new-cdc-study-finds-majority-of-those-infected-with-covid-19-always-wore-masks or scan the QR code to the right, and read the article. When you are finished, answer the five critical thinking questions.

1. Who is the author?
2. Who benefits from this text?
3. Who is disadvantaged by this text?
4. Whose viewpoint is missing from this text?
5. What does the writer want you to think or do after reading this text?

After reading this article, go to https://www.snopes.com/fact-check/cdc-report-majority-wore-masks on the Snopes.com website or scan the QR code to the left for a more objective view of this story.

Believe it or not, these questions are also important when we are reading about history. Historical events are usually written about long after they have happened. The basic facts about history—dates, people, and places—are usually agreed on by everyone but people may disagree about the reasons behind some historical events or the exact way they happened. Therefore, when reading about history, it's important to ask these critical thinking questions.

A good example of this is Genghis Khan. Older histories and those written in countries that were conquered by the Mongols tend to describe him in a negative way. However, many newer histories and those written in countries that benefited from Genghis Khan's rule have a very positive view of this historical figure. Can you think of any other examples from history?

14. Evaluating Sources - Final Project

Choose an interesting article from any reliable online or print source. Evaluate the source, any possible bias, and how you feel about the article. Post the full APA or MLA citation at the bottom of the Paper.

1. Title of Article:

_____

2. Author:

_____

3. Website Address: :_____

Is it a   a).com   b).org   c).edu   d.) other_____

4. Is the website reliable?   Yes   No   Maybe

Why? _____

_____

_____

5. Is the author: PRO   CON   NEITHER

6. What is the *main idea* of the article? *Quote* the main idea in APA/MLA format:

_____

_____

_____

7. What is your reaction to this article? (~30-50 words)

_____

_____

_____

_____

_____

_____

8. APA/MLA Reference:

_____

_____

_____

Index by Time

Index by Location

Answers to Quiz Questions

Section I - Monsters and Mysterious Creatures

What Happened to the Dinosaurs?
Vocab 1. e 2. g 3. j 4 b. 5 a. 6 c. 7 d. 8 h. 9 f. 10. i
Quiz 1. d 2. c 3. b 4. b 5. c

The Loch Ness Monster
Vocab 1. g 2. d 3. h 4. a 5. j 6. b 7. e 8. i 9. c 10. f 11. k
Quiz 1. c 2. b 3. a 4. d 5. d

The Elusive Ivory-billed Woodpecker
Vocab 1. d 2. e 3. a 4. j 5. f 6. g 7. c 8. i 9. h 10. b
Quiz 1. c 2. d 3. b 4. b 5. a 6. Their habitat was ruined

Bigfoot - Ancient Ape of The Northwest
Vocab 1.c 2. a 3.b 4.f 5.e 6.d 7.g
Quiz 1.d 2. b 3.c. 4.d 5.a

It's a bird? It's a plane? It's a Picasso
Vocab 1. g 2. j 3. a 4. b 5. i 6. c 7. f 8. h 9. d 10. e
Quiz 1. a 2. b 3. b 4, a 5. b

Section II - Heroes and Villains

Genghis Khan: Villain or Hero?
Vocab 1. h 2. c 3. f 4. a 5. e 6. b 7. g 8. j 9. i 10. d 11. l 12. k
Quiz 1.c 2.b 3.d 4.a 5.b

The Children's Crusade
Vocab 1. e 2. h 3. a 4. g 5. f 6. b 7. m 8. j 9. d 10. l 11. i 12. k 13. c
Quiz 1. b 2. a 3. c 4. c 5. d

Artist or Monster? Stop Adolf Hitler
Vocab 1. i 2. b 3. f 4. h 5. j 6. a 7. c 8. e 9. d 10. g
Quiz 1.c 2. a 3.b. 4.a 5.a

Lyuh Woon-hyung and the Division of Korea
Vocab 1. c 2. i 3. d 4. j 5. h 6. g 7. k 8. f 9. b 10. a 11. e
Quiz 1. a 2. c 3. d 4. a 5. b

Who Killed 2Pac?
Vocab 1. b 2. a 3. h 4. c 5. f 6. i 7. g 8. j 9. e 10. d
Quiz 1. c 2. b 3. c 4. a 5. d

Section III - Famous Unsolved Crimes and Criminals

Who Was Jack the Ripper?
Vocab 1. d 2. e 3. b 4. f 5. g 6. c 7. a 8. i 9. h
Quiz 1. b 2. c 3. b 4. d 5. a

The Osage Indian Murders
Vocab 1. c 2. a 3. i 4. j 5. e 6. g 7. f 8. h 9. k 10. b 11. d
Quiz 1. a 2. a 3. c 4. c 5. d

D. B. Cooper, Skyjacker
Vocab 1.b 2. e 3.a 4.d 5.c 6.f
Quiz 1.b 2. d 3.c. 4.c 5.b

Elizabeth Stewart Gardner Museum Heist
Vocab 1. c 2. d 3. i 4. a 5. b 6. e 7. g 8. k 9. j 10. h 11. f
Quiz 1. a 2. a 3. b 4. c 5. d

Floating Feet
Vocab 1.f 2. b 3.c 4.j 5.m 6.i 7.a 8.h 9.d 10.n 11.g 12.k 13.o 14.e 15.l
Quiz 1. c 2. b 3. d 4. d 5. b

Section IV - Disappearances

The Olmecs
Vocab 1. d 2. a 3. f 4. c 5. b 6. j 7. e 8. g 9. i 10. h
Quiz 1. d 2. a 3. c 4. c 5. b

Nan Madol: Pacific Megalith Mystery
Vocab 1. n 2. k 3. g 4. j 5. f 6. a 7. i 8. b 9. c 10. l 11. h 12. e 13. d 14. m 15. o
Quiz 1. d 2. b 3. a 4. b 5. b

The Disappearance of the "Lost Colony" of Roanoke Island
Vocab 1. i 2. f 3. h 4. j 5. a 6. c 7. b 8. e 9. g 10. d
Quiz 1. c 2. b 3. a 4. c 5. a

The Dyatlov Pass Incident
Vocab 1. c 2. e 3. d 4. b 5. h 6. g 7. j 8. i 9. a 10. f
Quiz 1. d 2. b 3. c 4. a 5. c

Help MH370!
Vocab 1. d 2. f 3. i 4. g 5. b 6. c 7. h 8. a 9. e 10. j
Quiz 1. c 2. b 3. d 4. b 5. d

Section V - Aliens and Other Worlds

Who Built the Pyramids?
Vocab 1. b 2. a 3. g 4. c 5. j 6. d 7. i 8. f 9. e 10. h
Quiz 1. a 2. c 3. b 4. a 5. a

The "Lost Cosmonauts"
Vocab 1. f 2. a 3. g 4. b 5. j 6. i 7. d 8. c 9. e 10. h
Quiz 1. c 2. a 3. b 4. d 5. b

Project Serpo
Vocab 1. j 2. i 3. c 4. a 5. d 6. e 7. f 8. g 9. b 10. h
Quiz 1. a 2. b 3. d 4. a 5. b

Crop Circles - Real or Hoax?
Vocab 1. b 2. c 3. f 4. d 5. e 6. h 7. g 8. a
Quiz 1. b 2. c 3. a 4. d 5. c

Stephen Hawking's Time Travel Cocktail Party
Vocab 1. c 2. b 3. i 4. e 5. a 6. d 7. g 8. h 9. j 10. f
Quiz 1. a 2. c 3. b 4. c 5. a

Section VI - Conspiracies and Secrets

Shakespeare, Marlowe, Spies, and Murder
Vocab 1. e 2. g 3. k 4. f 5. d 6. i 7. c 8. a 9. b 10. h 11. j

Quiz 1. b 2. a 3. c 4. b 5. b

The Illuminati: secret societies and conspiracy
Vocab 1. e 2. a 3. b 4. c 5. h 6. f 7. g 8. j 9. k 10. d 11. m 12. p 13. o 14. i 15. n 16. l 17.q
Quiz 1. c 2. a 3. b 4. b 5. d

Bessie Coleman
Vocab 1. g 2. a 3. b 4. e 5. f 6. h 7. i 8. c 9. d 10. j 11. k 12. l 13. m
Quiz 1. b 2. c 3. a 4. c 5. a

Save JFK
Vocab 1.h 2.f 3.c 4.g 5.d 6.b 7.e 8.a 9.j 10.i
Quiz 1.c 2.d 3.b. 4.c 5.a

The First Lady's Love Letters
Vocab 1. g 2. k 3. a 4. f 5. b 6. h 7. c 8. d 9. e 10. i 11. j
Quiz 1. c 2. a 3. b 4. a 5. d

Section VII - Screams - Murderers, Witches and Ghosts

The Salem Witch Trials
Vocab 1. b 2. e 3. c 4. a 5. i 6. k 7. f 8. d 9. j 10. l 11. m 12.h 13. n 14. g
Quiz 1.a 2.a 3.b 4.c 5.d

World's Fairs: World's Columbian Exposition
Vocab 1. k 2. j 3. a 4. c 5. i 6. b 7. h 8. d 9. e 10. l 11. f 12. g
Quiz 1. c 2. b 3. d 4. c 5. a

The Phantom Barber
Vocab 1. c 2. a 3. f 4. h 5. i 6.d 7. e 8. b 9. j 10. g
Quiz 1. a 2. b 3.d 4. b 5. a

The Haunting of The Geiser Grand Hotel
Vocab 1. e 2. g 3. d 4. c 5. a 6. h 7. f 8. j 9. b 10. i
Quiz 1. a. 2. b. 3. c. 4. b. 5. b.

Slender Man is Not Real!-
Vocab 1. j 2. h 3. i 4. a 5. c 6. e 7. g 8. b 9. d 10. f
Quiz 1F Slender Man is a character in a story. He does not live anywhere.

2T

3T

4F Peyton was stabbed 19 times.

5F Anissa and Morgan did not care about Peyton.

Discussion Question 3 How can you build empathy with the homeless?

Suggested answers: 1. Ask a homeless person about the good parts and struggles of everyday life. 2. Talk to someone who helps homeless people. 3. Read "Letters: Homelessness, from the perspective of a homeless man on Collegian.com, 9/21/2017. https://web.archive.org/web/20190909140947/https://collegian.com/2017/09/letters-homelessness-from-the-perspective-of-a-homeless-man/.

Discussion Question 4 How might the cyclist be in danger?

1) The attackers can come back. 2) Peyton might die. 3) The EMTs cannot find his location. 4) He is traumatized for life.)

Section VIII - Miscellaneous

Tsodilo Botswana and Ancient Art
Vocab 1. d 2. g 3. f 4. a 5. b 6. j 7. c 8. e 9. i 10. h
Quiz 1. b 2. a 3. d 4. c 5. c

"Fire!"
Vocab 1. j 2. f 3. h 4. i 5. b 6. g 7. c 8. d 9. a 10. e
Quiz 1. b 2. a 3. d 4. c 5. A

Discussion 1 Vocabulary

Nouns (12 words)

1. firemen
2. blaze
3. heat
4. fire engine
5. ashes
6. stove
7. matchsticks
8. furnace
9. smoke
10. lantern
11. gasoline
12. Hades

Verb (7 words)

1. melt
2. extinguish
3. burned
4. ignited
5. incinerated
6. exploded
7. set

Adjective (4 words

1. cooking
2. flammable
3. combustible
4. roaring

The 27 Club
Vocab 1. f 2. c 3. d 4. a 5. b 6. i 7. h 8. g 9. e
Quiz 1. a 2. b 3. c 4. a 5. c

The Number 23 Enigma
Vocab 1. b 2. e 3. c 4. f 5. d 6. a 7. i 8. j 9. g 10. h
Quiz 1. b 2. a 3. a 4. c 5. d

A New US Holiday?
Vocab 1. c 2. h 3. a 4. b 5. d 6. i 7. e 8. j 9. f 10. k 11. g
Quiz 1. c 2. a 3. c 4. b 5. a

Acknowledgments

Image Credits: 2, estebande/Depositphotos pg. 7, Marmaduke Wetherell/Wikimedia Commons (Public Domain) pg. 13, Butler, Amos W./A catalogue of the birds of Indiana/Internet Book Archive (No Copyright) pg. 18, ehrlif/Depositphotos pg. Red Panda pg. 23, J. Crocker/Wikimedia Commons (by permission) pg. 28, lub_lubachka/ Depositphotos pg. 28, Red Panda pg. 31, Gary Todd/Flickr (CC BY-SA 2.0) pg. 35, Furian/Depositphotos pg. 37, John Bonner/The Story History of France (No Copyright) pg. 44, Unknown/Wikimedia Commons (Public Domain) pg. 46, Bayerische Staatsbibliothek/ Wikimedia Commons (Public Domain) pg. 50, olinchuk & Red Panda/Depositphotos () pg. 55, r2hox/Flickr (CC BY-SA 2.0) pg. 61, R. Taylor/Wikimedia Commons (Public Domain) pg. 67, CrimsonEdge34/Wikimedia Commons (Public Domain) pg. 71, White House/Damming the Osage (CC0) pg. 72, FBI/ (Public Domain) pg. 74, FBI/FBI.gov (Public Domain) pg. 78, FBI/Wikimedia Commons (Public Domain) pg. 83, Red Panda/ Pixabay & Depositphotos/idea by Katie Kosma () pg. 90, Octavia Medellin/ Bywaters Special Collections, SMU (No copyright) pg. 92, Michael Everson/Wikimedia Commons (CC BY 3.0) pg. 93, Madman2001/Wikimedia Commons (CC BY-SA 3.0) pg. 96, CTSnow/ Wikimedia Commons (CC BY 2.0) pg. 97, aurbina /Wikimedia Commons (Public Domain) pg. 97, Raul AB/Fliker (CC BY-ND 2.0) pg. 101, William James Linton/Wikimedia Commons (No Copyright) pg. 107, Vadim Brusintsyna/Wikimedia Commons (No Copyright) pg. 112, Paul Rowbotham/Flickr (CC BY-SA 2.0) pg. 118, Wilhelm Joys Andersen/Flickr (CC BY-SA 2.0) pg. 123, Robert Couse-Baker/Flickr (CC BY-SA 2.0) pg. 129, Unknown /Wikimedia Commons (Public Domain) pg. 129, lighthouse/Depositphotos () pg. 134, Jabberocky/ Wikimedia Commons (Public Domain) pg. 139, NASA/Paul Alers/Wikimedia Commons (CC BY-SA 2.0) pg. 145, Unknown/Wikimedia Commons (Public Domain) pg. 145, /National Portrait Gallery (Public Domain) pg. 150, Cristoph Wilhelm Bock/Digitaler Portrait Index (Public Domain) pg. 150, Charles Thomson & Paddy.84/Wikimedia Commons (Public Domain) pg. 157, Unknown/Wikimedia Commons (Public Domain) pg. 159, Bill Larkins/Flickr (CC BY-SA 2.0) pg. 162, Cecil Stoughton, White House/NARA (Public Domain) pg. 164, Tos/Wikimedia Commons (Public Domain) pg. 168, FDR/ Wikimedia Commons (Public Domain) pg. 174, Joseph E. Baker/Wikimedia Commons (Public Domain) pg. 179, H. D. Nichols/Boston Public Library (CC BY-SA 2.0) pg. 180, Vitalliy/Depositphotos pg. 180, baibaz/Depositphotos pg. 180, arskajuhani/Depositphotos pg. 181, Unknown/University of Washington (Public Domain) pg. 183, tkasperova@mail.ru/ Depositphotos () pg. 189, Baker County Tourism/Flickr (CC BY-ND 2.0) pg. 194, shalunx13/Depositphotos pg. 200, Joachim Huber/Flickr (CC BY-SA 2.0) pg. 206, Marcin Wichary/Flickr (CC BY-SA 2.0) pg. 212, Rose Robin/Flickr (CC BY-SA 2.0) pg. 217, moussa81/Depositphotos pg. 222, monkey business/Depositphotos pg. 222, dovapi/Depositphotos pg. 222, imagesbykenny/Depositphotos pg. 222, VadimVasenin/ Depositphotos pg. 222, RawPixel/Depositphotos pg. 252, screenshot/Wikipedia

Made in the USA
Middletown, DE
21 October 2021